Contents

Acknowledgements

I would like to thank the many people who have helped in the preparation of this book.

My colleagues at Queen Margaret College showed me how to teach health care professionals. My research students, in particular Pauline Rafferty and Martin Dunbar, helped me clarify many psychological concepts. Penny Aittren and her library staff gave me help on many occasions. My colleagues and friends in the world of health psychology contributed through many discussions and arguments.

The Queen Margaret College students of Nursing, Speech and Language Therapy, Physiotherapy, and Dietetics stimulated me to think about the applications of psychology, and the BSc Podiatry students commented on some of the early drafts and demanded that I justify my discipline.

My family have been supportive throughout. My husband gave me relentless encouragement and a great deal of help.

I am grateful to Pergamon Press for permission to reproduce the Social Readjustment rating scale.

DEDICATION

In memory of my father, Robin Pinsent.

Preface

Psychology is of importance to health professionals for its own intrinsic interest, but also for its contribution to clinical practice. Knowledge of psychology may enable health professionals to improve their therapeutic skills, and it may help them to cope with professional demands and their own personal lives. There are many introductory texts written for first-year psychology undergraduates, but books on psychology that are suggested for health professionals are often multi-authored, intended for medical students, for researchers or for clinical specialists. They also tend to emphasise illness rather than health.

This book is intended for health professional students and practitioners who have had some introduction to psychology, and are perhaps in their second or subsequent years of study. It will be relevant to students and practitioners in Physiotherapy, Speech and Language Therapy, Dietetics, Occupational Therapy and Podiatry.

Students of Nursing may also find it useful and it will complement other books on introductory psychology written specifically for the nursing profession.

The book has been written for those who want to study psychology relevant to their own discipline. I have often assumed that the reader has had some clinical experience, but some of the activities can be carried out on fellow students or colleagues or even on willing family members in rôle play.

I have considered the concept of *health* rather than *illness* because of the current approach to holistic treatment. Most people are healthy most of the time and their aim is to stay healthy. In health care based on hospitals it is easy to have a distorted view of the health of the population. The current emphasis on community care has led to greater awareness of the social context in which people live, and ways in which this could affect their physical health and their health behaviour. When we consider health, we inevitably consider illness. Despite this, I have tried to discuss issues from a health perspective rather than from an illness perspective.

This book is about the psychology *of* health, not psychology *and* health. I have introduced health issues first and then I have discussed the psychological concepts that inform that issue. For readers with no background of psychology, I hope this book will give some insight into how psychology contributes to our understanding of health. I hope that they will then refer to an up-to-date introductory psychology text.

Although many such textbooks are written for American college undergraduates, they give much of the basic psychology that underpins health psychology, often in a readily accessible form. In this book some psychological background is summarised in boxes and these may lead the reader to look further at the topic in these introductory psychology texts. Activities are included so that the text can be issued for discussion groups, and further reading lists identify accessible texts for student-centred learning.

Case studies have not been included. The book is intended for a wide range of health professionals, and each discipline has particular angles on each of the issues discussed. It is hoped that case studies will be generated from the experience of readers themselves or of their tutors, and discussed, if possible, with colleagues. It is the active application of psychology to real life problems that will convince the reader of the value of psychology to their profession.

In my first week as an undergraduate student at Aberdeen University I bought *A Modern Introduction to Psychology* by Rex and Margaret Knight. I have a vivid recollection of reading it all the way through, lying on my bed (it had a pink bedspread – why do we remember visual details of significant events in our lives?), and I was irrevocably captured by psychology. If this book gives only a fraction of the inspiration that I experienced I will be well pleased.

Knight, R. and Knight, M. (1959) *A Modern Introduction to Psychology*, 6th edn, London: University Tutorial Press.

1

Introduction to the Psychology of Health

CONTENTS

1.1 INTRODUCTION

"Psychology can do a great deal to improve the quality of health care." Adler et al. (1979)

This book is about the psychology of health. In it we will discuss the application of theories and research findings in psychology that help us to understand and thereby improve health care. This first chapter will attempt to introduce what we mean by psychology and how psychology can be related to health. I will refer to issues that are raised in later chapters and show how findings from psychology can be applied to health.

1.1.1 The Assumptions of Psychology

My first assertion is that psychology is the scientific study of behaviour. It is arguable that some aspects of psychology may be best studied without using conventional scientific method, but the principles of theoretical understanding, hypothesis testing, data collection and analysis can be applied whatever the approach. The study of health is closely related to the study of medicine and the essential biological basis of human behaviour is particularly pertinent.

Secondly, psychology attempts to understand people and make sense of their emotions and feelings. We are often emotional about our health and we are sometimes irrational. Ill health in ourselves or others can arouse powerful emotions. We may act with anger about a young person suffering a fatal heart attack, with political zeal about social inequalities of health, and with grief about degenerative disease. We seek explanations for our behaviour and the behaviour of others and we try to understand what is happening when someone else is suffering. An enquiring mind seeks causal explanations and attempts to predict events. Ultimately we hope to control our health and reduce illness and disease. We can use the fundamental principles of psychology to study health behaviour and the experience of health and illness. Psychological knowledge can be applied to health, and the study of the healthy mind and body can inform psychological theories.

1.1.2 Questions of *Why* and *How*

Why are there individual differences in behaviour?

Why do some people behave in a healthy way and others do not? Are there consistent individual differences that persist in some people that lead them to behave in a healthy way? Do these individuals always behave in a healthy way or only in some aspects of their health?

Are there differences that are characteristics of groups? Does the gender or economic status of a group influence health? Why do groups differ in their attitudes and beliefs about health?

Why does health in adults differ from that in children? Is it just because they are more physically mature, or do children view health differently from adults? Do children learn about illness behaviour from their parents? If so, what implications does this have for health education?

How do these differences come about?

Questions that ask *how* tend to be those that are describing processes. They are often framed in a bio-physiological context and although this book is not about physiology, health professionals often have a thorough grounding in human physiology and therefore a basic knowledge will be assumed. A bio-psychosocial framework will be proposed. This means that the physiological basis of behaviour is often assumed and never ignored.

How do motivational states or drives influence behaviour? For example, in a simple way we can say that we eat when we are hungry. However, we also eat when we are not hungry if we want someone's company. If we are trying to lose weight, we will not eat even though we are hungry.

How do families influence the health of their children? To what extent is illness and health behaviour related to family norms and dynamics?

How do attitudes change? Attitudes to health have changed since the 1980's and people are now more aware of the consequences of smoking, high-fibre diets, and exercise.

How do people acquire control over their health or medical treatment, and what happens if they fail? How do we learn health behaviour habits and remember them? Are they learned in childhood, acquired as part of health education in school or are they influenced by media campaigns?

Activity 1.1

Some of these how and why questions are addressed under differ-ent headings in conventional undergraduate psychology texts. Select an undergraduate psychology textbook from the further reading list, and identify which of these questions might be covered in chapters on Learning, Motivation, Social psychology, Personal-ity, and Developmental psychology.

1.1.3 Applying Psychology to Health

This is a book about applied psychology, in the sense of using psychology to solve problems. This view of psychology is also shared by some under-graduate psychology textbook authors:

> *"No matter how interesting and intellectually stimulating, a text that fails to show the practical value of new ideas is irrelevant in a very basic sense" (Coon 1986 p xxiii)*

The study of psychology can be justified as being of intrinsic interest in its own right. If psychology is to have a place in the educational curriculum of health professionals, it must be demonstrated that it will help them to improve their practice. The study of psychology will then be worth the time spent by hard pressed health professionals. Improvement in therapeutic relationships and the effectiveness of therapy is discussed in Chapter 4.

Activity 1.2

This is the most important activity in the book.
Describe your own case studies and share with a colleague. We all know someone who is ill or we may have been ill ourselves.
Describe someone that you have cared for or you have known who has been ill. For example a child awaiting surgery, a bereaved elderly person, an aggressive youth, a stressed colleague. List the ways in which you think psychology can help you understand the problem. Do this from your present understanding, and then at the end of the book go back and see if you can add to your list. To some extent, knowledge of psychology helps us to identify and sort out the issues. It is unlikely to give us precise guidelines. To what extent do you think this is true of the case that you have described?

A knowledge of psychology will also help health professionals to understand patients' emotional state. In Chapter 3 and Chapter 7, we will discuss stress. Discussion of the concepts underlying stress and its measurement allows the health professional to make judgements about the influences on health. This will be based on psychological theories and research.

1.2 RESEARCH AND PSYCHOLOGY

Theories make sense of related observations and mean that we can ask questions that will give meaningful answers. Theories about why people smoke must take into account what people think are the positive aspects of smoking, as well as the ill health effects. Theories are often based on models, and these help us to predict behaviour. A model is a representation of variables linked together that predict an outcome. They are often shown in diagrams (Box 1.1). For example, a simple model of motivation suggests that we eat when we are hungry. Hunger can be defined as a sensation occurring when our blood sugar is low. However, this does not help to explain eating disorders such as obesity or anorexia. We may use pictures to illustrate our understanding (Figure 1.1).

Research into the psychology of health tests and extends our existing psychological theories and also generates new theories. Sometimes the

---

Box 1.1   Diagrammatic models in psychology
Motivation Need ⟶ drive ⟶ response goal ⟶ need reduction
Learning behaviour by imitation Attention → remembers → tries to → succeeds → shows behaviour (looks at   image   copy action model)

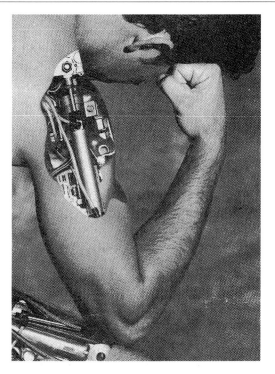

FIGURE 1.1   A mechanistic model
(Source: Health Education Board)

results of the research are only descriptive but often they lead to predictions. These may ultimately help health professionals to control behaviour.

All the techniques of psychological research probably have some rôle in research into the psychology of health, but some are used more extensively than others. There are many textbooks written about statistics and research methodology for medical and health researchers and these give a sound basis for planning and analysing health research (Altman 1991, Pilcher 1990).

1.2.1 Surveys, Questionnaires, and Interviews

We can learn a great deal about health from asking people questions. A large part of medical diagnosis is based on answers given by the person who is complaining of symptoms, and health professionals can become very skilled at taking a medical history. Often the diagnosis is confirmed by diagnostic tests carried out in the laboratory but we still rely on the perceptions of individuals. Verbal or written answers are also used in research into health. Psychologists are skilled in identifying key questions and phrasing them in such a way as to elicit precise, unambiguous answers. Construction of questionnaires is time consuming and harder than it first appears. However, we can learn a great deal from a large number of people about health problems and possible associated variables. The responses give us descriptive data. For example, we can learn about the severity and frequency of symptoms, how long it was before medical attention was sought, the demographic characteristics of the sufferers, and estimates of the amount of pain or distress experienced.

We may also use psychometric scales that have been through a careful set of psychometric steps to ensure that they are meaningful and can be used in statistical analysis (Rust and Golombok 1991).

Descriptive data derived from quantitative research can be very useful but often we want to ask more searching questions and we may want to test a theory. For example, we may have a theory that headaches are related to hormonal changes. To test this theory we form hypotheses. For example, suppose we hypothesize that headaches are more frequent in women than in men; that they occur more often in the premenstrual phases than in the post-menstrual phases of the menstrual cycle; and that they are less likely to occur in women taking the oral contraceptive pill.

We can test these hypotheses by collecting enough data to carry out statistical analyses. We can look to see if more headaches occur in one group than we would expect by chance. If the frequencies in the two groups are significantly different, we may feel we have enough evidence to set up physiological hypotheses, and maybe to design laboratory experiments. We could also take a quasi-experimental approach. In a true experiment we would allocate people into two groups, and then change the conditions in one of the groups (manipulate the independent variable). In a quasi-experimental approach we measure the relevant variables in two naturally occurring groups. We can do this by collecting data from a cross section of the population. In the case of the incidence of headaches, we could collect data from one group of women who were in their premenstrual phase, and from another group of women who were in their post-menstrual phase. We would record the number of headaches in each group and see if they were different.

Alternatively we could collect data from women longitudinally. This means that we follow the women over a period of time. They would record the number of headaches in their premenstrual phase and again in the post-menstrual phase. We would compare the frequency of headaches in the two phases in each woman. This is actually a more powerful design because each woman is her own control, but the data would take longer to collect and the women may change over time anyway.

1.2.2   Interventions

When we want to improve health we may want to see if a specific intervention or change has had any effect. The approach we use here is similar to the design of clinical trials. Subjects are randomly allocated to two groups. In one they are given the active intervention (such as a drug, psychological therapy or written information). In the other group they are given routine care or an attention control.

If we find a difference between the two groups in some outcome measure (the dependent variable) then we can conclude that it was a result of the intervention. In order to be more certain, such studies are often carried out 'blind'. This means that the researcher who assesses the outcome does not know into which group the subjects were allocated. In a drug trial it is possible to keep the subjects themselves blind so that they do not know whether they have taken the active drug or the inactive (placebo) drug. If the researcher does not know either, it is called a 'double blind trial'.

If we have two different groups there may be differences between them that may influence the results. For example, if one group was significantly heavier than the other, this might affect the metabolism of the drug. We can try to match the two groups so that the distribution of weight is the same in both groups but it is often difficult to match groups on very many variables. To avoid this problem clinical trials often use a crossover design. This means that one group takes the active drug first and then crosses over and takes the placebo drug. The second group takes the placebo drug first and the active drug second. This allows a within-subject comparison. In practice, crossover designs are very difficult to do in psychological research, and subjects are rarely blind.

Descriptive data can also be analysed by using correlations. We may suspect that one variable is related to another. For example, we may hypothesize that obesity is related to certain types of foot problems. If we assess the health of feet in a large number of people (subjects) and measure their weight, we can see whether there is an association between foot health and weight. If we do find an association it does not necessarily mean that excessive weight causes the foot problems, because having foot problems could itself reduce activity and so increase weight. It is also possible that a third factor such as poverty might lead to both a poor diet causing obesity and to wearing ill-fitting shoes that cause foot problems. Correlations do not tell us the direction of an association. To test whether obesity causes foot problems we would need to manipulate weight. In a sample of similar people, half could be given a weight-reducing diet. If this group were shown to have lost weight and had fewer foot problems than the other half who had not lost weight, then we would conclude that there was a causal relationship.

1.2.3 Case Studies

Much of health psychology is based on quantitative data that involves putting numbers to behaviour or feelings, and experimental methods such as the clinical trials described above. We can also learn much from the collection of qualitative data. Qualitative data is essentially descriptive. It gives us insight and may lead to new approaches or hypotheses. Data is often collected by interviews on a relatively small number of subjects. Single case studies have traditionally been used to describe unusual medical or psychological conditions. In some cases a treatment is tried out and reported on an individual and the patient is followed up, sometimes over a period of years. It may be difficult to generalize from one individual to other populations, but the demonstration of success of a treatment in one individual may be enough to justify a larger study. Qualitative research based on a single person is also appropriate when a topic is new or particularly sensitive. For example if little is known about the perception of miscarriage, then sensitive in-depth interviewing can identify issues that we would not get from written questionnaires or rating scales.

1.3 PSYCHOLOGY AND HEALTH

1.3.1 Goals of Health Psychology

Health Psychology originated in the late 1970s, and has grown rapidly since the early 1980's. In a recent textbook Sarafino (1994) described four goals of psychology derived from a definition given by Matarazzo in 1982.

The promotion and maintenance of health

Differences in health have been attributed to differences in behaviour. As we shall see in Chapter 2 there are many health behaviours and habits that contribute to health and illness, although social, demographic and genetic factors are also important. By understanding individual differences in behaviour, we may be able to encourage behaviour patterns that lead to good health, and reduce the frequency of those that lead to poor health. Smoking and the wearing of seat belts are two examples of differences in behaviour that can affect health.

Improving health care systems and health policy

Health care frequently takes place in institutions and most countries have a national health care service. Health psychologists look at the organization and the ways in which health professionals can improve their practice. Chapter 3 considers the application of psychology to improving practice.

The prevention and treatment of illness

Illness may be prevented by adopting healthy habits or avoiding unhealthy ones. Illness may also be prevented by attending screening programmes or taking up vaccination. The efficacy of treatment of illness can be increased by applying psychological principles. In Chapter 4 and Chapter 5 we look at how therapy can be facilitated.

Causes and detection of illness

There may be psychological factors that have contributed to individual differences in the occurrence of illness and its prognosis. Some people are more vulnerable to heart disease than others and this has been related to behaviour patterns such as Type A (see Chapter 7 for a definition) and to stress. This is discussed in Chapter 7.

The importance of developmental changes was not stressed by Matarazzo but we know that ill heath in adulthood often has its origins in childhood. Health behaviour, and probably illness behaviour, is learned in childhood. The pattern of health and illness and the response of individuals varies across the lifespan. In Chapter 5 we look at changing health over the lifespan. Reproductive issues affect our health directly and indirectly. Women are more often ill than men in terms of self-reported health and consultation rates, but they live longer then men. Some of the reproductive events that affect health are discussed in Chapter 6. Women have a particularly important role in influencing their family's health. The weekly shop will often be in the control of the mother even if she is working full time. Health has become a marketing issue, with increasing varieties of low-fat spreads, additive-free foods and low-calorie drinks.

Activity 1.3

Which of these topics do you consider most relevant to your profession or discipline? Are they all applicable? Which do you think could be most closely implemented by health professionals?

1.3.2   The Study of Health Psychology

The goals in the study of health psychology are to describe, understand and predict health behaviour.

- *Describing* implies quantifying, and quantitative approaches have usually been taken in health psychology. Qualitative techniques are being increasingly used, however, for example in understanding the spiritual needs of patients (Ross 1994).

- *Understanding* implies that we acquire meaning. It is hard to understand why people do not comply with treatment if they then get worse not better. It might be easier to understand, if it is realized that the person was afraid of dependence, worried about side effects or had not been givenclear instructions.

- *Prediction* allows us to say in advance what will happen. In therapy we might try to do this by telling patients that if this exercise is followed, their condition is likely to improve. We may be able to prepare patients for hospitalization and reduce their anxiety if we can predict the effect of the use of coping mechanisms or relaxation.

- We also seek to find ways of *controlling* behaviour; this is often what the patient wants. Reduction in smoking behaviour, the control of pain, and coping with stress may all benefit from psychological principles.

Health psychology differs from traditional academic psychology in that it may be of more interest to health professionals than psychologists. It attempts to fulfil the needs of health professionals studying psychology rather than the needs of psychologists studying health. However, it also attempts to contribute to psychological theory.

1.3.3   Medical Psychology

The medical model will be discussed in detail in Chapter 4. This model is essentially mechanistic and symptoms of illness are regarded as a failure of a system or its working parts. If these faults are identified and put right, then health will be restored. A close analogy is a car breakdown. We can replace the mechanism or tune the engine. However, the car still needs a driver and its operation is controlled by society. Its speed, where it can be parked and its condition are controlled by law. Similarly, our bodies can be mended and put into working order, but they still function in the context of society. This functional approach leads to a mechanistic view of health. For example, at the time of the menopause there is a reduction in ovarian activity and a reduction in levels of output of the hormone oestrogen. These levels can be restored by replacing the oestrogen by hormone replacement therapy. The menopause could thus be regarded as a hormone deficiency disease, that can be treated by doctors. However, the transition through the menopause is also a cultural event, and society has expectations and norms that it applies to middle-aged women. This will be discussed in Chapter 6.

The biological basis of health and illness is often closely linked to the medical model and if we reject the medical model we may inadvertently also reject the biological foundations of health. For example, in the field of sexuality there have been conflicts of interpretation between feminist theories and biological explanations, but these should be seen as complementary rather than contradictory (Choi and Nicolson 1994). A biological scientific explanation may be seen as masculine, while holistic or cultural views may be favoured by feminists. However, we need both types of explanation if we are to understand fully the influences on health (Alder 1994).

Health psychology and introductory psychology textbooks usually describe physiological processes. I recommend that the reader looks at the sections on the nervous system, the endocrine system, the immune system, the digestive system and the respiratory system. All these systems form the biological basis of behaviour and knowledge of them is essential to understand the psychology of health.

Activity 1.4

Consider the relevance to health and illness of some of these systems in your own discipline or profession. Has anything been omitted?

1.3.4   Behavioural Medicine

Behavioural medicine is concerned with health problems and is closely linked to clinical medicine. Behavioural medicine has been defined as 'the interdisciplinary field concerned with the development and integration of behavioural and biomedical knowledge and techniques relevant to health and illness, and the application of this knowledge and these techniques to prevention, diagnosis, treatment and rehabilitation' (Schwartz and Weiss 1978, p 250).

Activity 1.5

Compare this definition with the goals of health psychology described in section 1.3.1.

Behavioural medicine tends to be more concerned with illness than with health. Pearce and Wardle (1989) suggest that behavioural medicine places emphasis on interdisciplinary connections, whereas health psychology concentrates on the specific contribution of psychology. However, in their book, Pearce and Wardle concentrate on medical problems and organize their discussion of psychological factors under the headings of medical conditions such as diabetes and obesity.

Particular diseases have received attention from behavioural psychologists: asthma, cancer, diabetes, cardiovascular diseases, arthritis and renal failure. Many of these are related to stress. Chapter 7 discusses some of the psychological research linking stress to illness.

Activity 1.6

There are other medical conditions that have received less attention, e.g. back pain, and dermatology. Can you add to this list?

Behavioural medicine also has its roots in behaviourism. This approach suggests that behaviour results from two types of learning: classical conditioning and operant conditioning. These are discussed in Chapter 4. Behavioural medicine thus also includes problems of emotion such as fear, and many health problems are associated with behaviour problems. Clinical psychologists share many of these interests.

Activity 1.7

List some health behaviour problems that may be helped by changing behaviour, e.g. over-eating.
List some emotional problems that might be helped, e.g. fear of flying.

1.3.5   Psychosomatic Medicine

The term 'psychosomatic' is often taken to imply the influence of the mind over the body. A psychosomatic illness may be regarded as less real than an organic-based illness. The term 'psychosomatic illnesses' was often used as a rag-bag in which to put any illness that was difficult to explain. Most illnesses have a psychological component and to that extent they can all be described as psychosomatic. Psychosomatic does not mean that people are malingering or that they are hypochondriacs.

Christie (1983) describes the historical background to psychosomatics and relates it to psychophysiology. Much of the research was carried out in the 1970s and the more recent use of multivariate statistical analysis and model building in health psychology has, to a great extent, taken its place. A group

Box 1.2 The holy seven psychosomatic illnesses (Christie 1983)		
asthma	rheumatoid arthritis	ulcerative colitis
essential hypertension	neurodermatitis	thyrotoxicosis
	peptic ulcer	

of illnesses known as the 'holy seven' were thought to have their origin in childhood (Box 1.2). The specific disorder was thought to relate to specific conflicts that were often thought to be unconscious. The term 'psychosomatic' (mind and body) was thus confused with the term 'psychogenic' (arising from the mind). It will be argued throughout this book that all illnesses have psychological components and that the prognoses of all illnesses are affected by psychological factors. There is no direct evidence that the holy seven diseases are particularly closely related to individual differences in personality or behaviour.

The term is less used today, but it is sometimes used dismissively, particularly when the condition is not understood. If a person is described as having a psychosomatic illness, it is an indication that there is a psychological angle to the problem. It may also indicate a lack of professional understanding. The term psychosomatic may be best regarded as a descriptive term rather than as an explanation.

1.3.6   Medical Sociology or the Sociology of Health and Illness

The ways in which we understand illness and react to symptoms of illness are influenced by the norms and expectations of society. Similarly, our expectations and standards of health and our attitudes to health behaviour may depend on a number of social factors. People in different cultures suffer from different illnesses even when the physical conditions are similar.

Understanding about the membership of groups is essential to understanding health and illness. There is a close relationship between sociology and psychology and you may find some concepts that are discussed in both disciplines (Scambler 1991). The concepts of illness behaviour, grief reaction and roles are all considered by both medical sociologists and health psychologists. Families and kinship are very important in health and are discussed in Chapter 5. Although the psychological approach taken in this book emphasizes the behaviour of the individual, we know that social factors can make it practically impossible to behave in a healthy way (Chapter 2). For example, the healthy practice of eating fresh fruit may be very difficult if none is sold on the housing estate, and if public transport is expensive or non-existent.

Activity 1.8

Suggest some behavioural risk factors for the four leading causes of death: heart disease, cancer, stroke and accidents.
After reading Chapter 2, complete your list.

Risky behaviour has received attention from both health psychologists and medical sociologists (Plant and Plant 1992). Alcohol abuse and smoking are major causes of death and illness in our society today. Most smokers know that they are increasing the risk of smoking-related diseases and reducing their life expectancy, but still continue to smoke. Excessive drinking also carries health risks and alcoholism has itself been regarded as a disease. Substance abuse carries health risks and illegal drug-taking has social as well as physical and psychological consequences.

Medical sociology also considers the institutions that treat and control our health. Health professionals are themselves part of small teams and larger professional bodies. The professionalization of health care has been a contentious issue. The status (and pay) is often linked to the activities and public image of the groups. Some health professions dedicate one week in the year to promoting the work of their profession. Why do they do this when other groups, such as dentists and lawyers, do not?

Activity 1.9

Where does your profession or discipline stand in its search for professional identity? Has this changed in the past ten years? Is it likely to change in the next ten years?

1.3.7 Community Health

Concepts discussed in medical sociology are also used in health promotion and health education. They both apply the principles of sociology and psychology to the community. For example, the health belief model has been applied to attempts to change behaviour, although with limited success (Chapter 2).

Immunizing children against whooping cough, using condoms to avoid HIV infection, and exercise are all health behaviours that are promoted by health professionals. Health education seeks to give information about health and the ways in which it can be maintained.

Unhealthy living may be related to social class, housing, or unemployment. Some of the origins of differences in health are discussed in Chapter 2. For those people who are working, ill health may result from accidents or poor working conditions. A change in health may come from enabling individuals to take steps to change their circumstances or even to change social policy (see Matarazzo's goals of health psychology). Groups of individuals can be very powerful when they are brought together by the experience of a medical condition.

Two other related fields are medical anthropology and epidemiology. There are few texts written for health professionals in these areas but Rose and Barker (1986) and Holden and Littlewood (1991) give some background.

Activity 1.10

How can we avoid blaming the victim when we encourage individual responsibility for health? For example, if we stress that diet can influence health, what does this mean for those that are socially or financially unable to provide a healthy diet? Discuss this in the context of unemployment, and in the context of educating school leavers.

Mothers are also likely to be the first to respond to symptoms of ill health and may encourage or discourage illness behaviour. They are also more likely than men to report illness even when allowing for obstetric and gynaecological problems, and to experience hospitalization, Radley (1994). The relationship of reproduction to health is discussed in Chapter 6.

In the future, more health care may take place in the community as day surgery becomes more common and diagnostic skills improve. The influence of social factors on therapy and recovery may become even more evident. This will contrast with the isolation of patients in a hospital ward separated from their families and from their role in society.

1.4   CONCLUSION

The study of psychology can offer much to the understanding of health. If we understand about the process whereby an individual avoids being ill, becomes ill or recovers from illness we may be able to improve health care. If, in addition, we understand why someone remains healthy or recovers from illness quickly, we should be able to improve the quality of life. The study of the psychology of health will help us to fulfil both these aims.

1.5   SUMMARY

The study of psychology in relation to health is based on a number of assumptions and asks why there are differences in health behaviour and how these come about. Our understanding is based on an extensive body of research which uses the research techniques of the social sciences. Health psychology can be distinguished from medical psychology, behavioural medicine, psychosomatic medicine and medical sociology.

1.6   FURTHER READING

Pearce, S. and Wardle, J. (1989) *The Practice of Behavioural Medicine.* Oxford: BPS Books Oxford University Press

This is comprehensive and gives many references. There is an emphasis on medical conditions and also practical guidelines for practice.

Sarafino, E.P. (1994) *Health Psychology: Biopsychosocial Interactions,* 2nd edn. Chichester: John Wiley & Sons

An up-to-date American health psychology text that emphasizes prevention and care, and links material well to physiology. It includes many interesting vignettes that illustrate issues.

Broome, A. and Llewelyn, S. (Eds.) (1995) *Health Psychology. Processes and Applications*, 2nd edn. London: Chapman and Hall

This gives clear accounts of theoretical perspectives, followed by chapters by experts who discuss specific areas or disorders.

1.7   REFERENCES

Adler, N.E. (1979) Themes and professional prospects in health psychology. In *Health Psychology – A Handbook* Ch. 22, p 589, edited by G.C. Stone, F. Cohen and N.E. Adler. San Francisco: Josey-Bass

Alder, B. (1994) Postnatal sexuality In *Female Sexuality. Psychology, Biology and Social Context,* edited by P.Y.L. Choi and P. Nicolson New York: Harvester Wheatsheaf

Altman, D.G. (1991) *Practical Statistics for Medical Research*. London: Chapman and Hall

Choi, P.Y.L. and Nicolson, P. (Eds.) (1994) *Female Sexuality. Psychology, Biology and Social Context*. New York: Harvester Wheatsheaf

Christie, M. (1983) Psychosomatics; an historical approach. In *Psychology Survey No 4* edited by J. Nicholson and B. Foss. Leicester: BPS Books

Coon D. (1986) *Introduction to Psychology. Exploration and Application*, 4th edn. St Paul, USA: West Publishing Company

Holden, P. and Littlewood, J. (1991) *Anthropology and Nursing*. London: Routledge

Pearce, S. and Wardle, J. (1989) *The Practice of Behavioural Medicine*. Oxford: BPS Books Oxford University Press

Pilcher, D.M. (1990) *Data Analysis for the Helping Professions*. Newbury Park: Sage

Plant, M. and Plant, M. (1992) *Risk Taking: Alcohol, Drugs, Sex and Youth*. London: Routledge

Radley, A. (1994) *Making sense of illness*. London: Sage

Rose, G. and Barker, D.J.P. (1986) *Epidemiology for the Uninitiated*, 2nd edn. London: British Medical Association

Ross, L. (1994) Spiritual aspects of nursing. *Journal of Advanced Nursing,* **19**, 439–447

Rust, J. and Golombok, S. (1989) *Modern Psychometrics. The Science of Psychological Assessment.* London: Routledge

Sarafino, E.P. (1994) *Health Psychology: Biopsychosocial Interactions,* 2nd edn. New York: John Wiley and Sons

Scambler, G. (1991) S*ociology as Applied to Medicine,* 3rd edn. London: Bailliere Tindall

Schwartz, G.E. and Weiss, S.M. (1978) Behavioral medicine revisited: An amended definition. *Journal of Behavioral Medicine,* **1**, 249–251

2

Differences in Health

CONTENTS

2.1 INTRODUCTION

All of us will have been ill at some time in our lives, even if with only a headache or a cold. We are also aware that our state of health is not the same from one week to the next, even though we may not think of ourselves as being ill. Why should some people hardly ever appear to be ill and yet others seem to be in perpetual chronic ill health? The difference can be understood in terms of models. These are derived from psychological theories and have been investigated in many studies in health psychology. There is no one correct model and all of them make some contribution to our understanding of differences in health.

2.2 SOCIOCULTURAL MODELS

Health status is unequal across different groups in society and there are consistent discernible patterns in health that are related to geography, sex, age and socio-economic status. Although we may be interested in health, we find that theories of differences in health are often theories about differences in the incidence of illness.

The main causes of death in the UK today are accidents, heart disease, cancer and respiratory disorders.

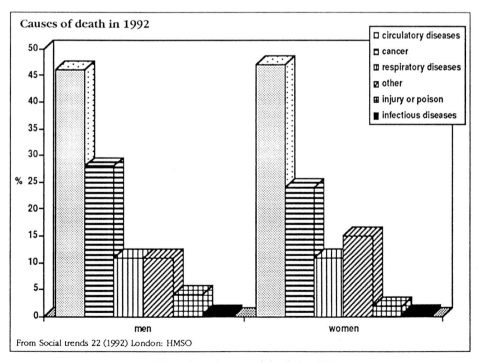

FIGURE 2.1   Causes of death in 1992

The data for the UK are published annually in *Social Trends* (HMSO). These overall statistics hide many differences between groups and there are many factors influencing morbidity statistics. All health professionals will be aware that some groups of people are more vulnerable than others. Patients who attend an NHS podiatry clinic will be predominantly elderly. More boys than girls may be brought to a preschool speech therapy clinic, and more middle-aged men than young women will be in cardiac rehabilitation programmes. There are cultural factors that influence both the morbidity and the uptake of health services. We may find many correlations between social factors and health statistics but it is often difficult to establish causal relationships.

2.2.1   Socio-economic Status

We can learn a great deal from statistics, and the National Health Service in the UK probably has unique records of illness and mortality. Publication of the 'Black Report' (Townsend and Davidson 1982) and the 'Health Divide' (Whitehead 1988), showed that although health had improved dramatically since 1900, it was still clearly associated with socio-economic status assessed by occupational class (Box 2.1). The reports highlighted the problems of distinguishing between individual and corporate responsibility for health and caused much debate in the lay and medical press (Townsend *et al.,* 1988). Sociologists have found it very difficult to agree on a measure of social class and health psychologists have found it just as difficult to measure health. This makes it very hard to draw conclusions about the causes of health, although the relationships between socio-economic status and mortality rates are clearer.

Box 2.1   Social class

In response to the question 'what is your occupation'? most people will have a ready answer. However, some people may find it difficult. Consider an unemployed draughtsman or a postgraduate student; a woman who becomes a childminder because there are no jobs for computer programmers; a company director whose board is made up of close family members and has no employees; someone who is between jobs; a 'resting' actress who is waitressing; those with two jobs – the list is endless. Thus the first problem is one of reliability and this may be overcome by asking about the main occupation in the last five years. The second problem is that the job description may not be valid. If we hope to have a global measure of social position, education and income, the current job description may not reflect this. Thirdly, the proportion of people in each group is rapidly changing. In 1971, 30% of the working population were employed in manufacturing industries

---

Box 2.1   Social class (*cont.*)

compared with 20% in 1991 (Social Trends 1992). Classification becomes particularly problematic in Social Class V (unskilled manual) where job descriptions are difficult to define and people may frequently change jobs.

In some Government statistics (e.g. the General Household Survey) married women are classified by the occupational class of their husband whereas single women are classified by their own occupation.

The majority of married women now work outside the home and their income may be a significant contribution to the family income. The notion of women working for 'pin money' has long since gone.

Social class groups

Professional
Employers and managers
Intermediate non-manual
Skilled manual
Semi-skilled manual
Unskilled manual

Other indices used include:
Household tenure (owner occupier or tenant)
Educational level
Car ownership
Bathroom index

The 'Black Report' (1982) and 'Health Divide' (1988) both concentrate on the effect of the uneven distribution of wealth on health. Inequalities in health are, of course, based on statistical relationships and we still need to explain how they have arisen. Four possible explanations have been suggested:

Artefact explanation

The measures of health and social class are artificial variables. The proportion of people in the poorer classes has declined and those that remain are more likely to be unhealthy than those that have been upwardly mobile.

Theories of natural or social selection

Social class I contains the strongest and healthiest people. The poorest and the weakest drift downwards. The genetic contribution to poor health would further increase the differences.

The materialist explanation

Health inequalities arise because of inequalities of wealth and income. The concept of poverty is relative and we are now more aware of poor sections of society. It may be more important to identify groups such as those caring for elderly relatives, disabled adults, or single mothers rather than those identified in terms of occupational class.

Cultural behaviour explanations

This suggests that health inequalities are due to inappropriate patterns of behaviour, e.g. smoking. Health behaviour patterns are based in a cultural context and the same factors may not be equally applicable in all social groups.

The indices of social deprivation that have been used in research studies have consistently shown that social gradients in health persist. In the Whitehall study of the health of civil servants, Marmot *et al.* (1984) found that the incidence of coronary heart disease and lung cancer was almost three times greater in the lowest employment grades than in the highest. This difference could not be accounted for by differences in smoking, body weight, cholesterol levels, blood pressure or exercise. The inequalities of health reported in 1982 in the UK were found to be even greater ten years later (Davey-Smith *et al.* 1990). Wilkinson (1992) found that health differences were least in those countries that had the least material inequality. Interestingly, he suggests that health does not get better with increasing wealth, so the relationship between health and wealth must be very complex. Wilkinson (1992) also suggests that material inequalities may affect the quality of social relationships and psychosocial stress. General social policy may only directly affect the maintenance of social relationships in specific instances such as housing policy, divorce law or contraceptive policy.

However, we should remember that in general, health has improved. Although there may be some sectors that are more healthy than others, by raising the standard of living and health of all social groups we are still increasing the standard of health for the more socially deprived groups.

The data analysed in the 'Health Divide' are based on those aged under 65. We know from demographic data that a large proportion of deaths occur in people aged over 65. An average man aged 60 in 1961 could expect to live until the age of 75, but a man aged 60 in 1991 can expect to reach the age of 77.6 years. A woman aged 60 in 1961 could expect to reach the age of 79 but if aged 60 in 1991 can expect to live to 82.7 years (*Social Trends* 1992). Of course, deaths in the younger age groups may be more distressing, and have more economic impact than death in old age. We also know that the proportion of people needing health care in old age is rising rapidly and it is therefore important that the influences of health are studied in this age group.

2.2.2 Life Events

It would seem that background stressors such as social deprivation or poor housing can affect health, but so can change. Life events are events that cause significant change. They can be either positive or negative, but they all demand adjustment to new circumstances. Life events appear to precede a number of physical and psychological health problems. They can trigger or exacerbate psychological disorders and may lead to clinical anxiety or depression.

In the late 1960's, Holmes and Rahe (1967) developed a scale to measure the impact of life events. They asked a group of people from the general population to rate the amount of adjustment that each life event would require. They identified 43 items and constructed a schedule of recent experiences (social readjustment rating scale; SRRS) that allocated the maximum of 100 life change units to the death of a spouse (Box 2.2). The total score of the scale was regarded as a measure of the degree of stress. The events were familiar and experienced by most people at some time in their lives, but not all the events would be regarded as negative or obviously stressful. Holidays are positive events but they are also times of change.

Box 2.2	Social readjustment rating scale (Holmes and Rahe 1967)	
Rank	**Life event**	**Mean value**
1	death of spouse	100
2	divorce	73
3	marital separation	65
4	jail term	63
5	death of close family member	63
6	personal injury or illness	53
7	marriage	50
8	fired at work	47
9	marital reconciliation	45
10	retirement	45
11	change in health in family member	44
12	pregnancy	40
13	sex difficulties	39
14	gain of new family member	39
15	business readjustment	39
16	change in financial state	38
17	death of close friend	37
18	change to line of different work	36
19	change in number of arguments with spouse	35
20	mortgage over $10,000	31

Box 2.2	Social readjustment rating scale (Holmes and Rahe 1967) (*cont.*)	
Rank	**Life event**	**Mean value**
21	foreclosure of mortgage or loan	30
22	change in responsibilities at work	29
23	son or daughter leaving home	29
24	trouble with in-laws	29
25	outstanding personal achievement	28
26	wife begins or stops work	26
27	begin or end school	25
28	change in living conditions	24
29	revision of personal habits	23
30	trouble with boss	20
31	change in work hours or conditions	20
32	change in residence	20
33	change in schools	19
34	change in recreation	19
35	change in church activities	19
36	change in social activities	18
37	mortgage or loan less than $10,000	17
38	change in sleeping habits	16
39	change in number of family get-togethers	15
40	change in eating habits	15
41	vacation	13
42	Christmas	12
43	minor violations of the law	11

Reprinted with permission from *Journal of Psychosomatic Research* 11 Holmes TH, Rahe RH, 1967 Elsevier Science Ltd Pergamon Imprint Oxford England

There may not be a clear and direct relationship between life events and health. Firstly, the life events may be related to each other, and loss of a job may lead to financial hardship, changes in housing, and changes in social and church activities. Secondly many of these life events are not discrete events. Retirement is ongoing, and trouble with in-laws may never end. Thirdly, one major disaster such as bankruptcy may have an effect on several of the other events all at once. The most important criticism of this 'dictionary approach' is that the meaning of the event was ignored in the original studies (Craig and Brown 1984). Gain of a new family member would have a different meaning depending whether it was a new stepfather or a new baby.

An unexpected life event may be followed by a period of cognitive adaptation (the extent to which they can adapt or change). Taylor (1983) suggests that there may be a search for *meaning*, a search for *mastery* (controlling or preventing its recurrence) and *self enhancement* (preventing fall in self esteem). People will differ in the extent of their cognitive adaptation and this may be related to their subsequent health. A number of studies have found relationships between life events and illnesses, but the correlations are rather low. Some of the relationships between life events and health may occur because of psychiatric disturbance following the event (Murphy and Brown 1980). The important studies of Brown and Harris (1978) on depression in women showed that those life events that were described as having long-term threatening implications were significantly related to depression. The importance of life events should not be underestimated, but it should not be assumed that any one event will necessarily have an effect on health.

In practice many of us have few life events but we may have many minor events or hassles, and these may be just as important. In a study of married women with young babies, I found that almost no major life events had occurred in six months. However, many minor life events had occurred which caused much distress (Alder *et al.* 1986). One mother found that her baby's pram had been stolen and another was very upset when her television blew up. Hassles are distressing daily annoyances (Kanner *et al.* 1981). They include being late for an appointment, having an argument, or losing some-thing. Kanner *et al.* (1981) found that frequent and severe hassles were better predictors of health than major life events. In a study of women receiving hormone replacement therapy (HRT), it was found that reported psychological symptoms were more closely related to frequency of hassles than to levels of circulating oestrogen (Alder 1992). This was so even though vasomotor symptoms (hot flushes and night sweats) are oestrogen related. There are also corresponding uplifts that are pleasant life events, but these have received less attention from researchers.

Activity 2.1

Which of the life events in the SRRS (Box 2.2) would you regard as having long-term effects for your particular patient group? Would you expect differences between men and women?

2.2.3   Environmental Factors

The extent to which people are ill and the length of time that they are ill, may be more important to health professionals than the mortality rate, but mortality rates are, at least, based on reliable data. Mortality rates have fallen dramatically this century and there have been great advances in medical knowledge leading to cures of diseases, and to preventive medicine. Some of the advances like antibiotics, psychotropic drugs, and surgical operations were supported by great advances in scientific knowledge. However, much of the reduction in illness in the community (or rather the increase in health) has come about from public health measures. Improvements in housing, hygiene, and immunization programmes have changed the pattern and causes of death, but there are still potential environmental factors such as noise, crowding and pollution that influence health. Legislation is often needed to control these and individuals may feel unable to do anything to avoid them. The degree to which we may be able to avoid environmental pollution is also linked to economic conditions.

The crowded housing conditions of the nineteenth century in the UK were associated with the spread of disease. It is known from studies of rat populations that crowding leads to stress and this may inhibit some individuals from breeding. In humans, perceived crowding may be more important than the actual density. Cohen and Spacapan (1978) carried out a field experiment to look at the effects of crowding on behaviour. Women psychology students were asked to list and price large or small items in a shopping centre that was either crowded or uncrowded. They then met a woman who had apparently lost a contact lens. Those subjects who had more items to buy or who were in a crowded centre were less likely to help. The effects of being in a crowded centre may mean that they thought someone else would help and so they were not needed. Alternatively the effect of crowding itself may have been stressful. However, there were no differences between the situations and the subjects' rating of the success or pleasantness of the situation.

We know that people can be very reluctant to help a stranger. In 1964, Kitty Genovese was murdered in a respectable suburb in New York City. Thirty-eight residents admitted that they had witnessed the attack but no one went to help her. Latane and Darley (1970) suggested that "bystander apathy" explained why no one helped her. If there are other people around then no one person may feel that they have responsibility. If others are not responding then the individual may think that the situation is not serious. If the bystander cares what others might think of him if he does not go and help, then he may be more likely to intervene. There is evidence that people on their own are more likely to help. In a classic study, Latane and Rodin (1969) arranged that subjects apparently heard someone in the next room fall off a ladder and moan. Seventy per cent of subjects who were in the room alone responded within 65 seconds. Those that were in the room with strangers were slower and less likely to respond. The presence of a collaborator who showed no concern was the most inhibiting.

The characteristics of the victim may also influence how people react. The greater the similarity between the victim and the onlooker the more likely it will be that help is forthcoming.

Activity 2.2

Have you ever been in a similar situation? What happened? If there was an identifiable health professional present (e.g. in uniform) what would you predict would happen?

2.2.4   Social Conditions

Being unemployed has many negative effects, and it is also associated with poor health. Those in poor health may find it hard to get permanent employment, so it is not easy to tell whether unemployment is the cause of ill health or whether it is the effect of ill health. Subjective impressions of health may be more sensitive measures than morbidity rates. There may be many reasons why people might consider themselves ill. A sample of men who had been unemployed for between 18 and 24 months or longer than 6 months before being re-employed was compared with a control group (McKenna and Payne 1989). The Nottingham Health Profile (Hunt and McEwen 1980) is a very useful, valid and easily completed measure of perceived health and it was used to compare the unemployed men with a control group. Unemployed workers had higher scores than employed men on all variables except pain and these differences were consistent across social classes. Well-being was lower in those who were long-term employed than it was in those who became re-employed.

To be without a job must be hard enough, but to be without a home must be a very distressing experience, especially for those with young children. A family who is officially homeless in London may be housed in bed and breakfast accommodation. Victor (1992) compared the health of over 300 homeless families with residents in a regional health survey. The homeless were mostly female (61%) and under 34 (72%) compared with 18% female and 32% young people in the resident group. Most of the homeless were not working and most had dependent children. There were no differences in the rates of acute illness but the homeless had a significantly higher rate of long-term illness. Of the homeless, 41% smoked compared with 29% of the resident group. They were twice as likely to be mentally ill. Not only does this group need housing, but they also need appropriate health services.

When we try to unravel the causes of inequalities in health we find that both genetic and environmental factors are important and that they interact with each other. There is no better example of the interaction between nature and nurture than differences in health between men and women. No one would deny that there are biological differences between the sexes that make their health patterns different. At the same time there are cultural differences in life-style and health-related behaviour that may also contribute to different health patterns. Women have a longer life expectancy than men but they have higher morbidity, especially in old age. Differences in health that are related to gender are fascinating (Niven and Carroll 1993) but many of these differences may be strongly influenced by differences in reproductive experience (see Chapter 6). There are considerable differences between the health of males and females throughout the world and many of these can be related to poor maternal health (Smyke 1991).

2.2.5   Demographic Differences

Another problem that makes it difficult to relate social conditions to health
is that the relationship may not be the same for all groups. Elderly people
may suffer some of the worst material deprivation in the country. Yet the
evidence suggests that although non-health life events affect health status to
some extent, the state of health before the life event is more important in
influencing health (Wan 1982). In a careful three-wave study of an elderly
population in Aberdeen, Frischer *et al.* (1991) found that there was not
necessarily an increase in the prevalence of health events with increasing
age, but there was an increase in non-health events. However, health events
had more effect on psychological health than did non-health events. Here
we see the very complex relationships between health and psychological
well-being. There are higher mortality rates in Scotland than in England
and Wales but when controlled for deprivation (household density, male
unemployment, social class and car ownership), the difference largely
disappears (Carstairs and Morris 1991).

When we start to gather statistics about health and illness, we find that the
first recorded illness behaviour is likely to be a consultation with the family
doctor. Since the early 1960s this has been the basis for much epidemiologi-
cal research, and has given us information about health behaviour in the
general population rather than in hospital clinic attendees (Fry *et al.* 1983). A
comparison of consulting behaviour between 1970/71 and 1981/82
(McCormick *et al.* 1990) showed that women in all social class groups were
more likely to consult for serious illnesses in the 1980's compared with the
1970's. The likelihood of children and elderly people consulting for any
illness also increased. For trivial diseases and conditions the likelihood of
consulting increased by 12% for both sexes and every age group and social
class group. The increase was greatest in the manual social classes. There
were increases in consultations for diabetes in manual social classes, and
increases in diseases of the circulatory system, hay fever and asthma, acne
and diseases of the musculo-skeletal system. There were decreases in iron
deficiency anaemia and chronic bronchitis. Some of these changes can clearly
be related to changes in medical practice (e.g. prevention of anaemia) and
others to social conditions (e.g. chronic bronchitis).

Some of the relationships between socio-economic circumstances and
whether people consulted, are interesting from a psychological perspective.
Are there more consultations for acne because there is now a higher incidence (more atmospheric pollution, more fatty foods) among young
people? Is it because there is a recognition that acne is a medical problem
and people expect a cure, or do we just have higher expectations of health
and so are less inclined to tolerate unhealthy skin? Adults who were single
were less likely than married adults to consult for intermediate or trivial
illnesses and single women were less likely to consult for serious illnesses.
We might therefore wonder how important social support is in influencing

our consulting behaviour. Without a spouse with whom to discuss health problems would someone be more or less likely to consult a general practitioner? People living in council houses and in urban areas were more likely to consult for serious illnesses. People seeking work were more likely to consult for minor illnesses, but not for less serious illnesses.

Activity 2.3

List as many as possible environmental factors that you think could influence health. How many of these could health professionals change?
Consider the studies on homelessness (Victor 1992). Why is it difficult to interpret correlational data?

2.3 HEALTH BEHAVIOUR

2.3.1 Health and Ill Health

Kasl and Cobb (1966) define *health behaviour* as *any activity undertaken by a person believing himself to be healthy for the purposes of preventing disease or detecting it at an asymptomatic stage.* This definition is, of course, very much influenced by a medical perspective. We might also wish to include behaviours that increase health in the sense that they may make us fitter, stronger or more attractive.

We act to promote health by getting enough sleep, eating a balanced diet, and we act to avoid ill health by not smoking or practising safe sex. We use seat belts and crash helmets and teach our children to cross roads safely. We take up offers of cervical screening and have our babies immunized. We also practise health habits that we are scarcely aware of, such as washing our hands, or brushing our teeth. We try to avoid exposure to pollutants such as cigarette smoke or additives in food, but of course we do not do all of these things all of the time!

So how do we make sense of the very obvious variation in health around us? Poor health may be seen as an unfortunate affliction and the sufferers are to be treated with compassion and sympathy. For some conditions such as leukaemia this may be easy, but if someone suffers from an alcohol-related disorder we may not see it in quite the same way. We may also see ill health as being related to a lifestyle that may have some level of individual control. There are many diseases related to smoking and yet we may regard smoking as an unhealthy habit that can be overcome. The attribution of illness is very complex and while encouraging people to lead a healthy lifestyle we may imply that if they follow the golden rules then they will remain healthy. If, as can happen, someone who doesn't smoke or drink alcohol and who is not overweight suffers an early heart attack he will seek some other explanation.

Other people that know him may feel that there is no point in living a healthy lifestyle if heart attacks can happen to anyone. This is a consequence of drawing implications for the individual from what are essentially statistical relationships based on large populations. By adopting healthy habits we are only reducing the statistical risks of ill health, we are not ensuring health and a long life.

2.3.2   Health Behaviour

All the illnesses in Figure 2.1 are influenced by lifestyle factors such as diet, alcohol intake, smoking and exercise. If we want to increase our chances of remaining healthy we may be able to adapt healthy behaviour into our life-style. This would mean having a balanced and low-fat diet, taking exercise, drinking in moderation and not smoking. Health professionals are frequently involved in helping people to change their lifestyle.

Backett (1990) carried out in-depth interviews with a sample of 28 healthy middle-class married couples with two children. They were well informed about basic health principles but were less sure about carrying them out. They were aware of what made up a healthy diet, but they did not always put their knowledge into practice because of pressures of time, finance, work or social obligations, or individual preferences. In this study many respondents saw 'scientifically based' knowledge as being incompatible with daily life, and rather moral in tone. If we are not sure that experts are certain about the relationship between health and healthy behaviour, we may be less likely to behave in a healthy way.

Healthy behaviour does not guarantee good health, and there are many reasons why people do not enjoy good health in spite of behaving in a healthy way. The physical health of an individual is influenced by biology, psychology and culture. When we attempt to change health behaviour we must also take into account the degree to which these other factors influence behaviour. We tend to practise some health habits but not others. We may think that if we do not smoke we can then allow ourselves to eat or drink more. Unfortunately this is not based on statistical logic, however tempting it may be. People are not consistent in their health habits. They make resolutions but fail to keep them, or they postpone attempts at giving up smoking or losing weight. Weight lost as a result of dieting is only too easy to regain. People give up smoking and then resume when they are under stress.

A number of reasons have been suggested for these changes in health habits (Taylor 1986):

*   Different health habits are controlled by different factors. Smoking may be related to stress, but exercising may be related to access to health facilities. Seat belts may only be worn because of legislation.

*   There are individual differences in factors controlling health habits. One

individual attempts to lose weight because of fashion trends, and another because of fear of a second heart attack.

- Controlling factors may change. Alcohol may be taken to overcome shyness initially but later becomes necessary for social interaction.

- Factors controlling health habits may change with age. Exercise may be part of a young person's school programme but in middle age the social context of exercising has changed.

Health behaviours or habits are not closely interrelated and so we can look more closely at why some people lead a lifestyle that is a mixture of good and bad health habits. Currie *et al.* (1991) interviewed a sub-sample of individuals living in a small Scottish town who had taken part in a postal survey. The most commonly reported behaviour change was towards positive dietary habits and the least was towards more exercise. On the basis of a model of health-related behavioural change, it was possible to identify predisposing factors such as occupation, concern about health, weight or ageing and triggers such as illness in family or friends (Figure 2.2).

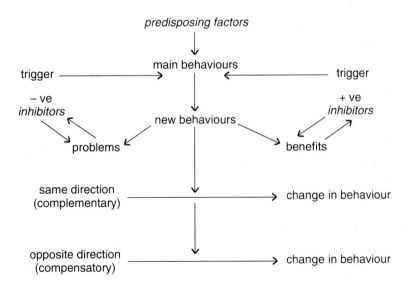

FIGURE 2.2   The process of health-related behavioural change (after Currie, Amos and Hunt 1991)

There are also barriers to change such as family obligations and demands, and feeling worse after the change. These have different influences on different behaviour patterns. Triggers to change diet habits were likely to be concerns about health, whereas illness in relatives would trigger changes in smoking habits. Similarly, barriers to weight control included family eating patterns and preferences, and barriers to smoking included cravings and the function of smoking activity. It would be unrealistic to persuade people to adopt a 'healthy lifestyle' and attempts to change health habits will need to be more specific. Behavioural programmes to reduce smoking, increase screening uptake or to change dietary habits can be very successful but they may carry an implication of victim blaming for those that do not change and become ill. As we have seen from the research on socio-economic status, health programmes need to take into account the social context of health change.

Activity 2.4

In your own discipline identify a health behaviour or habit that would maintain health
e.g. Podiatry students suggested that foot care was important for healthy feet. A healthy foot was defined as being asymptomatic, having perfect mobility, no pain or discomfort and with a good circulation. (They didn't comment on appearance!)

Smoking has many influences on health. In a cohort study of over 1000 mothers of five year olds it was found that mothers who smoked were less likely to take their children to health clinics. The more they smoked the stronger was the relationship. The effect of smoking was independent of poor housing, lack of support or social status (Butler and Golding 1986). This was one health behaviour (clinic attendance) related to another health behaviour (not smoking). Changing parental behaviour is seen as a practical way in which health professionals may be able to improve health, whereas social change on a grander scale may require a revolution. Health promotion has become a recognized professional discipline, drawing on many of the psychological principles outlined in this book.

2.3.3   Health Behaviour, Cancer and Heart Disease

It is often suggested that there is a link between cancer and psychological factors, but recent research has come up with conflicting findings. The development of cancer once it has been diagnosed has been associated with such psychological concepts as anal fixation or separation from parents. Cohen (1980) reviewed the literature and concluded that there were no consistent findings that supported a relationship between specific psychological factors and the causes of cancer. Cancer has its own stigma. It may be feared as carrying a fatal prognosis and dreaded because of association with unpleasant treatment and side effects. Cancer differs from many diseases in that it may not involve just one operation or a specific course of treatment. Not only may there be surgery and drugs but there is also the fear that the cancer might recur. Drug therapy may have unpleasant side effects and the patient may have to take a long time off work. There may be adverse effects on sexuality and anger at the prospect of premature death. It is not surprising that measures to preserve health and avoid cancer receive much attention. The psychological effects of having cancer will be considered in Chapter 3.

There can have been few more lively controversies than those surrounding the relationships between psychosocial and organic factors in cancer and cardio vascular disease. It has been suggested that some people have particular personality characteristics than make them more prone to cancer. Gossarth-Maticek *et al.* (1984) carried out a series of intervention studies that showed a beneficial effect of therapy. A sample of 1353 elderly Yugoslavian patients was assessed and monitored over ten years. Significant characteristics of those dying of cancer included "rational and anti-emotional behaviour" and a high level of "traumatic life events involving chronic helplessness". On the basis of the assumption that "the development of cancer was related to disturbances of interpersonal relationships" (Gossarth-Maticek *et al.* 1984, p 321) they undertook intervention studies. 'Creative notation therapy' was given in a controlled study to 98 patients with regional lymph metastases treated with radiotherapy, and the patients were followed up for 94 months. The mean survival time of those treated by Gossarth-Maticek was 9.39 months (s.d. 12.36) greater than the survival time of matched controls. This and other studies have been severely criticized by Pelosi and Appleby (1992). It is not clear what constitutes 'Creative notation therapy'; most of the therapy in the studies appears to have been given by Gossarth-Maticek himself; the definition of personality types is imprecise, and the methodology and analyses are unclear. The numbers in the studies are very high, and in one study (Gossarth-Maticek *et al.* 1984) a 100% follow up was claimed after ten years. Some of these points have been addressed by Eysenck (1992), but the link between cancer, coronary heart disease, personality and therapy remains unclear.

Highly stressed executives may be perceived as being at risk of heart attacks. Friedman and Rosenman (1974) described characteristics of those who were at risk of heart attacks. Type A are typically highly competitive: they are often in a hurry, being impatient with delays and trying to do several things at once, and they tend to be easily aroused to anger. Those he described as Type B did not show these characteristics. These are described in Chapter 7 and will be considered in the context of stress-related illness (Box 7.3).

Would psychological intervention to change Type A behaviour reduce the risk of coronary heart disease? Friedman *et al.* (1984) assessed a group of people who had suffered a previous heart attack and randomly assigned them to a rehabilitation programme that included either group therapy or the standard cardiac rehabilitation programme. By the end of the third year of follow up, the annual recurrence rate was 3% in the therapy group compared with 6.6% in the control group. Of course people who have had one heart attack will be highly motivated to change their behavior. It may be

harder to persuade healthy people to modify their behaviour by stress management if they are rewarded by society for Type A behaviour.

2.4   PERSONAL CONTROL MODELS

People differ in their views about their health. Some people see it as something over which they have a great deal of control and others may be content
to leave the control of their health in the hands of health professionals.
Personal control is made up of a person's beliefs about how well he or she
can bring about good events and avoid bad events. Personal control is both
a cause and a consequence of the way in which people respond to their
environment, and can be influenced by experience. (Box 2.3)

Box 2.3   Personal control

*A composite theory of personal control (after Peterson and Stunkard
1989)*

1. It is one of the most important ways in which people differ from one
   another
2. It is an interaction between the person and the environment
3. It is a belief about how one can interact with the world
4. It can be measured by self-report questionnaires
5. It is desirable encouraging intellectual, emotional, behavioural and
   psychological vigour in the face of challenge
6. It is prompted by novel and challenging events
7. It can be thwarted by failure and encouraged by success

People with a high level of personal control are more likely to have a
healthy lifestyle, more likely to seek and follow medical advice when ill, are
better at coping with life's crises, have more social support that buffers them
against illness and may have a more competent immune system (Peterson
and Stunkard 1989).

2.4.1   Locus of Control

The concept of locus of control suggests that people differ along measurable
dimensions. Rotter (1966) devised a scale that measured people along an
internal–external unipolar dimension. At the high end of the internal scale
people believe that they are responsible for their own destiny and can control it by their own behaviour. At the other end of the scale, people believe
that their lives are controlled by external events beyond their control, such
as the behaviour of others or fate. This scale was later revised by Levenson
(1981) who developed a multidimensional scale. In this the external locus of

control was divided into two concepts: a belief that eve
controlled by fate (chance locus of control) and a be
under the control of powerful others (powerful othe
Wallston *et al.* (1978) developed their original health l
(Wallston *et al.* 1976) into a multidimensional health l
which measured internal locus of control (IHLC), pov. ...
control (PHLC) and chance locus of control scale (CHLC) (Box 2.4),

These are separate theoretical and empirically differentiated dimensions, although they found a negative correlation between IHLC and CHLC. These measures have been described as personality traits and patients may be portrayed as either internals or externals (Kent and Dalgleish 1986, p 193). Although people probably do stay the same, the degree of internality can be changed by intervention programmes (Rafferty 1993, see Chapter 3), so it may be misleading to describe control as a kind of personality trait.

Box 2.4   Multiple health locus of control (Wallston *et al.* 1978)

Items are rated on a five-point scale

Examples of items measuring *Internal locus of control*
If I get sick, it is my own behaviour which determines how soon I get well again
I am in control of my own health
If I take care of myself, I can avoid illness

Examples of items measuring *Chance locus of control*
Most things that affect my health happen to me by accident
My good health is largely a matter of good fortune
Luck plays a big part in determining how soon I will recover from an illness

Examples of items measuring *Powerful others locus of control*
Having regular contact with my doctor is the best way for me to avoid illness
Whenever I don't feel well I should consult a medically trained professional
Whenever I recover from an illness, it is usually because other people (for example doctors, nurses, family, friends) have been taking good care of me

---

Some people may have a belief in control by chance and powerful others but have little belief in personal responsibility for their own health. In contrast, other people may be low in their belief that they can control their health but believe strongly that powerful others can affect their health. Wallston and Wallston (1981) consider that this represents the most adaptive of all combination of beliefs.

Activity 2.5

In a group, role play a person with a high level in one locus of control and low in the others. How difficult was it for the others in the group to recognize the high locus of control? Did it feel uncomfortable? What did this exercise tell you about your own locus of control?

2.4.2 Applications

A series of studies that have looked at the locus of control measure and health variables has had mixed results (Wallston and Wallston 1992). Control has been shown to be related to smoking reduction, but not to weight loss and probably does not account for very high levels of influence on actual behaviour. Patients who have high internal scores are more likely to seek information, whereas those who believe their health is due to chance are less likely to seek information (Wallston *et al.* 1978). It was originally thought that there was a generalized perception of control of health but then evidence began to suggest that people could have different perceptions about control over different aspects of health. People may believe that they have a high level of control over their weight but no control over disability from arthritis.

Attempts have been made to develop separate locus of control scales for specific disorders. Bradley *et al.* (1984) devised a scale of perceived control of diabetes and this has been used in a number of studies on diabetic management (Bradley *et al.* 1991). Georgiou and Bradley (1992) devised a smoking locus of control scale. They used three sets of items based on internal, powerful others and chance locus of control concepts, and added a fourth set of significant others. They did not find separate factors of internal and chance and produced a final version of eleven items of three dimensions: internal chance (ICLCS), powerful others (POLCS), and significant others (SOLCS). They found a number of interesting associations. Younger smokers were more likely to believe in control by powerful others. Those with high chance scores were more likely to expect that they would still be smoking in ten years' time. Those that had wanted to stop were more likely to have high scores for internal beliefs and significant others.

People with an internal locus of control believe that they can influence their health, but people with an external locus of control believe that it does not matter what they do, others or fate will decide. The degree of influence of the concept of locus of control has been questioned. Calman and Downie (1989) found few relationships between multidimensional health locus of control and exercise, smoking and alcohol use in a large community study. Eacchus (1990) found that the locus of control scores of physiotherapy students were little different from the general population, although they were somewhat more likely to believe in internal control. However, they also had lower scores in the powerful others scale. Those with more information are usually more likely to have an internal locus of control and so it is surprising that the internality scores were not higher. There were no changes in scores over the three years of a graduate course.

Health locus of control tells us more about illness than health and does not include dimensions such as fitness and activity which, as we shall see in Chapter 3, are part of the lay person's concept of health. If we assume that control influences exercise behaviour, then interventions could be directed at increasing perceptions of control as well as providing access and incentives to exercise. Of course it is possible that the very act of participating in exercise could make people feel more in control and they would therefore be more likely to rate themselves highly on an internal scale.

In a series of studies on elderly residents in nursing homes, control was found to be important. Schulz (1976) looked at the effect of visits by volunteers. The residents were divided into four groups:

- *Group A* were visited by volunteers and the residents chose when the visit would take place, how long it would last and the visits were expected.

- *Group B* did not choose when the visits would take place, or the duration but the visits were expected. The number and frequency of visits was matched with Group A.

- *Group C* had the same visits but they were not expected.

- *Group D* were not visited at all.

The residents were assessed before and after the experiment and it was found that Group A and B were no different from each other but they did better than Groups C and D. They had less medication and less variety of medicines; they were rated as being in better health by nurses who were blind to the allocation of groups, they were positive and had more zest for life, and they reported being more hopeful and useful, less lonely and less bored. Unfortunately the effects did not last after the visits by the student volunteers stopped, and 42 months later Groups A and B who had had control and then had lost it experienced more deterioration in their health compared with Groups C and D.

Langer and Rodin (1976) carried out a study on residents of nursing homes who were encouraged to take more control over their lives. The residents all had a speech from the director about changes that were going to take place. Group A were told that they could make changes such as rearranging their furniture, and deciding whether or not to attend a movie and each was given a plant if they wanted (all did), and told that they could take care of it. In Group B the residents were also told about the changes but the decisions were to be made by the nursing staff and the pot plant would be cared for by the nurses. The two groups were on different floors of the same nursing home and were similar in age, socio-economic status and health. Three weeks later, 93% of Group A had shown overall physical and mental improvement, whereas in Group B 71% had worsened. In a follow up 18 months later, Group A were more healthy, vigorous, sociable and self-initiating and mortality was lower (Rodin and Langer 1977).

The effects of pollution can act directly on health but they may also cause stress because they are perceived as being uncontrollable. Rotton *et al.* (1979) exposed subjects to an unpleasant smell coming from a bottle of liquid. One group was told that they could cork it if they wanted to, the other was told to leave it alone. They were then all given insoluble puzzles, providing a frustrating experience. Those who had been told that they could not stop the smell were less persistent in attempting the puzzles. Those that had been able to cork the bottle were no different from those who had not been exposed to any smell at all.

Activity 2.6

Predict the differences between professional groups, laymen, chronically ill, or unemployed on each of the scales of locus of control.

2.5   MODELS OF HEALTH BEHAVIOUR

Everybody has their own ideas about why they or other people are healthy. To be the possessor of good health is a source of pride, especially in old age. The reason why some people are more healthy than others is a combination of biological, social and psychological factors.

2.5.1   Health Belief Model (HBM)

Healthy behaviour undoubtedly contributes to health and the health belief model is probably the most important model that has been proposed to explain health behaviour.

Susceptibility

The health belief model suggests that whether or not someone practises health behaviour depends on whether they believe that they themselves are likely to be threatened (*susceptibility*). I may think that it is very unlikely that I will get malaria in the UK, but highly likely that I will get burnt in strong sun. I may consider myself vulnerable because I am fair-skinned. I will not use a mosquito net but I will use a sunscreen.

Severity

My behaviour will also depend on whether I believe that sunburn is serious and my beliefs about the risks of cancer (*severity*). I may have acquired

beliefs about the relationship between exposure to th
skin cancer from reading magazines. I will also be ir
about the consequences of skin cancer, and my own
tance of my health. Although I may perceive that m
because I do not think I am at risk, it does not affec

Benefits

I may also believe that a sunscreen will prevent sunburn, and that the benefits in reducing the risk outweigh the financial cost and inconvenience of
applying it (*benefits*). The inconvenience of using a mosquito net in Scotland
would outweigh any benefits of reducing the risk of being bitten by a ma-
laria-infected mosquito (even though it might protect against midges!). The
balance could change with the context. We have seen a dramatic increase in
the use of sunscreens as people (and the media) have become more aware
of health risks from ultra violet light (Borland *et al.* 1990). Context is also
important and the decision to use a sunscreen will depend on whether I am
in the North of Scotland or the South of France.

Cues to action

Action may only be taken if there is a cue or trigger. The health belief may
not be directly related to behaviour and there may be no change in behaviour unless there is a trigger or cue to action. If a family member dies of heart
disease or breast cancer, this might well make other members of the family
feel vulnerable. Other triggers might come from twinges of pain in their
chests or reddening of the skin (perception of internal cues). Media head-
lines may also increase awareness, and remind people of the dangers of

FIGURE 2.3   Health Belief Model
based on Becker and Rosenstock 1984

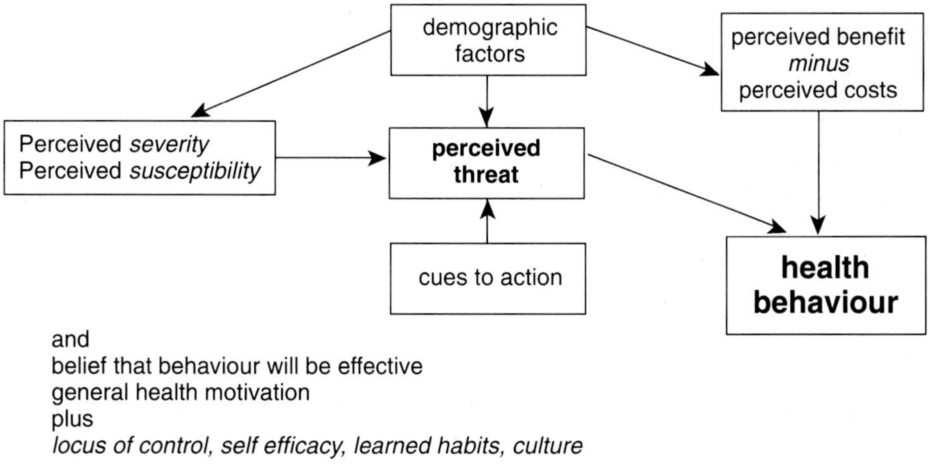

and
belief that behaviour will be effective
general health motivation
plus
locus of control, self efficacy, learned habits, culture

burn. Health professionals are likely to encounter those who already perceive themselves as vulnerable and they may be asked for more information about preventive effective health behaviour. A cue to action could be formalized by sending out a postal reminder to attend a clinic.

Further modification of the health belief model, (Becker *et al.* 1977) includes the motivation of people to practise health-related behaviour (Box 2.3). Early studies supported the health belief model, but other factors such as social circumstances may be more important. The model predicts medical preventive behaviours such as screening but has been widely extended to other health behaviours or habits. A meta analysis of studies of the health belief model with adults (Harrison *et al.* 1992) suggested that there is a relationship between the dimensions measured by the model, but that retrospective studies are more likely to find a significant effect. Some studies found a very strong relationship, e.g. on the use of child safety restraints in cars, but others none at all, e.g. weight loss.

Activity 2. 7

Give an example of a health behaviour. Then substitute sentences to fit the beliefs in the model as in Figure 2.3.

2.5.2. Model of Reasoned Action

Many of us have good intentions about healthy behaviour and it has been argued that we will only behave in such a way if we want to. If intentions do predict behaviour then we need to look at factors which influence intentions. Fishbein and Ajzen's model (Fishbein and Ajzen 1975) is based on a model of reasoned action (Figure 2.4). The intention to behave in a particular way is made up of attitudes towards the behaviour and subjective norms

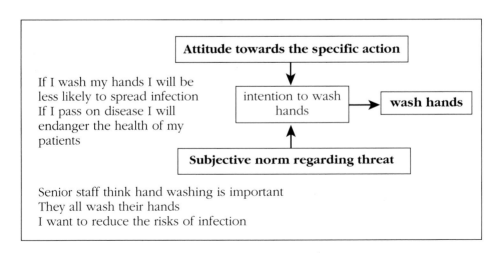

FIGURE 2.4   Model of reasoned action

about the appropriateness of the action. Attitudes are, i
of beliefs and values (Box 2.5).

Box 2.5 Attitudes

An attitude is an abstract concept and we can only
attitude by their words or behaviour. Attitudes consist of beliefs, value
and actions. If a person has a negative attitude towards diets he may
believe that they don't work. The belief may be based on first-hand
experience or from study of the dietetic literature. He may feel that diets
are useless and of little value. Finally, he may behave in a negative way
towards diets by ignoring them or abandoning them after a few days. In
attempting to change attitudes all these components must be addressed.
Attitudes can be measured by open-ended interviews or more usually
by attitude scales. These must be carefully designed but can be made
specific to any health issue (Henerson *et al.* 1987).

Subjective norms are made up of what one thinks that others think one
should do, particularly if they are significant others like family, colleagues or
health professionals. We also differ in the extent to which we are motivated
to do as others think we should. Adolescents may be deliberately eager to
do the opposite of what they think their parents want them to do.

The attitude and beliefs can be measured more easily in the model of
reasoned action than in the health belief model, but of course there are situational factors that influence the relationship between intention and practice.

2.6. HEALTH RELATED CONCEPTS

2.6.1 Hardiness

Not all individuals react by being ill when stressed. A factor that may help
people to resist stress is 'hardiness' (Kobasa *et al.* 1982; Kobasa *et al.* 1985).
Hardiness is made up of three characteristics:

- *Control* – belief that they can influence events

- *Commitment* – people's sense of purpose or involvement in events, activities and other people in their lives.

- *Challenge* – seeing changes as incentives or opportunities for growth
rather than threats to security

In a series of studies on business executives it was found that those who
were hardy had high levels of commitment to their work. They enjoyed
challenges and change rather than feeling threatened by them. They perceived that they had a high level of control over their lives and over the

nount of stress that they would encounter at any one time. They felt that they had chosen to be in stress-producing situations. In a prospective study of male business executives, Kobasa *et al.* (1985) found that hardiness, as well as exercise and social support, acted as a protective factor against illness. Hardiness may act as a buffer to resist illness if there are stressful events. This is known as 'the buffering effect' and can also come from social support (see Chapter 7).

2.6.2 Self Efficacy

The belief that we can succeed at something that we want to do is known as self efficacy (Bandura 1977). We decide whether or not to carry out a healthy behaviour by deciding whether it will achieve the desired effect and then whether we are capable of doing it. We might know that exercise will help us to be fit but we might not feel capable of doing it. Seligman *et al.* (1979) suggest that if someone prone to depression experiences uncontrollable failures he may attribute them to internal factors such as lack of ability. If they consistently attribute their ill health in this way they may experience learned helplessness. Seligman and his colleagues carried out a series of experiments on dogs who were placed in laboratory situations from which they could not escape. They were able to experimentally induce a state of learned helplessness and the dogs became apathetic and listless. Cognitive therapy seeks to challenge these negative attributions and has shown some success.

Self efficacy may underlie much of our health behaviour and is closely linked to the concept of self esteem. It may be a general concept that we hold about ourselves but it is more likely to be specific. Someone may believe that they are capable of reducing the fat in their diet, but not believe that they are capable of giving up smoking. Someone with high perceived self efficacy is more likely to persevere with activities such as exercise to restore limb function. They are less likely to worry about failure and of course people who think that they are going to succeed are more likely to do well.

In a study of a smoking control programme Condiotte and Lichenstein (1982) found that self efficacy predicted which smokers would relapse, how soon they would relapse, and in what situations relapse was likely to occur. If they started smoking again, those who were high in self efficacy were more likely to try again to give up than those who were low.

> **Activity 2.8**
> *Consider the problems in attending a specialized clinic in your own discipline for the following groups. How could they be improved?*
>
> - *Disabled people*
> - *Elderly people*

- *Single mothers*
- *Those with reading difficulties*
- *Those with hearing or visual difficulties*

2.7 SUMMARY

The use of models has influenced the direction of preventive health behaviour. Social factors may be very important but they may be difficult or impossible to change. Individual differences in perception of control may influence health behaviour and adherence to treatment regimes. Interventions can change behaviour and there seem to be few stable personality characteristics that influence health behaviour. Beliefs about health behaviour are also open to change but they may have a less direct effect on actual behaviour. The decision whether or not to engage in health behaviour may be based on a cost–benefit analysis, but one of the best predictors of health behaviour is previous health behaviour. This has led to much interest in health education of children, as evidenced by recent campaigns to reduce smoking and to promote safe sex in order to reduce the risks of HIV infection.

2.8 FURTHER READING

Abraham, C. and Shanley, E. (1992) *Social Psychology for Nurses*. London: Edward Arnold

An up-to-date and well referenced book. It deals with complex psychological concepts in social psychology and applies them to nursing, but it also has wider relevance to health care.

Carroll, D. (1992) *Health Psychology: Stress, Behaviour and Disease*. London: The Falmer Press

The social context of health and illness is explored and clearly applied. A number of research studies are summarized

Fiest, J. and Brannon, L. (1988) *Health Psychology*. Belmont California: Wadsworth

This American health psychology text is clear and very comprehensive. It deals with many of the topics in this book in greater depth.

Scambler, G. (1991) *Sociology Applied to Medicine,* 3rd edn. London: Bailliere Tindall

An easy to follow text on sociology applied to health issues.

2.9   REFERENCES

Alder, E.M., Cook, A., Davidson, D., West, C. and Bancroft, J. (1986) Hormones, mood and sexuality in lactating women. *British Journal of Psychiatry,* **148**, 74–79

Alder, E.M. (1992) The effects of hormone replacement therapy on psychological symptoms. In: *Reproductive Life.* edited by K. Wijma and B. Von Schoultz. Carnforth: Parthenon Publishing

Backett, K. (1990) Image and reality: health-enhancing behaviours in middle class families. *Health Education Journal,* **49**, 61–63

Bandura, A. (1977) Self efficacy: towards a unifying theory of behavioral change. *Psychological Review,* **84**, 191–215

Becker, H.M., Hawfner, D.P., Kasl, S., Kirscht, J.P., Maiman, L.A. and Rosenstock, I.M. (1977) Selected psychosocial models and correlates of individual health-related behaviors. *Medical Care,* **15**, (supplement) 27–46

Borland, R., Hill, D. and Moy, S. (1990) Being sun smart. *Behaviour Change,* **7**, 126–135

Bradley, C., Howe, P., Christie, M. (Eds) 1991 *The Technology of Diabetes Care: Converging Medical and Psychosocial Perspectives* Chur: Harwood Academic Publishers

Bradley, V., Brewin, C.R., Gamsu, D.S. and Moses, J.L. (1984) Development of scales to measure perceived control of diabetes mellitus and diabetes-related health beliefs. *Diabetic Medicine,* **1**, 213–218

Brown, G.W. and Harris, T. (1979) *The Social Origins of Depression.* London: Tavistock

Butler, N.R. and Golding, J.C. (1986) *From Birth to Five: a study of Britain's five-year olds.* Oxford: Pergamon Press

Calman, K.C. and Downie, R.S. (1988) Education and training in medicine. *Medical Education,* **22**, 488–491

Carstairs, V. and Morris, R. (1991) *Deprivation and Health in Scotland* Aberdeen: Aberdeen University Press

Cohen, S. (1980) After-effects of stress on human performance and social behavior: A review of research and theory. *Psychological Bulletin,* **88**, 82–108

Cohen, S. and Spacapan, S. (1978) The after-effects of stress: an attentional interpretation. *Environmental Psychology and Non Verbal Behaviour* **3**, 43–57

Condiotte, M.M. and Lichenstein, E. (1982) Self efficacy and relapse in smoking cessation programs. *Journal of Consulting and Clinical Psychology,*
  49, 648–658
Craig, T.K.J. and Brown, G.W. (1984) Life events, meaning and physical illness: a review. In: *Healthcare and Human Behaviour* edited by A. Steptoe
  and A. Mathews. London: Academic Press
Currie, C.E., Amos, A. and Hunt, S.M. (1991) The dynamics and processes
  of behavioural change in five classes of health-related behaviour.
  Findings from qualitative research. *Health Education Research,* **6**, 443–
  453
Davey-Smith, G., Bartley, M. and Blane, D. (1990) The Black report on socio-
  economic inequalities in health 10 years on. *British Medical Journal,*
  301, 373–7
Eacchus, P. (1990) Health locus of control in student physiotherapists. *Physi-
  otherapy,* 76, 366–370
Eysenck, H.J. (1992) Psychosocial factors, cancer and ischaemic heart dis-
  ease. *British Medical Journal,* **305**, 457–459
Fishbein, M. and Ajzen, I. (1975) *Belief, Attitude, Intentions and Behavior:
  An Introduction to Theory.* Reading, Massachussetts: Addison-Wesley
Friedman, M. and Rosenman, R.H. (1974) *Type A Behavior and Your Heart.*
  New York: Fawcett Books
Friedman, M., Thoresen, C.E., Gill J.J., *et al.* (1984) Alteration of Type A
  behavior and reduction in cardiac reoccurrence in post-myocardia
  infarction patients. *American Heart Journal,* **108**, 237–248
Frischer, M., Ford, G. and Taylor, R. (1991) Life events and psychological
  well-being in old age. *Psychology and Health,* **5**, 203–210
Fry, J., Hunt, J.H.J. and Pinsent, R.J.F.H. (1983) *A History of the Royal College
  of General Practitioners.* Lancaster: MTP Press
Georgiou, A. and Bradley, C. (1992) The development of a smoking-specific
  locus of control scale. *Psychology and Health,* **6**, 227–246
Gossarth-Maticek, R., Schmidt, P., Vetter, H. and Arndt, S. (1984) Psycho-
  therapy research in oncology, In: *Health Care and Human Behaviour,*
  edited by A. Steptoe and A. Mathews. London: Academic Press
Harrison, J.A., Mullen P.D. and Green, L.W. (1992) A meta-analysis of the
  health belief model with adults. *Health Education Research,* **7**, 107–116
Henerson, M.E., Morris, L.L., Fitz-Gibbon, C.T. (1987) *How to Measure Attitudes.* London: Sage
Holmes, T.H. and Rahe, R.H. (1967) The social readjustment rating scale.
  Journal of Psychosomatic Research, **11**, 213–218
Hunt, S. and McEwen, J. (1980) The development of a subjective health
  indicator. *Sociology of Health and Illness,* **2**, 231–246
Kanner, A.D., Coyne, J.C., Schaeffer, C. and Lazarus, R.S. (1981) Comparison
  of two modes of stress management. Daily hassles and uplifts versus
  major life events. *Journal of Behavioral Medicine,* **4**, 1–39

Kasl, S.A. and Cobb, S. (1966) Health behavior, illness behavior, and sick role behavior. *Archives of Environmental Health,* **12**, 246–266

Kent, G. and Dalgleish, M. (1986) *Psychology and Medical Care* London: Baillere Tindall

Kobasa, S.C., Maddi, S.R. and Kahn, S. (1982) Hardiness and health: A prospective study. *Journal of Personality and Social Psychology,* **42**, 168–177

Kobasa, S.C.O., Maddi, S.R., Puccetti, M.C., and Zola, M.A. (1985) Effectiveness of hardiness exercise and social support as resources against illness. *Journal of Psychosomatic Research,* **29**, 525–533

Langer, E.J. and Rodin, J. (1976) The effect of choice and enhanced responsibility for the aged: a field experiment in an institutional setting. *Journal of Personality and Social Psychology,* **34**, 191–198

Latane, B. and Darley, J.M. (1970) *The Unresponsive Bystander: Why Doesn't He Help?* New York: Appleton-Century-Crofts

Latane, B. and Rodin, J. (1969) A lady in distress: inhibiting effects of friends and strangers on bystander intervention. *Journal of Experimental and Social Psychology,* **5**, 189–202

Levenson, H. (1981) Differentiating among internality, powerful others and chance. In: *Research With the Locus of Control Construct,* vol. 1, edited by H.M. Lefcourt. New York: Academic Press

McCormick, A., Rosenbaum, M., and Fleming, D. (1990) Socio-economic characteristics of people who consult their general practitioners. *Population Trends,* **59**, 8–10

McKenna, S.P. and Payne, R.L. (1989) Comparison of the General Health Questionnaire and the Nottingham Health Profile in unemployed and re-employed men. *Family Practice,* **6**, 3–8

Murphy, E. and Brown, G.W. (1980) Life events, psychiatric disturbance, and physical illness. *British Journal of Psychiatry,* **136**, 326–338

Niven, C.A. and Carroll, D. (Eds) (1993) *The Health Psychology of Women.* Chur: Harwood Academic Publishers

Pelosi, A.J. and Appleby, L. (1992) Psychological influences on cancer and ischaemic heart disease. *British Medical Journal,* **304**, 1295–1298

Peterson, C. and Stunkard, A.J. (1989) Personal control and health promotion. *Social Science Medicine,* **28**, 819–828

Rafferty, P. (1993) *Recovery Following Gynaecological Surgery. An Evaluation of Pre-Operative Intervention by Physiotherapists.* PhD Thesis, Open University, Queen Margaret College, Edinburgh

Rodin, J. and Langer, E.J. (1977) Long-term effects of a control-relevant intervention with the institutionalized aged. *Journal of Personality and Social Psychology,* **35**, 897–902

Rosenstock, I.M. (1974) The health belief model and preventive health behavior. *Health Education Monographs,* **2**, 354–386

Rotton, J., Yoshikawa, J. and Kaplan, F. (1979) Perceived control, malodorous air pollution and behavioral after-effects. South-eastern Psychological Association, New Orleans, USA, quoted in: Fiest, J. and Brannon, L. (1988) *Health Psychology*. p. 229. Belmont CA: Wadsworth Publishing Company

Rotter, J.B. (1966) Generalized expectancies for internal versus external control of reinforcement. *Psychological Monographs, 80*, (Whole part 609)

Schulz, R. (1976) Effects of control and predictability on the physical and psychological well-being of the institutionalized aged. *Journal of Personality and Social Psychology, 33*, 563–573

Seligman, M.E.P., Abrahamson, L.Y., Semmel, A. and von Baeyer, C. (1979) Depressive attribution style. *Journal of Abnormal Psychology, 88*, 242–247

Smyke, P. (1991) *Women and Health*. London: Zed Books

Social Trends 24 (1994) London: HMSO

Social Trends 22 (1992) London: HMSO

Taylor, S. (1986) *Health Psychology*. New York: Random House

Taylor, S.E. (1983) Adjustment to threatening events: a theory of cognitive adaptation. *American Psychologist, 38*, 1161–1173

Townsend, P. and Davidson, N. (1982) *The Black Report* In: *Inequalities of Health*, edited by P. Townsend, N. Davidson, M. Whitehead. (1988) Harmondsworth: Penguin

Victor, C.R. (1992) Health status of the temporarily homeless population and residents of North West Thames region. *British Medical Journal, 305*, 387–391

Wallston, B.S., Wallston, K.A., Kaplan, G.D. Maides, S.A. (1976) Development and validation of the Health Locus of Control (HLC) scale. *Journal of Consulting and Clinical Psychology, 44*, 580–585

Wallston, K.A., Wallston, B.S. Devellis, R. (1978) Development of the Multidimensional Health Locus of control (MHLC) Scales. *Health Education Monographs, 6*, 160–170

Wallston, K.A. and Wallston, B.S. (1981) Health locus of control scales. *Research with the Locus of Control Construct*, vol. 1, edited by H.M. Lefcourt New York: Academic Press

Wallston, K.A. and Wallston, B.S. (1992) Who is responsible for your health? The construct of health locus of control. In: *Social Psychology of Health and Illness* edited by G.S. Sanders, and J. Suls. Hillsdale, NJ: Erlbaum

Wan, T.T.H. (1982) *Stressful Life Events, Social Support Networks and Gerontological Health*. Massachusetts: Lexington Books

Whitehead, M. (1988) The health divide In *Inequalities of Health* edited by P. Townsend, N.Davidson, M. Whitehead, (1988) Harmondsworth: Penguin

Wilkinson, R.G. (1992) Income distribution and life expectancy. *British Medical Journal, 304*, 165–168

3

Improving the Outcome of Treatment

CONTENTS

3.1   INTRODUCTION

As we have seen, illness can be regarded as the absence of health, but it is as hard to define 'being ill', as it is to make a definition of 'being healthy'. How do we know when someone is ill? How do we know when we ourselves are ill? How do we know that we are feeling better? How can we encourage someone to get better?

The health professional may have to decide whether someone is ill enough to need further treatment or specialist consultation. They may contribute to discussions about when someone should be discharged from hospital. It may be assumed that people go home when they are 'better'. What does 'well enough to go home' mean? It may be relatively easy for occupational therapists to assess the home environment, but less easy to assess the emotional state of the patient or the extent to which they believe themselves to be well. Health professionals may be in the first line of medical care and may see people in their own homes before any illness behaviour has occurred, or after the illness is considered to be over. They may have to decide whether someone should return for further check ups or proceed with a programme of further rehabilitation.

3.1.1   Illness Behaviour

Kasl and Cobb (1966) described *illness behaviour* as being *when the individual feels ill and behaves in particular way.* Illness is a psychological concept and has different meanings for different people. It is difficult to decide objectively whether someone is ill or not. In psychiatry the concept of *caseness* suggests that illness can be defined on the basis of a total score of symptoms, and there are many methods of establishing diagnostic criteria. These have given rise to a number of widely used screening scales for psychiatric disorders (e.g. the Hospital Anxiety and Depression scale, Zigmond and Snaith 1983; the Edinburgh Postnatal Depression Scale, Cox *et al.* 1987). These are often used by health professionals. Yet from our discussion of health and illness we have seen that illness is a relative concept, and is often functionally based.

Illness is recognized because of the presence of symptoms. Some people hate to admit that they are ill, whereas others notice every symptom. If we experience unusual symptoms, which are severe enough and last for long enough, we may feel that we are ill and then behave in certain ways – like complaining.

In a fascinating series of experiments, Pennebaker and colleagues showed that our awareness of symptoms depends on what else is going on around us (Pennebaker 1982). The perception of symptoms depends on what we expect. In one experiment subjects were told either that ultrasonic noise might cause an increase in skin temperature, or that it might cause a decrease (Pennebaker and Skelton 1981). They were then told that they were to listen to a tape of ultrasonic noise, although in fact it was blank. Actual skin temperature did not change, but fluctuations in temperature were reported as being cooler or warmer according to whether they had been told that skin temperature might decrease or increase.

We are also generally not very good at reporting physiological states such as heart rate but some people are more accurate than others. Attempts to describe symptom reporters in terms of personality (Chapter 4, Box 4.7) suggest that there may be *stable dispositions* as well as *situational changes*. This means that there may be some characteristics of a person that are part of them and do not change with time, but others that depend more on the situation that they are in. We don't necessarily report all our symptoms and certainly choose to whom we report them. Mechanic (1978) suggested a number of factors that influence symptom reporting:

1. The number and persistence of symptoms

The perception of symptoms may bear little relation to the medical opinion of severity.

Women's estimates of menstrual blood loss are unreliable when compared with objective measures of haemoglobin. The reported blood loss may be the main symptom used for deciding whether the woman should have a hysterectomy for dysfunctional bleeding. If objective measures are taken and they do not agree with the reported loss, she may be dismissed as not having a gynaecological problem. Although the haemoglobin content of blood in sanitary towels or tampons is a convenient and reliable measure of blood loss, it may not be the same as the volume of fluid loss. The woman may be more aware of the fluid loss and certainly more concerned about it. The amount of fluid that needs to be collected in tampons and towels is a salient symptom to the woman, but the loss of haemoglobin is salient to the gynaecologist (Granleese 1989).

2. The extent of the social and physical disability resulting from the symptoms

A headache may or may not interfere with social activities. Nausea in pregnancy may not affect everyday life unless it reaches a certain threshold. Hot flushes and night sweats in menopausal women may be perceived as normal, yet in some cases they cause severe social distress.

3. The recognition and identification of the symptom

This will depend on the cognitive schemata that the patient has of the symptom. This means that we can only report a symptom if we have some name for it (see Chapter 4). The more we know, the more our awareness increases. Health professionals themselves may be very aware of physical symptoms and this may contribute to professional stress (see Chapter 7).

4. The perceived severity of the symptoms

These may be related to a threshold or to a change. A sudden increase in urinary frequency, or an increase in frequency of headaches may be seen as a symptom. Of course, illness behaviour also depends on the nature of the symptoms. Diarrhoea is an obvious example. In adults it is unlikely to be fatal but it causes great inconvenience. People want immediate relief, and although clinical investigations may identify the cause, by the time the results are known the patient has usually recovered.

Having recognized that they have symptoms what do people do?

As we saw in Chapter 2 there are cultural and demographic influences on health and these also affect illness behaviour. Cultural influences are very important and the transcultural study of health is rapidly developing (Jansen and Weinman 1992). The contrast between cultures is clearly demonstrated by comparing Chinese traditional medicine with Western medicine. Chinese traditional medicine is based on the forces of Yin and Yan and the interaction of the five elements (metal, wood, water, fire and earth). This contrasts with Western medicine that looks for causes and gives appropriate symptomatic treatment (Cheung 1992). In Chinese traditional medicine, help with psychological problems would be sought from family or friends unless the symptoms were thought to derive from a physical illness in which case they would go to a medical physician.

In both America and Great Britain there are many ethnic minorities and their cultural definitions of illness need to be understood. Differences in morbidity may reflect differences in illness behaviour. Zborowski (1952) showed that illness behaviour differed between Americans of Italian descent and those of Irish descent. Italians reported more symptoms and more pain than the more stoical Irish or English and these cultural differences have been supported by more recent research (Friedman and DiMatteo 1989, pp 47–49).

There are other sociological and demographic factors that influence illness behaviour. Although more illness is found in community surveys in lower socio-economic groups, people in higher socio-economic groups are more likely to seek health care. Older people consult their doctors less than younger people in relation to their level of illness (Cartwright 1990).

Even though treatment may be free under the NHS there will be costs of travel, taking time off work and the implications of further investigations or treatment. Lower income groups may also have less information about health care provision, although we should not underestimate the role of informal networks. In an early study of women who had had elective sterilization operations, I was struck by the number of women who had worked in hospitals (from cleaners to consultants). They knew first hand that sterilization was a quick and safe operation and could be carried out for contraception purposes (Alder *et al.* 1981, Alder 1993).

Sometimes people may discover that they are ill even though they have no symptoms. Fibroids may be discovered from a pelvic examination and though they give no immediate problems, hysterectomy may be suggested. Some symptoms may not be apparent to the patient. In some psychiatric disorders the person may not be aware that their behaviour is abnormal and may perceive it as rational.

Activity 3.1

List some physical problems that may be discovered by medical tests but give no immediate symptoms, although they could be problematic in the future.
Discuss whether the patient is 'ill' or not.

Activity 3.2

Work together with another student or a colleague. Each of you should try to describe a behaviour pattern that would be considered abnormal under any circumstances. Your partner should try and think of a rational explanation for the behaviour that you have described.

3.2   SELF MEDICATION

In an Australian study, a panel of six general practitioners evaluated the actions taken by 360 people who had had a minor symptom or condition in the previous two weeks. The actions included using left-over prescription medicines, home remedies and over-the-counter medicines (Wilkinson *et al.* 1987). Most people keep some medicine in the home.

Activity 3.3

Look in your medicine cupboard at home. What medicines or over the counter preparations do you have? How old are they? Why have you kept them?

Elderly people were found to be twice as likely to treat a minor illness with an over-the-counter medication than to do any thing else (Coons *et al.* 1988). Because drugs are available without prescription they may be thought to be harmless. Poly pharmacy among elderly people is very common: non-prescribed drugs may be taken in combination with over-the-counter preparations and the combination may change their effectiveness. The practice of taking of over-the-counter medicines may begin in early adulthood. Headaches are common in all age groups and in a study of adolescents it was found that most of them had used medication to cope with headaches (King and Sharpley 1990).

Self medication is extremely common and it has been suggested that those who take non-prescribed medicine may be less likely to consult doctors. Kleinman (1985) suggests that there are two kinds of medicine in addition to traditional, institutional medicine. There is *popular medicine* that includes self care, self medication and self help groups. When we buy aspirin and cough medicine or follow health advice in a magazine we are operating outside institutional medicine. *Folk medicine* includes alternative medicine and includes acupuncture and homeopathy. It is not clear whether the increase in folk medicine has arisen from dissatisfaction with traditional medicine, from inadequate provision of health services, or from a desire for autonomy.

Activity 3.4

When did you last take non-prescribed medicine? Would you count vitamin pills as medicine? Did you think of yourself as ill when you last bought a medicine over the counter at a supermarket or chemist? Look at the discussion on illness behaviour at the beginning of this chapter.

3.3 THE SICK ROLE

The concept of the *sick role* is closely related to illness behaviour. Kasl and Cobb (1966) define the *sick role* as *an activity undertaken for the purpose of getting well by those who consider themselves ill.* Talcott Parsons (1951) suggested that a patient who has entered the sick role has both rights and obligations. The person is no longer expected to take on social responsibilities like going to work, shopping or even attending lectures and sitting exams. They are not expected to will themselves better by effort, and illness is not considered to be their fault (we view self-inflicted illness very differently). Sick people are expected to want to get better and to seek medical help if needed. Someone who is 'really ill', by definition, needs medical attention. There are also obligations for the person who has entered the sick role. The symptoms must accord with a medical diagnosis to be recognized by society. There is much sociological debate about the concepts of diseases such as alcoholism or dyslexia.

There must be overt symptoms before the illness will be recognized by others. It is interesting that when these are not visible, as in back pain, the sufferer must present signs such as groaning or an awkward gait to justify its reality. Similarly menstrual problems may not be accepted as real because social taboos prevent them being openly discussed. Finally, the sick role must be accepted by the individual, and the sick person is expected to take steps to get well.

Not everyone is willing to 'act sick' and some people may conceal their symptoms to avoid becoming dependent. In some conditions this is seen as desirable. A diabetic patient who is determined to lead a normal life will receive social approval but a flu sufferer who staggers around the office will encounter disapproval. Another obligation suggested by Lazarus (1984) (quoted in Fiest and Brannon 1988, p 86), is that sick people should remain optimistic and cheerful. An obituary may refer to a long illness bravely borne and sick people are not expected to display distress. Most people believe that being ill is temporary and in most cases this is true. Chronic diseases bring about different responsibilities and the person cannot stay in the sick role for ever. Most of us have symptoms of one sort or another at any one time, but whether or not we enter the sick role may be only loosely related to the severity and persistence of symptoms.

3.4   HOSPITALIZATION

In the 1940's hospitals were thought of as somewhere where people died. A mark of the severity of illness was that one had to 'go to hospital'. Today many healthy people go to hospital, and nearly all first births in the UK take place in maternity hospitals. This means that about 90% of women will experience a stay in hospital. Many tests and investigations take place in outpatient clinics and routine day care operations are becoming more common. Many people go to hospitals for check ups to ensure that they remain healthy and many rehabilitation programmes and health education programmes are run from hospitals. A hospital is a microcosm of human society and employs many people not directly concerned with patient care. Entering a hospital in the UK today may seem like entering a shopping centre. The National Health Service (NHS) is a major employer in the UK, employing millions of people. Probably all NHS staff would agree that their goal was to treat patients' illness but they also care for patients' welfare. The relative value of these two goals may cause conflicts between professions. Hierarchies and professional boundaries are very important in hospitals and may to some extent be necessary to maintain an efficient system.

Abraham and Shanley (1992) discuss the ways in which social rules operate within a hospital. *Social rules* are shared rules or expectations that shape our behaviour towards others in social situations. There are also *special rules* that apply in games and they may be debated and agreed at international levels, and they may even extend to non-participants such as football fans.

The rules that apply in institutions may be informal or formal. *Informal social rules* are often broken, e.g. keeping someone waiting. In this case we are expected to apologize and give a reason. *Formal social rules* may be imposed by others such as car parking, use of specific lavatories, or wearing a particular uniform. If these are broken there may be punishment. The social rules in relationships may be defined by social rôles. In the rôle of a physiotherapist you can invade personal space and inflict pain, which would not be acceptable in your rôle as a commuter on a train. We can often be confused when rôles are changed. A male patient in pyjamas and dressing gown was met walking down a gynaecological ward. He turned out to be an eminent medical professor who was an in-patient in the neighbouring ward and wanted to visit a colleague.

Activity 3.5

Identify some rules of your own professional group. Now select another professional group and do the same. Are the rules identical? If not, where might conflict arise?

3.4.1. Being a Hospital Patient

Even a healthy person visiting a hospital for a routine test may find it stressful. If a person is admitted for a day or overnight stay, then they enter the rôle of a *hospital patient*. This is not the same as the sick rôle because it is partly defined by the expectations of the hospital. Goffman (1961) suggested that the person becomes invisible, leaving only the illness visible. This gives a rather spooky image of disembodied wounds or diseased spleens floating round the ward. Health professionals and doctors may talk to each other about 'the ulcer in the second bed'. The patient becomes a non-person and the treatment may be discussed at the bedside as if they were not present. In practice patients are not expected to be completely inanimate. They must answer when spoken to and comply with requests to cough or move their position. Once in hospital the patient perceives their rôle as pleasing the doctors and nurses by being co-operative. The 'good' patient does not ask questions; he obeys instructions, makes no demands and never complains. They get better quickly and have no complications. However being a good patient is not necessarily good for your health. Good patients are appreciated by staff, but Taylor (1986) points out that good patients may not ask for information that may help their recovery, and may not report symptoms that could be clinically relevant. Taylor (1979) suggests that the hospital environment may actually encourage patients to become helpless. The more that patients feel they cannot control the environment around them the more helpless they will feel; this is called learned helplessness. The longer a patient is in hospital the worse they do on cognitive tasks that are related to learned helplessness, Box 3.1 (Raps *et al.* 1982).

The 'bad' patient asks questions, demands attention and complains. 'Bad' patients may not be seriously ill and still complain, in which case they are seen as 'difficult' patients. The patient may be feeling angry and this is unexpected when they are perceived by staff to be surrounded by high quality medical care and attentive nursing.

Box 3.1   Learned helplessness

Seligman and co-workers (Seligman 1975) studied the effect of perceived control in a series of classic experiments on dogs. In one experiment (Seligman and Maier 1967), the dogs were divided into three groups that were given different conditioning experiences.

One group was constrained and then given a tone followed by an electric shock which they could turn off. The second group were yoked to the first group so that they experienced the same amount of shock but they were unable to turn it off. The third group were constrained but had no shocks. The groups were then placed in a shuttle box. In this there were two compartments separated by a low barrier. In one side there was an electric grid that could deliver a mild shock. The shock could be avoided by jumping over the barrier into the next compartment. This escape avoidance task presented no problems to the dogs that had been able to switch off the electric shock in the prior conditioning or to the dogs that had had no shock. The dogs that had previously been unable to escape the shock did not attempt to avoid the shock by jumping over the barrier after the tone. Seligman (1975) explained this in terms of learned helplessness (the inability to control one's environment).

The model of learned helplessness was extended to explain apathy and depression in people. People become depressed because they believe that nothing that they do will help. If they have an *internal locus of control* they are more likely to become depressed if they fail because they attribute failure to internal causes. If they have had a *history of failure* they may expect to fail and not take any action to avoid failure. If they *generalize* from the specific experience they are more likely to be depressed because they think that they are ineffective in general.

Anger many arise because of anxiety. The patient may also resent the loss of freedom. He may be forbidden to get out of bed, visits are restricted, and eating and sleeping must take place at set times. Being seen naked may further disturb the patient, and bedpans are hard to use with dignity. There is a loss of privacy and the lack of opportunity for private conversations. These rules are set by others and so the patient experiences a loss of control.

The patient may assert his sense of control and independence by breaking the rules. Taylor (1979) describes this as *reactance*. The feelings of anger may be accompanied by a physiological reaction which may make some conditions such as hypertension worse. Being a bad patient could be good for health. If more questions are asked, more information will be given, and if symptoms are reported they may help diagnosis.

Activity 3.6

From your clinical experience or from your reading, describe a 'difficult patient'. Now identify the issues and consider to what extent the behaviour can be explained by feelings of loss of control.

Although health professionals themselves cannot easily change the hospital system and may themselves feel helpless, this picture of the hospital environment should be contrasted with the hospice movement.

A hospice was originally a place to provide comfort and care for travellers. A hospice aims to give personal care to terminally ill patients and to improve the comfort and quality of life (Saunders *et al.* 1981). Medical care is custodial and palliative, and the hospice attempts to provide an informal, home-like atmosphere. There is very little invasive therapy and care is aimed at reducing pain and discomfort. Psychological support is given by staff, clergy and counsellors. Visiting is encouraged and families may spend whole days with the patient, eating with them and being involved with their care. Some hospices also provide day care or short-term respite care. The emphasis on holistic care in which psychological, physical and spiritual needs of patients are all considered has meant that many of the ideas once only found in hospices are spreading throughout health care. Ross (1994) found that nurses were able to identify patients' spiritual needs, but many found it difficult to respond to them.

3.4.2 Control

There are some ways in which control could be given to the patient and they may prevent the extremes of 'good' or 'bad' patient behaviour.

Privacy

This will be determined to some extent by the architecture of the hospital or clinic. Maybe architects should spend some time as hospital patients in order to appreciate fully the hospital patient role. Large Nightingale wards may be easier to run with limited staff, but in a single-bedded ward patients have more control over their own activities. Most people are sociable when they are not seriously ill and a ward can be friendly place. The patients may form lasting friendships and return to visit remaining patients and staff after discharge. In large wards patients often compare symptoms and feel less isolated.

The ward environment

The hospital environment has other aspects that make staying in hospital stressful. Noises such as moaning or crying can be disturbing and prolonged snoring can be irritating and fatiguing. Gurgles and cutting noises behind curtains present alarming images, and laughter in the sluice room remind patients of the loss of the outside world. Hospital smells may become familiar to the staff but may have associations for the patients. While cigarette smoke or stale urine may be unpleasant, even strong disinfectant can create an unfamiliar atmosphere. Health professionals have an important part to play in the recognition of these problems and attempts to reduce them.

The professional role

The social role of the health professional also carries expectations of behaviour and sustained social identity. A nurse will have a different social identity and rôle from a doctor and different again from a dietician. Each social rôle has rôle-related rights such as being allowed to inflict pain, to ask intimate questions, or to constrain movement. Each rôle also has obligations to be respectful, to be caring and to preserve confidentiality. Uniforms help to maintain rôle relationships and to give signals to others about their behaviour. Uniforms can also be a barrier and some professional groups choose not to wear them.

Activity 3.7

Consider a professional group that does not have a traditional uniform, e.g. speech therapist, dieticians. Would it make any difference to their therapy if they wore uniforms? See also Chapter 4 on therapeutic relationships.

3.4.3   Stereotypes

Kelly and May (1982) reviewed studies of 'good' and 'bad' patients and found that it was not the type of patient or the personality that mattered. Particular kinds of illnesses and behaviour were viewed negatively. Patients who were incontinent or who had long-term illnesses, and those who were uncompliant or uncooperative were viewed negatively. The 'bad patients' are difficult to care for, and may be unrewarding. This is not to imply a judgement but to recognize that not all people behave in the same way when they are sick. A cognitive coping approach regards difficult patients as a challenge. Health professionals may expect people who are ill to be friendly, cooperative and appreciative. These expectations may come from the professionals' own needs to be appreciated. That said, we all need to be rewarded by positive feedback in order to maintain our motivation. If health professionals are consistently warm, cheerful and competent it is only too easy to think that they do not need reassurance and positive feedback. If these needs are not met, then professional stress may follow (see Chapter 7).

Activity 3.8

Discuss your experience of men and women as patients. Have you observed differences? To what extent does this relate to the reason for treatment. Do you think there are sexist stereotypes in health care?

3.5   PREPARATION FOR SURGERY

There have been many studies that have shown that patients are highly anxious before operations. Johnston (1980) found very high scores on a standard anxiety measure (The state trait anxiety inventory, STAI; Spielberger *et al.* 1970). She suggested that going into hospital itself was worrying as well as the operation itself. Day surgery can be worrying but may cause less anxiety than being admitted as an in-patient. Jennings and Sherman (1987) assessed over 300 patients admitted for a variety of surgical procedures. There was no significant rise in STAI scores from the initial pre-operative evaluation and the scores just before surgery. Women may be more anxious than men and this may be because they are more likely to admit to negative feelings. They may be worried about how their husbands and children will cope without them at home. Johnston (1987) found that gynaecological patients were mostly worried about whether the operation would be successful, how long it would take to get back to normal and how they would feel after the operation. 'Worrying' as measured from a list of 25 possible worries was closely related to the scores on the STAI (Speilberger *et al.* 1970).

Initially post-operative care takes place in hospital and nurses play a central role. As the patients recover, they increasingly become the focus of care by other health professionals. After surgery most patients will be visited by a physiotherapist and rehabilitation exercises are an important part of care. Patients recover at different rates and there are also individual differences in psychological state after surgery. Although clinical experience may identify a post-hysterectomy syndrome that is characterized by depression (Richards 1974), prospective studies have not found an increase in psychological disorder following hysterectomy operations (Gath and Cooper 1981). The high incidence of cases *after* hysterectomy can be mostly explained by the high incidence of psychiatric disorders *before* surgery (Ryan *et al.* 1989).

This means that although it may appear that after surgery patients are depressed and anxious, it is not necessarily the operation that caused the depression or anxiety. Indeed, Gath and Cooper (1981) found that many women who were psychiatric 'cases' before the hysterectomy operations were no longer cases after surgery. In the post-operative ward, patients may continue to be anxious as they cope with the experience of hospital itself, pain, loss of independence and the anticipation of convalescence. Johnston (1980) found that anxiety did not reduce significantly until six days after the operation. Ryan *et al.* (1989) found that mood (although measured by a psychiatric diagnostic interview) had improved over a year later. Reassurance about progress of recovery and 'return to normal' may be crucial.

Even healthy patients recover at different rates after identical surgery and attempts have been made to investigate the reasons and to increase the recovery rate by preparation beforehand. If we expect a change we may find that it occurs. This may the basis for the 'placebo effect' (Box 3.2). The effectiveness of a therapy may depend on the expectations of the patient. If a patient believes that the therapy will be effective then they may stop worrying and stop paying attention to the symptom. This may explain the placebo effect on pain. It follows that anxiety reduction could act as a placebo and this should be regarded as something to be encouraged. It is often the health professional who provides emotional reassurance and this may be an important part of the treatment.

Box 3.2   The Placebo effect

A placebo is any type of therapy (often a pill) which is deliberately used for its psychological effect. Placebos are used in double blind clinical trials of drug therapy where an active drug is compared with an inert substance. Placebos can also be in the form of saline injections or even mock operations. The placebo effect of technology can be demonstrated by not switching the apparatus on.

It is estimated that about a third of patients in severe clinical pain will respond to a placebo with the degree of relief normally associated with 10 mg of morphine. (Beecher 1955). The placebo effect can also be negative, and a patient given an inert substance may report side effects.

Any therapy can have a placebo effect that is non-specific, and just knowing that therapy is being given can be beneficial.

One of the most frequently performed operations is actually carried out on healthy young women. Elective sterilization for contraceptive purposes is now the most popular form of contraception for women over 35. In November 1990 it was estimated that, worldwide, 138 million women were protected from unwanted pregnancy by voluntary female sterilization, representing about 16% of all married women of reproductive age (Population reports 1990). In developed countries it is particularly popular. The number of women relying on sterilization to prevent pregnancy in the USA rose from 17% in 1982 to 23% in 1988. Laparoscopic sterilization became widely used in the 1970s. It became popular because it was a simple and effective surgical procedure, involved one post-operative check, no provision of supplies, few side-effects and had a low failure rate. From the woman's point of view the operation can be done on a day care basis, leaves only two small scars and is safe. However, sterilization operations are effectively irreversible and it is very difficult to repair fallopian tubes successfully. Even so, follow-up studies of women after sterilization have generally reported favourable results. In a retrospective study of over 500 patients, only 2% complained about physical problems (Lawson *et al.* 1979). Women who had previously taken the oral contraceptive pill may have more menstrual problems once they return to normal menstrual cycles. Alder *et al.* (1981) found that women who had been sterilized reported more menstrual changes, both positive and negative, compared with the wives of vasectomized men.

3.6   PREPARATION FOR CHILDBIRTH

It is arguable that childbirth is neither stressful nor a medical procedure and women are certainly not ill when giving birth. In the UK most deliveries take place in hospital under medical supervision.

Preparation for childbirth has been offered to women since the pioneering relaxation classes of Grantley Dick-Read in the 1930's (Dick-Read 1942) which aimed for 'childbirth without fear'. There have been relatively few evaluations of antenatal programmes, but some studies have looked specifically at the effect of antenatal preparation on pain and analgesic use. One difficulty in interpreting the results of preparation classes that tend to show very positive effects, is that mothers attending antenatal classes tend to be older and to be from higher social classes. However, one study randomly allocated mothers to classes and found that class attenders were more likely to have a normal vaginal delivery than non-class attenders. It seems that information given in preparation for childbirth is less effective in reducing anxiety than information given to prepare surgical patients. This may be because the emotional and experiential aspects of giving birth are particularly important and it is difficult to prepare for this. Of course if they are positive experiences, then it does not matter, but a negative reaction to delivery can be very distressing and many mothers complain that they were ill prepared for the emotional impact. In a study of 132 mothers, ratings of self efficacy were found to be related to ratings of labour as a positive experience (Byrne-Lynch 1990).

3.7   STRESSFUL MEDICAL PROCEDURES

3.7.1   Minor Procedures

In small hospitals, outpatient clinics, general practitioners' surgeries and podiatry clinics many people undergo minor, but potentially stressful, medical procedures. The procedures could have different functions. Removing corns in a podiatry clinic or reducing the frequency of a stutter *improves health*; a cervical smear *prevents ill health*; having an X ray *diagnoses* the state of health. Some procedures may only be loosely defined as concerning illness. Artificial insemination using donor semen might be carried out in a gynaecological out-patient clinic and routine antenatal care takes place at the hospital or general practice antenatal clinics. Yet in both cases the patient is healthy. It is difficult to separate the stress of the actual procedures from the worry about the outcome of the procedure and its long-term consequences. A diagnostic procedure such as a laparoscopy or a mammogram may be the cause of anxiety because of the fear of what might be found. The fear of the consequences of the operation was found to be the most important source of anxiety in a study by Johnston (1982) Other procedures may be painful, e.g. pelvic floor repairs or tonsillectomy. In most surgical procedures a general or local anaesthetic is given. Although this removes pain it also means that there is a loss of control. The strange sensation after a local anaesthetic for a dental filling is enough for some people to refuse a local anaesthetic and accept the pain. The pain following surgery is often severe and prolonged and fears about the unknown may be great. In contrast, minor medical procedures such as an injection may not take very long. The patient is conscious, and may even watch the procedure. Recovery may be very quick and the pain is usually soon forgotten.

> ### Activity 3.9
>
> *In your own profession identify minor medical procedures that you consider would be distressing. Compare with colleagues. What were your criteria for your choice?*

3.7.2   Preparation

Some studies of preparation for stressful procedures in adults have shown benefits (Mathews and Ridgeway 1984) Information given about the procedure beforehand can reduce anxiety experienced in a vaginal examination. People's rating of the stress of a procedure may be influenced by the benefits that might come from the outcome. In a study of 20 patients undergoing attempts to conceive by *in vitro* fertilization in an early programme, we found that they were positive about the very stressful and invasive procedures (Alder and Templeton 1985). Even though they were unsuccessful in conceiving, they thought that it was their only chance, and some felt that they could then begin to accept their childlessness *because* they had made an effort.

In a study of cervical screening we found that anxiety could be reduced by giving information, reassurance and the opportunity to ask questions (Foxwell and Alder 1993). Many women find the procedure of taking a cervical smear distressing and do not fully understand the purpose of the meaning of a negative result. One group of 30 patients (the study group), was given routine care plus an extra ten minutes of information, reassurance, and an opportunity to ask questions. The control group was given brief information and a leaflet. The two groups were no different in STAI anxiety scores (Spielberger *et al*. 1970) before the smear was taken, but when they received the results three to four weeks later, anxiety levels were significantly reduced in the study group, but not in the control group. Cognitive coping has also been found to be an effective method in reducing anxiety (Rafferty 1993, Box 3.3).

Box 3.3   Cognitive coping

In an experimental study, Rafferty (1993) showed how easily the principles of cognitive coping can be incorporated into clinical practice. The study compared the effectiveness of two types of preparation to improve the recovery of gynaecological surgery patients. Both types of preparation were in the form of a pre-admission class led by a physiotherapist and a nurse, in which the women were given a short talk, a discussion and an information booklet. One group received a booklet that gave information about the procedures and sensations that they could expect to experience in hospital, and instructions on exercises to be performed after surgery. The booklet given to the second group contained cognitive coping instructions in addition to this information. Both groups were given an opportunity to ask questions in the class. Although the recovery of the two groups did not differ significantly four days after surgery, the group who received cognitive coping instructions had significantly lower State Anxiety scores (Spielberger *et al*. 1970), significantly fewer symptoms, and significantly lower scores on the General Health Questionnaire (Goldberg *et al*. 1970): a measure of psychiatric disorder.

Booklets are relatively easily to produce and may receive sponsorship from hospitals or charities. There have been a number of reports of the effectiveness of booklets in reducing anxiety, increasing knowledge and increasing recovery rates. In an experimental study, 215 patients waiting for a course of radiotherapy were sent a booklet which described radiotherapy and follow up care. They were compared with a control group of 210 who did not receive the booklet (Eardley 1988). The response rate was extremely high in this study, 89% in the control group and 88% in the experimental group. There were no differences in overall worry about the treatment but twice as many of those who received the booklet were satisfied with the amount of information they now had. Reactions to the booklet were positive: 66% felt less worried after reading it, 80% thought it a good idea and 68% felt that it should be given to patients at the time that they are first told of the need for radiotherapy.

3.8   CONTROL

The concept of control is important in understanding individual differences in coping with the stress of being in hospital or undergoing some unpleasant medical procedure (Taylor 1986, p 329). Feelings of losing control are themselves unpleasant and, together with the pain and discomfort of a medical procedure, may cause anxiety. Interventions to increase control increase feelings of self efficacy (Bandura 1977) which is a feeling of being able to achieve things. Taylor divides control into behaviour control, cognitive control, decision control and information control.

- *Behaviour control* involves being able to influence the procedures in some way. Allowing a patient to control the progress of a painful procedure can reduce anxiety. If anxiety before an unpleasant event can be reduced, the unpleasant event will be more tolerable.

- *Cognitive control* is used in cognitive therapy and is very effective. In cognitive control the idea is to think about something neutral or irrelevant (distraction technique) or to concentrate on the positive aspects of the procedure.

- *Decision control* involves the option of choice, which appears to be beneficial. If patients can choose when to have an unpleasant procedure, e.g. an injection, then they will experience less discomfort. Cognitive dissonance theory (see Box 3.4) suggests that if a choice is made, then subsequently that choice will be seen positively. A decision to have a mastectomy would be confirmed by selective attention to positive accounts in magazines.

- *Information control* involves the assumption that the more information the better. It is expected that informed consent means just that, but some procedures may be very complex and it may be difficult to decide on the appropriate level and extent of information needed. Information may be reassuring because it may enable coping strategies to be used, e.g. in rehearsal and it gives predictability.

Taylor (1986) discusses the difference between these types of control and stresses the importance of cognitive and behavioural control, and she also describes some examples of increasing control on health outcomes.

Box 3.4   **Cognitive dissonance**

Festinger (1957) suggested that behaviour could also lead to change in attitudes

If there are two attitudes (or cognitions) that are in conflict with another then the discomfort caused will lead the person to change one of the attitudes. For example if someone enjoys a high-calorie diet (positive attitude towards ice-cream) but also believes that obesity leads to increased risk of heart attack, (positive attitude to health) he will feel uncomfortable holding these two attitudes. He can reduce the dissonance and discomfort by changing one of his attitudes. He may decide that ice-cream is really for children or is junk food, or he may change his attitude to the importance of the risk of heart attack.

Festinger predicted that people would change their attitudes rather than their behaviour especially if there are no other 'consonant' reasons for changing the behaviour.

Festinger and Carlsmith (1959) recruited subjects for an experiment in which they were told to tell another subject that a series of tasks that had actually been dull were interesting and fun. Those that had been paid $20 an hour (in 1959) and a control group paid nothing rated the tasks low on interest and scientific value. Those who had been paid only $1 rated the tasks more highly. Why did those who had been paid less change their attitudes and lie rather than those who had been paid more?

Cognitive dissonance theory explains that those who had been given a good reason to lie (paid $20) could justify their lie because they were being paid so much. Those who had been paid little had no such reason, so they had to change their attitudes to avoid dissonance.

Dissonance theory can also explain why when faced with two choices we subsequently find reasons for justifying our choice.

If our nearest and dearest express attitudes that are different from ours we have two opposing cognitions, liking for the people themselves, but disliking their attitudes. Either we like the person less or our attitude changes.

If smoker has feelings of like and respect for a health professional who also has negative attitudes towards smoking, they may change their attitudes to avoid dissonance.

Activity 3.10

Consider your example of stressful medical procedures in Activity 3.9.
Could you devise a cognitive coping approach? If not, can you think of a stressful medical procedure that you have encountered which would be suitable?

3.8.1 Worry work

Janis (1958) suggested that people differ in their approach to surgery. Some people worried a great deal, felt very vulnerable and had difficulties sleeping. A second group showed moderate levels of anxiety. They were somewhat anxious, worried about specific procedures, but they asked for information. The third group were unconcerned about the operation. They slept well and denied that they felt worried. After the surgery the 'very worried' and the 'unworried' groups had the poorest post-operative reactions. The patients with moderate levels of anticipatory fear recovered best. The 'very worried' groups were still anxious and concerned about the future. The 'unworried' groups were more likely to complain. Janis (1958) suggested that the group with moderate fear were mentally prepared because they had asked for information about their treatment. The mental rehearsal of solutions to real problems and working through the consequences, helped subsequent coping. Those who were over-anxious were too frightened and those with low anxiety were not motivated.

Janis claimed a *curvilinear* relationship between fear level and outcome but this has not been confirmed by other studies. There were methodological problems with Janis's two studies. In the first the same interviewer assessed anxiety both before and after the operation, and the second study of students was retrospective.

Mathews and Ridgeway (1981) identified a *linear* relationship between anxiety and recovery. The greater the level of fear before surgery, the poorer was the recovery. Those who are anxious beforehand have more pain, medical complications and slower recovery.

Some patients are described as *monitors*. They prefer getting stress-related information and thinking about danger. *Blunters,* on the other hand avoid getting stress information and use distractions (Miller 1980). Miller (1980) found that in patients about to undergo colposcopy, procedural and sensory information reduced heart rate in monitors but not in blunters. One reason for this could be because if a patient copes by avoiding (blunters) then they would be unable to cope with being given information by avoiding. Monitors are used to coping with adverse information and therefore cope better.

The implication of this research for health professionals is that it is not enough to give information alone, although this may be the easiest way. A more effective strategy would be to allow for coping style. Coping strategies can be given alongside information and these may be more easily conveyed in a face-to-face discussion. Mathews and Ridgeway (1981) conclude that although behavioural instructions are most likely to be given and may be the most readily given by health professionals they may only work indirectly. Cognitive coping methods may be more effective but may be seen as more 'psychological'.

3.8.2 Applications

The studies on preparation for surgery or medical procedures have been carried out in many different settings, and although all interventions have some effects, not all effects are achieved by all interventions. Kincey and Saltmore (1990) and Kendall and Epps (1990) discuss the problems of the research carried out on preparation for surgery. It is easy to assume that all patients would benefit from information. However, for some it would increase anxiety. If the health professional decides whether the patient should get the information or not, then the patient loses control. One solution is to give brief information and then give an opportunity to the patient to ask for more information. This would allow those who feel that they can cope to benefit, while protecting those who feel unable to handle more information. If it is considered essential that information is given, then cognitive coping strategies can be suggested at the same time (Box 3.5).

Box 3.5   Coping techniques

1. Information
procedural: what will happen, e.g. after the operation you will go to the recovery room
sensory: what it will feel like, e.g. it is normal to feel pain at the site of the incision

2. Modelling
e.g. a film of a model experiencing the procedure. The model is shown as anxious but successfully overcoming anxiety.

3. Relaxation
e.g. controlling breathing during contractions in labour.

4. Cognitive coping
e.g. replace negative thoughts with positive ones, e.g. replace 'I may die under the anaesthetic' with 'hundreds of people have anaesthetic every day and survive'.

In summary, successful information should have the following character-istics:

- It should be realistic and specific

- It should be given sufficiently in advance for review of problems and worry work

- There should be an opportunity to ask questions and for the information given to make allowances for differences in coping styles

Kendall *et al.* (1979) studied patients about to have cardiac catheteriza-tion. This is a procedure where a catheter is inserted into a blood vessel and threaded through to the heart. One group was given a cognitive coping package that included coping statements. The control group had support and information on procedure but no specific coping skills. Patients' self reports of anxiety and physical ratings of adjustment were better in the cog-nitive group.

3.9   MEDICAL TREATMENT FOR CHILDREN

Many adults find attending a hospital clinic or admission to a ward worrying and most children probably find it a stressful experience. Improving treat-ment outcome by reducing anxiety in children requires special skills. Early studies suggested that children do suffer adverse reactions to a hospital stay. Children may not understand the reasons for admission or the separation from parents and home. If the child has a negative early experience then this may have long-term consequences. Palaquist *et al.* (1986) found that young children who had previously had a negative hospital experience showed more distress during a routine medical examination than those whose previ-ous experiences had been neutral or positive.

The distress of a medical procedure or admission to hospital may be less-ened by some kind of preparation. All kinds of preparation have been used with children, ranging from playing with dolls to watching video films. Often both the child and the parents are involved and the preparation may do as much to reduce anxiety in the parents as in the children. Saile *et al.* (1988) carried out a meta-analysis of 125 studies of interventions (a statistical method of combining the results from a number of different studies). They found that if the procedure was severely stressful (such as cardiac catheterization) the preparation had a greater effect. Repeated intervention and active par-ticipation by the child also increased the effect. The analysis also found that modelling films were popular because they could be used with many children and were economical. However, their effects were moderate.

Emotional support given to significant others may be helpful although more expensive.

3.10   PAIN

Pain is an experience that is closely related to stress. In the context of health we can describe it as an emotional and sensory experience usually associated with damage to the body. There is also emotional pain and we talk about the pain of bereavement, or the pangs of jealousy, but there is also a concept of real pain in medicine that can be measured or at least reported.

Everyone experiences pain at some time of their life, and most illnesses are associated with pain. We can also experience pain when we are not ill. Childbirth is undoubtedly painful, but the mother is not ill and may see the experience of pain in giving birth very positively. When we look at why people seek medical attention, we find that pain is one of the most common reasons. Severe or chronic pain can be debilitating, tiring and depressing. Even minor headaches can be disruptive and in Western countries, painkillers are used widely.

Pain is difficult to measure. It can be sharp or stabbing, like a needle, or dull or aching like lower back pain. The experience of pain results from an interaction between physiological and physical factors. A headache may arise as a result of muscle tension, but the reasons for the tension may be psychological. An injury may not be noticed by an athlete or sports enthusiast until some time after the event.

Some people experience pain without a noxious stimulus. Phantom limb pain occurs when a person who has had a limb amputated feels pain even though there is no limb. In contrast, some people may have severe injuries but not experience pain. Soldiers in the Second World War who were having surgery were found to report less pain than a comparable group of civilians (Beecher 1956). For the soldiers, the pain was associated with having survived battle and the prospect of leaving the war. For the civilians, this pain was the start of a painful episode of their life.

The meaning of pain is very individual, and people show a number of differences in pain behaviour (Sarafino 1994). Pain behaviour is part of the sick role (see Section 3.3).

- *Facial/audible expressions of distress.*
  These can be shown as grimacing, moaning or crying out.

- *Distorted ambulating or posture*
  Moving in an awkward way, limping or holding the affected part of the body

- *Negative affect*
  Being irritable, depressed, or anxious

- Avoidance of activity
  Lying down frequently, staying off work, avoiding doing certain tasks or movements

  Activity 3.11

  From your own experience or from your experience of patients, make a list of pain behaviours. How can you tell if they are being exaggerated? Is this a meaningful question to ask?

3.11   SUMMARY

Illness behaviour has a specific meaning in psychology. It depends on symptoms. Symptom reporting depends on the number, severity and persistence of symptoms, as well as social and psychological factors. People enter the sick role and then take on obligations and rights. Admission to hospital or attendance at a medical clinic has psychological and social implications and the person may take on the patient role.

The anxiety and stress of surgery can be reduced by psychological preparation and this can have effects on surgery. Medical procedures other than surgery can also cause stress. Control and coping are key concepts, both of which contribute to the outcome of treatment. The studies of Janis (1958) led to the investigation of the relationship between worry and recovery. It is now established that there is a linear relationship between anxiety and recovery. Pain is a distressing experience and is an interaction of psychological and physiological processes. Pain behaviour is part of the sick role.

3.12   FURTHER READING

Johnston, M. and Wallace, L. (1990) *Stress and Medical Procedures*. Oxford: Oxford University Press

An edited book of theoretical views of stress and their application to medical practice.

Niven, C. and Carroll, D. (1993) *The Health Psychology of Women*. Chur: Harwood Academic Publishers

Redresses the balance in health psychology.

Pennebaker, J.W. (1982) *The Psychology of Physical Symptoms.* New York: Springer-Verlag

Describes their series of experiments on reporting symptoms.

Taylor, S. (1986) *Health Psychology.* New York: Random House

An American text particularly applied to health care

Sarafino, E.P. (1994) *Health Psychology Biopsychosocial Interactions.* New York: John Wiley & Sons

An up-to-date American health psychology text that emphasises prevention and care and links material well to physiology. It includes many interesting vignettes that illustrate issues.

3.13   REFERENCES

Abraham, C. and Shanley, E. (1992) *Social Psychology for Nurses.* London: Edward Arnold

Alder, B. (1993) Contraception In: Edited by C. Niven and D. Carroll *The Health Psychology of Women,* Chur: Harwood Academic Publishers

Alder, E.M., Cook, A., Gray, J., Tyrer, G., Warner, P. and Bancroft, J (1981) The effects of sterilization: a comparison of sterilised women with the wives of vasectomised men. *Contraception, 23,* 45–54

Alder E.M. and Templeton, A.A. (1985) Patient reaction to IVF treatment. *The Lancet,* 1 no. 8421, 168

Bandura, A. (1977) Self efficacy: towards a unifying theory of behavioral change. *Psychological Review,* **84**, 191–215

Beecher, H.K. (1955) Relationship of significance of wound to pain experienced. *Journal of the American Medical Association,* **161**, 1609–1613

Byrne-Lynch, A. (1990) Self efficacy and childbirth (Abstract). *Journal of Reproductive and Infant Psychology,* **8**, 300

Cartwright, A. (1990) Medicine taking by people aged 65 or more. *British Medical Bulletin,* **46**, 63–76

Cheung, F.M. (1992) Health psychology in Chinese societies in Asia. In: *The International Development of Health Psychology.* Edited by M. Jansen, and J. Weinman. Chur: Harwood Academic Publishers

Coons, S.J., Hendricks, J. and Sheahan, S.L. (1988) Self-medication with nonprescription drugs. *Generations,* **12**, 22–26

Cox, J.L., Holden, J.M. and Sagovsky, R. (1987) Detection of postnatal depression: Development of the 10-item Edinburgh Postnatal Depression Scale. *British Journal of Psychiatry,* **150**, 782–786

Dick-Read, G. (1942) *Relaxation in Childbirth*. London: Heinemann

Eardley, A. (1988) Patients' worries about radiotherapy: evaluation of a preparatory booklet. *Psychology and Health*, **2**, 79–89

Festinger, L. (1957) *A Theory of Cognitive Dissonance*. Evaston, Ill: Row, Peterson

Festinger, L. and Carlsmith, J.M. (1959) Cognitive consequences of forced compliance. *Journal of Abnormal and Social Psychology*, **58**, 203–210

Fiest, J. and Brannon, L. (1988) *Health Psychology: An Introduction to Behavior and Health*. Belmont, CA: Wadsworth Publishing Co.

Foxwell, M. and Alder, E. (1993) More information equates with less anxiety: reducing anxiety in cervical screening. *Professional Nurse, 9*, 32–36

Friedman, H.S. and DiMatteo, M.R. (1989) *Health Psychology*. Englewood Cliffs, NJ: Prentice Hall

Gath, D. and Cooper, P. (1981) Psychiatric disorder after hysterectomy. *Journal of Psychosomatic Research, 25*, 347–355

Goffman, E. (1961) *Asylums: Essays on the Social Situation of Mental Patients and Other Inmates*. Harmondsworth: Penguin

Goldberg, D., Cooper, B., Eastwood, M.R., Kedward, H.B. and Shepard, M. (1970) A standardized psychiatric interview for use in community surveys. *British Journal of Preventative and Social Medicine, 24*, 18–23

Granleese, J. (1989) Personality, sexual behaviour and menstrual symptoms: their relevance to clinically presenting with menorrhagia. *Personality and Individual Differences, 11*, 379–390

Janis, I.L. (1958) *Psychological Stress*. New York: Wiley

Jansen, M. and Weinman, J. (Eds) (1992) *The International Development of Health Psychology*. Chur: Harwood Academic Publishers

Jennings, B.M. and Sherman, R.A. (1987) Anxiety, locus of control and satisfaction in patients undergoing ambulatory surgery. *Military Medicine, 152*, 206–208

Johnston, M. (1980) Anxiety in surgical patients. *Psychological Medicine, 10*, 145–152

Johnston, M. (1982) Recognition of patients' worries by nurses and other patients. *British Journal of Clinical Psychology, 21*, 255–261

Johnston, M. (1987) Emotional and cognitive aspects of anxiety in surgical patients. *Communication and Cognition, 20*, 245–260

Kasl, S.V. and Cobb, S. (1966) Health behaviour and illness behaviour. I. Health and Illness Behaviour. *Archives of Environmental Health, 12*, 246–266

Kelly, M.P. and May, D. (1982) Good and bad patients: a review of the literature and theoretical critique. *Journal of Advanced Nursing, 7*, 147–156

Kendall, P.C., Williams, L., Pechacek, T.F., Graham, L.E., Shisslak, C. and Herzoff, N. (1979) Cognitive behavioural and patient education interventions in cardiac catheterisation procedures: the Palo Alto medical psychology project. *Journal of Consulting and Clinical Psychology,* **47**, 49–58

Kendall, P.C. and Epps, J. (1990) Medical treatments. In *Stress and Medical procedures* edited by M. Johnston, and L. Wallace, Oxford: Oxford University Press

Kincey, J. and Saltmore, S. (1990) Surgical treatments In *Stress and Medical procedures* edited by M. Johnston, and L. Wallace, Oxford: Oxford University Press

King, N.J. and Sharpley, C.F. (1990) Headache activity in children and adolescents. *Journal of Paediatric and Child Health,* **26**, 50–54

Kleinman, A. (1985) *Patients and Healers in the Context of Culture.* Berkeley CA.: University of California Press

Lawson, S., Cole, R.A. and Templeton, A.A. (1979) The effects of laparascopic sterilization by diathermy or silastic bands on post operative pain, menstrual symptoms and sexuality. *British Journal of Obstetrics and Gynaecology,* **86**, 659–663

Mathews, A. and Ridgeway, V. (1981) Personality and surgical recovery a review. *British Journal of Clinical Psychology,* **20**, 243–260

Mathews, A. and Ridgeway, V. (1984) Psychological preparation for surgery. In *Health Care and Human Behaviour* edited by A. Steptoe, and A. Mathews, London: Academic Press.

Mechanic, D. (1978) *Medical Sociology* 2nd edn. New York: Free Press

Miller, S.M. (1980) When is a little information a dangerous thing? Coping with stressful events by monitoring and blunting. In *Coping and Health* edited by S. Levine and H. Ursin, New York: Plenum Press

Palaquist, L.N., Gil, K.M., Armasting, D., DeLawager, D.D., Green, P. and Wvori, D. (1986) Preparing children for medical exam. The importance of previous medical experience. *Health Psychology,* **5**, 249-259

Parsons, T. (1951) *The Social System.* London: Routledge and Kegan Paul

Pennebaker, J.W. (1982) *The Psychology of Physical Symptoms.* New York: Springer-Verlag

Pennebaker, J.W. and Skelton, J.A. (1981) Selective monitoring of physical sensations. *Journal of Personality and Social Psychology,* **41**, 213–223

Population Reports (1990) Voluntary female sterilization. *Population Reports* series C number 10

Rabinowitz, H.S. and Zimmerlin, W.H. (1976) Teaching-Learning mechanisms in Consumer Health Education. *Public Health Reports,* **91**, 211–217

Rafferty, P. (1993) *Recovery following gynaecological surgery. An evaluation of pre-operative intervention by physiotherapists.* PhD Thesis, Open University, Queen Margaret College, Edinburgh

Raps, C.S., Peterson, C., Jonas, M. and Seligman, M.E.P. (1982) Patient behavior in hospitals: helplessness, reactance or both? *Journal of Personality and Social Psychology,* **42**, 1036–1041

Richards, D.H. (1974) A post-hysterectomy syndrome. *Lancet,* ii 983–985

Ross, L. (1994) Spiritual aspects of nursing. *Journal of Advanced Nursing,* **19**, 439–447

Ryan, M.M., Dennerstein L. and Pepperell, R. (1989) Psychological aspects of hysterectomy: a prospective study. *British Journal of Psychiatry,* **154**,156–522

Saunders, C., Summer D.H. and Teller, N. (1981) *Hospice: The Living Idea.* London: Edward Arnold

Saile, H., Burgmeir, R. and Schmidt, L.R. (1988) A meta analysis of studies on psychological preparation of children facing medical procedures. *Psychology and Health,* **2**, 107–132

Seligman, E.P. (1975) *Helplessness.* San Francisco: Freeman

Seligman, M.E.P. and Maier, S.F. (1967) Failure to escape traumatic shock. *Journal of Experimental Psychology,* **74**, 1–9

Spielberger, D., Gorusch, R.L. and Lushene, R. (1970) *The State Trait Anxiety Inventory Manual.* Palo Alto, CA: Consulting Psychologists Press

Taylor, S.E. (1979) Hospital patient behavior: Reactance, helplessness or control? *Journal of Social Issues,* **35**, 156–184

Taylor, S. (1986) *Health Psychology,* New York: Random House

Wilkinson, I. F., Darby, D.N. and Mart, A. (1987) Self care and self medication: an evaluation of individuals' healthcare decisions. *Medical Care,* **25**, 965–978

Zborowski, M. (1952) Cultural components in response to pain. *Journal of Social Issues,* **8**, 16–30

Zigmond, A.S. and Snaith, R.P. (1983) The Hospital Anxiety and Depression scale. *Acta Psychiatrica Scandinavica,* **67**, 361–370

4

Therapeutic Relationships

Contents

4.1 INTRODUCTION

A social interaction occurs whenever one person asks another for advice or practical help, whatever the nature of the problem. In spite of the increased paperwork of today much of the working day of a health professional consists of social interaction.

The nature of the relationship between a patient (client) and a therapist depends on many factors. The discipline of the health professional, the place where the interaction takes place, and the purpose of the interaction are all very important. There may be differences in approach between doctors and nurses, or between health professionals such as podiatrists or physiotherapists. It will be shown, however, that their interactions with their patients have much in common.

Therapy is any technique that is used to facilitate positive changes in a person's personality, behaviour, adjustment or physical health. The term is usually applied to work with individuals, and the use of the verb 'to facilitate' is important. Therapy *per se* will not make anyone better. Most health professionals are therefore therapists and the term will be used to include nurses, dieticians, and podiatrists, as well speech and language therapists, radiotherapists, occupational therapists and physiotherapists. Most therapy used by health professionals is individual therapy, in which there is one patient and one therapist. This contrasts with the educational system where there is usually a large group of students and one teacher. Therapy can be carried out in groups: for example, physiotherapy sessions, rehabilitation groups, ante-natal classes or exercise classes. Most research studies into therapeutic relationships have looked at one-to-one situations, but there are also therapist–client interactions in group therapy.

4.2 THE THERAPY

All therapies have similar goals, but the methods of arriving at these goals will depend on the model of therapy used.

Goals may be explicit or implicit. Insight or understanding of the health problem and its implications is an important goal, yet this may not be explicitly addressed. The explicit goals for behaviour psychotherapy are changes in unacceptable or inappropriate patterns of behaviour, but these are also the aims of speech therapy, where the purpose is to improve communication. Improvement in personal relationships may be a direct goal of marital or family therapy but it is also an indirect goal for rehabilitation after acute illness, or in the management of chronic or terminal illness. A direct improvement in general health is an explicit aim but may be difficult to define. Usually there are specific health aims such as an improvement of mobility or an increase in fluency. Most therapy will also improve self image and psychological well being.

4.2.1   Common Factors in Therapy

The therapeutic approach may vary but successful therapy will share the following common factors:

A caring relationship

A caring relationship between therapist and patient is one in which there is mutual respect and regard. The therapist is expected to show sympathy, warmth and understanding, and the patient is expected to have confidence in the therapist's abilities.

Reassurance and support to the patient

The problems may seem unique to the patient and relatives, but to the therapist they may be routine. The therapist can therefore give the patient reassurance that similar problems have been solved in the past and can be solved again.

Desensitization

If the problem is discussed in an accepting environment then it will lose its threatening quality. Much of behaviour therapy, but also psychotherapy, depends on associating anxiety-provoking thoughts with reassurance and acceptance. If a stroke patient makes clumsy attempts to carry out a task in the sympathetic presence of an occupational therapist, he is more likely to progress than if he makes his attempts in the presence of his family. Attempts at speech following laryngectomy can be tried out with a speech therapist who will not only be skilled at understanding the attempts, but will also be able to give appropriate feedback. Much of this is based on behavioural learning theory (Box 4.1).

Box 4.1   Principles of learning theory

Certain principles of learning were derived from many experiments carried out by B.F. Skinner. These led to the principles of operant conditioning.

Extinction
If there is no reinforcement following a response then the rate of responding will decline and eventually stop. This is known as extinction of the response.

Box 4.1 Principles of learning theory (*cont.*)

Stimulus generalization

If a stimulus becomes associated with a response (i.e. conditı
may generalise. Fear of pain may be associated with a nurse iı
and the response may generalise to all health professionals in u
even though they may never induce pain.

Reinforcement

This is not the same as reward. Something is only a reinforcer if it
increases the probability that the response will occur again. Rewards do
not always do this. Reinforcers may be specific to the individual and
vary in importance. Cigarettes may be very effective in reinforcing
behaviour in patients who smoke but not at all in non-smokers.
Reinforcement may be verbal and praise will be more effective if the
therapist is perceived as being important and competent.
Negative reinforcement acts to remove unpleasant conditions by a
response. People adjust their position or gait to avoid pain, so pain acts
as a negative reinforcer.

Shaping

Some responses may not appear spontaneously but can be achieved by
small steps. Reinforcement is given in small steps, gradually increasing
the requirement. If a behaviour change is desired by the therapist the
patient will be reinforced, often orally, at a first inaccurate attempt. As
the therapy proceeds, reinforcement is withheld until the response is a
bit closer to the desired response and then it is reinforced. By proceed-
ing in small steps the desired response is eventually reached.

Understanding

In all therapeutic interactions it is important to give understanding and explanation of the health problem to the patient or client. An explanation of
the causes of the problem, a description of what is happening now and
some idea of how it could change with therapy will give a rationale for the
subsequent therapy.

Reinforcement

All therapists reinforce adaptive responses. Adaptive responses are those
that make the goal more likely to occur. The patient depends on positive
feedback, whether they are recovering speech after a stroke, or learning to
walk with a prosthesis. The feedback involves both verbal and non-verbal
behaviour which expresses approval of desirable behaviour and ignores or

expresses disapproval of maladaptive behaviour. Its effectiveness will also depend on the level of motivation (Box 4.2).

Box 4.2 Motivation

A simple model of motivation suggests that there is a need (e.g. hunger) that leads to a state of arousal. This state of arousal or drive leads to appetitive behaviour or goal-seeking behaviour. When the goal is reached then the drive is reduced and homeostasis is restored.

Motivation can be understood from a biological perspective. Biological (or primary) needs such as hunger, thirst, need to rest, or to urinate are very apparent when caring for people who are unwell. We may be less aware of them when we feel healthy. Secondary drives are thought to be acquired through learning (see Box 4.1). The desire to please others, or a need for affection and physical contact can be acquired over years of social conditioning.

We can increase motivation by using incentives, by giving knowledge or skills in order to attain goals, or by reducing anxieties or fears. Motivation to take part in therapy may be reduced if there are conflicts such as listening while in pain, being in a hurry or wanting to urinate.

4.3 MODELS OF THERAPY

The therapeutic technique will depend on the model of illness adopted. The model depends on the theoretical approach, and, to some extent, on the professional discipline.

4.3.1 The Medical Model

This is the model that is most likely to be operating in hospitals and possibly in the layman's view of health and illness.

The medical model assumes that abnormal behaviour or illness can be classified into syndromes (see Chapter 2). The syndrome is then given a label, and this constitutes a diagnosis. Patients place great importance on the diagnosis. If a syndrome is given a name, preferably using medical vocabulary, it gains reality and recognition. It is extremely hard for couples with fertility problems to be told that they have unexplained infertility (Pfeffer and Woollett 1988). Many couples continue to seek more and more diagnostic tests, even though there may be no treatment.

In the medical model the symptoms are assumed to reflect an underlying disease process that is physiological in nature. This may relate to the immune system, a biomechanical problem, a chromosomal abnormality, an endocrine dysfunction or a change in the biochemistry of the brain. If the disease process can be identified then it is assumed that it can be treated. This is a very mechanistic model and implies that if something is missing it can be replaced and health will be returned. We often use terms like 'on the mend', 'restored to health' or 'gone to pieces'.

Using this model, treatment is given to *patients* (not clients), in *hospitals* or *clinics*, by *doctors* or *medically trained* staff. Treatment by health professionals is considered to be best supervised by a medical practitioner and self referrals are discouraged.

The model suggests that if a syndrome has an organic basis, then a physical treatment is appropriate. This leads on to a further assumption that if physical treatment is effective then there must have been a physical basis for the problem.

The medical model is clearly illness based and so the psychological aspects would be considered in the study of *medical psychology* or *behavioural medicine* rather than *health psychology* (see discussion in Chapter 1).

Activity 4.1

Think of as many common words or colloquial expressions as you can that represent illness or healing. At the end of this section try to identify the models that underlie the use of these words.

4.3.2 The Psychodynamic Model

This is based on the theory of psychodynamics developed by Sigmund Freud (see Box 4.3). Freud had a medical training and the psychodynamic model is essentially a biological deterministic model. It is not obvious that this kind of model should have any bearing on physical health. However, Freud has had such a great influence in our understanding of mental health, that many medical practitioners and health professionals have incorporated his ideas. Pelvic pain may therefore be seen to result from repressed anger, infertility from conflicts about sexuality, and dermatological problems from problems arising from deep-seated conflicts. It is assumed that psychic energy (libido) must be kept in equilibrium, like a hydraulic system. If there is no outlet for an emotion like aggression, then this can spill over and manifest itself in physical symptoms. If the conflicts are uncovered and resolved then the symptoms will disappear.

Box 4.3   Freud and psychoanalytic theory

Sigmund Freud made a significant contribution to the understanding of psychological disorders and many of his ideas have become incorporated into health professional education, particularly in psychiatry. Like behaviourism, with which it is often contrasted, Freudian theories are discussed in all introductory psychology tests.

Box 4.3   Freud and psychoanalytic theory (*cont.*)
His theory is based on the assumption that the unconscious mind affects everyday behaviour. Using an iceberg analogy he described the part above water as representing the conscious experience, and the bulk below as representing the unconscious experience. The unconscious is accessible through the technique of free association and is revealed in dreams and memories of early childhood.   Freud's theory of personality describes three major systems. The ego is conscious and is in touch with the real world. The ego has to reconcile impulses from the id and the super ego. The id is childlike, imperiously demanding that its needs be fulfilled. The super ego is the individual's conscience and tends to be authoritarian. The three work together to result in behaviour but they may also be in conflict.   Freudian theory is at once very complex and yet intuitively meaningful. However there are many scientific arguments against its acceptance. There is little scientific data, no statistical analysis, and the patients on which the theory was based were rich middle-class women.

Therapy based on a psychodynamic model does not mean full-blown psychoanalysis but may influence the choice of therapy. If the therapy is based on a dynamic energy model, the therapist might use non-directive therapy or encourage the patient not to bottle up emotional feelings.

4.3.3   The Behavioural Model

The behavioural model has been more extensively applied in health psychology. Behaviour therapy is based on the assumption that if a behaviour is a result of learning then it can be unlearned. This approach suggests that understanding or insight is not necessary and only the outward behaviour needs to be changed. This approach has been very effective for some specific health problems such as stopping smoking or acquiring social skills (Box 4.4). The principles are based on learning theory (Box 4.1). Although strictly only overt behaviour should be considered, this is often taken to include speech. It would be a very extreme behaviour therapist that didn't listen to what his patient had to say. Motor skills can be acquired through a series of small steps, but most therapists would also involve some cognitive processing as well. All introductory textbooks have extensive chapters on learning theory, although it can be hard to extract the principles that are particularly useful for improving health

Learning can be defined as a relatively permanent change in behaviour. Behaviourist theories of learning assume that there are laws of learning that are fundamental to living organisms. Many experiments have been carried out on rats and even pigeons to determine these laws. Learning is seen as resulting from stimulus–response associations. A stimulus can be any change such as the sight of food or a moving ball, and a response may be a reflex action such as salivation, or a muscular response such as catching the ball. Operant conditioning (associated with B.F. Skinner) increases the likelihood of a response occurring again by following the behaviour with a reinforcement. If a goal results from an accurate kick, then the motor responses leading up to the kick will be reinforced. In this case the reinforcement would be in the form of satisfaction and approval by the team and fans. This form of learning is contrasted with classical conditioning (associated with I Pavlov), in which an initially neutral stimulus (like a bell), becomes associated with a reflexive response such as salivation.

Box 4.4   Behaviour Therapy Techniques

There are a number of techniques that can be used in the context of changing health behaviour, although they may have been derived from treating psychological disorders.

Systematic desensitization
The person is gradually exposed to the feared object or situation. Relaxation is incompatible with feeling anxious, so patients are taught to relax and gradually the threatening aspects of the situation are increased.

Modelling
Children learn quickly by imitating adults and many professional skills are learned by watching skilled practitioners. Patients can be taught some techniques by demonstration, but there are limits to passive learning. Role playing is a kind of modelling. The therapist helps the individual to rehearse his behaviour by taking on the role of a family member or rehearsing an activity like shopping. An occupational therapist might use role play and modelling extensively in rehabilitation.

Positive reinforcement
Operant conditioning (see Box 4.1) can be used to change maladaptive behaviour. The following steps are applied whether the goal is to control obesity or to encourage patients to dress themselves.
1. Identify desired behaviour (response)
2. Select appropriate reinforcement
3. When the response occurs, follow with the reinforcement immediately. Use shaping (reinforcing successive approximations) if the response is not given.
4. Inappropriate behaviour is ignored but not punished.
The reinforcement may need to be continued, but the achievement of the goal, e.g. toilet training, may be self-reinforcing itself.

4.3.4   The Cognitive Model

The cognitive model of therapy includes not only behaviour but also internal cognitive states, or ways of thinking. Beck (1976) used a combination of insight and behavioural therapy that has become known as cognitive behavioural therapy (Box 4.5). It attempts to change inappropriate ways of thinking by altering selective perception. When health suffers the patient may focus on the bad things that have happened and on negative aspects of the future. A cognitive therapy approach focuses on positive aspects, and avoids over-generalization by presenting the patient with realistic prognoses to replace irrational fears and worries. An example of this approach is described in Chapter 3.

Box 4.5   Cognitive therapy

Cognitive therapy is problem centred and the therapist helps the client to identify and correct faulty thinking or reasoning. In contrast behaviour therapy emphasises observable events (stimuli) and overt behaviour (responses)

Cognitive behaviour therapy incorporates aspects of both and regards specific problems as learned behaviour. By changing inappropriate ways of thinking, behaviour also changes. The technique monitors the person's behaviour over time, sometimes using diaries. Cognitive behaviour therapy uses techniques of behaviourism. Positive and adaptive behaviour and ways of thinking are reinforced by the therapist. If change does not take place then a different set of behavioural contingencies will be applied. This means that there is a continuous dialogue between client and therapist.

For example, a woman with PMS would be asked to keep a record of her symptoms and their occurrence. Her feelings, thoughts, behaviour (e.g. exercise, diet) and life events would also be recorded. Eventually patterns may emerge and attributions might be identified. Once the problem is defined, the situation may be changed, e.g. by changing her expectations of herself as having to have a constant mood state or by changing behaviour such as reducing fluid or caffeine intake to reduce fluid retention.

4.3.5   The Sociocultural Model

This has become incorporated in the discipline of medical sociology or the sociology of health and illness. The distinctions between medical sociology and health psychology are discussed in Chapter 1. This model emphasizes the importance of differences in patterns of health in relation to poverty, unemployment or housing (see Chapter 2). In this therapeutic approach, the therapist might work closely with a medical social worker and attempt to improve health by changing living conditions. Health professionals may find themselves increasingly taking this approach as we become more and more aware of environmental influences on health.

Many health professionals use a variety of approaches but their education and training may reflect one or more to a greater or lesser extent.

Activity 4.2

Which model do you think is dominant in your own profession? Which others are also used?

4.4 THE THERAPIST

The characteristics of the therapist are very important to the patient. Some people prefer the therapist to be a member of their own sex or an older person, while others prefer the opposite sex, or someone of similar age or younger. There is no ideal combination and no general principles that we can apply to suggest ideal age differences between client and therapist, or matching gender, class or race. Therapists vary in their choice of model and their therapeutic approach. The hypothetico-deductive method or scientist-practitioner approach is common to all therapists, but is called the 'nursing process model' by nurses. To put it simply, the therapist assesses the condition and the patient, analyses the problem, applies a selected therapy and evaluates the outcome of the therapy. If the patient does not change in the expected direction the process is repeated.

The relationship between patient and the therapist is essentially unequal. The patient does not have the specialized medical knowledge of the therapist and the main source of information that the patient has about the skill of the therapist is the quality of the interaction. A number of studies suggest that patient satisfaction is greatest if the therapist or doctor shows concern and interest, and when the patient is treated as a person (Ben-Sira 1976).

4.4.1 Physician Styles

In a classic paper, Szasz and Hollander (1956) described a number of physician styles.

The active–passive style

The physician is active and the patient is passive. Decisions about treatment are made by the physician.

Guidance cooperative

The patient is guided by the physician whom it is assumed knows best, although the patient's wishes are taken into account. The doctor asks questions and the patient replies.

Mutual participation

The consultation is a negotiation and although the patient acknowledges the doctors' skills and knowledge, he retains the right to decide on his treatment.

> **Activity 4.3**
>
> *Which style do you think is dominant in your profession? Is this desirable?*

The choice of style depends on the theoretical approach and personality of the doctor or therapist, the expectations of the patient and the nature of the condition. In an accident or emergency, mutual participation and negotiation of treatment would be inappropriate (or fatal), but for an elective hysterectomy it might be highly desirable.

4.4.2   Non-Verbal Behaviour

Therapists convey much of their empathy by using non-verbal behaviour. Facial expressions and emotions have been studied for over a hundred years (Darwin 1872), but non-verbal communication is not all visual. We cannot communicate without including non-verbal signals even when speaking on the telephone. Non-verbal communication includes the volume, tone and pitch of the human voice. It depends on how loudly you speak, how fast and how emphatic. The style of speech can also convey information. Mothers use 'motherese' when talking to their infants and sometimes old people are spoken to as if they were children. Non-verbal communication includes facial expressions, eye contact, proximity and posture. There may even be olfactory communication. There is evidence for menstrual synchrony in women who live together which may be conveyed by pheromones. The smell of starch on hospital clothing, or the smell of antiseptic hand washes may convey messages. The smell may also become a conditioned stimulus (Box 4.1).

Argyle (1972) identifies the rôles of non-verbal communication as being: communicators of attitudes and emotions; supporting verbal communication; agreement signalling desire to interrupt and attentiveness; and replacement for speech, such as sign language.

> **Activity 4.4**
>
> *Consider the following emotions: Pain, anger, fear, embarrassment, impatience.*

Repeat the statement "Why are you doing this?", while attempting to convey one of these emotions. Ask a partner to identify the emotion. What cues were you using? How did you vary the emphasis?

Touch

Many therapies involve touch as part of the process. Whitcher and Fisher (1979) carried out an experiment in which nurses either touched the patient lightly on the hands while giving them information about their operation or did not touch them in any way. The two groups were compared and it was found that female patients described the hospital more positively and had lower levels of anxiety and lower blood pressure levels than those not touched. However the results for the male patients were in the opposite direction. Touching may be seen by men as threatening but by women as showing warmth and caring.

Facial expressions

Gaze is when someone fixes their eyes on another person and mutual gaze reflects love and affection. However, *staring* which is when one person continues to gaze irrespective of the other's response, produces a negative effect. We use eye movements extensively during speech and it can be disconcerting when someone does not follow the expected pattern. Avoidance of eye contact can indicate lying or embarrassment.

Posture

Mehrabian (1969) suggests that we interpret posture in terms of positive and negative attitudes. Leaning forward indicates attention and leaning back withdrawal or boredom. Depression is often conveyed by downcast eyes and bent shoulders, and anxiety by tenseness and stiffness.

Proximity

If someone stands too close to you it can feel very uncomfortable. Hall (1963) described four zones of interpersonal distance:

Intimate	0–18"	only intimate friends
Personal	1.5'–4'	personal space, if violated causes anxiety
Social	4'–12'	formal interaction and with strangers
Public	12'–15'	distance from important public figures

Yet health professionals often have to be physically close in order to carry out their tasks. We acknowledge circumstances in which the professional rôle (which may be designated by the wearing of a uniform) allows social rules to be broken. There are other circumstances in which we may be physically close, such as being in a lift on a crowded bus, dancing, or queuing. In these circumstances we avoid eye contact and this helps to preserve our personal space.

Activity 4.5

Stand in a room and ask another person to move slowly up to you until you feel comfortable with the distance. This will define your personal space. Now ask them to approach more closely and ask them to attempt a conversation.

What does it feel like? Change your height relative to your partner. What differences does it make? Select the tallest person and the short-est person in the group and reverse the height difference. What does it feel like?

Finally, sit down (as if in a wheel chair) and attempt a conversa-tion in which you are dominant, with someone standing up.

In a therapeutic interaction the rules may be broken and in certain con-texts we may invade personal space. This needs to be done sensitively and with the permission of the patient. One way to do this is to give the patient control over the timing of an invasive procedure and to move to a comfort-able distance once the procedure is over.

Korsch and Negrete (1972) taped interviews of 800 consultations with paediatricians at paediatric out-patient clinics. One fifth of the mothers were not given a clear statement or diagnosis and nearly half were not given a clear prognosis. Most mothers had expected that interest would be shown in their concerns and worry. Only 5% of the taped interviews of interactions were rated as friendly or empathetic, and the rest were rated as being tech-nical, ignoring the patient's view of illness. Three hundred out of the 800 mothers held themselves responsible for their children's illness. The doctors themselves felt that they had been democratic but analysis showed that they had taken a very active role and talked more than their patients. This study was carried out 20 years ago, and it needs to be replicated. We would expect that changes in the education of medical students would have had some effect.

If the patient sees the same doctor or nurse on successive visits, the prob-ability that appointments will be kept increases (Cartwright 1964). Presum-ably this is also true for therapists. There are many differences in how clinics are run, and different professions operate different systems. A speech thera-pist will have continuous care of one patient, whereas the nurse or physi-otherapist at an outpatient clinic may change between visits. In some areas continuity would clearly be of benefit; for example, midwives have shown the benefit of continuity of care.

A frequent problem for therapists is the breaking of appointments. A study of appointment keeping in a paediatric clinic found that appointments were broken by those who felt that they could not talk easily or intimately with their doctor (Alpert 1964). Demographic factors alone may not explain non attendance, but there may be more broken appointments in areas of deprivation.

Activity 4.6

Consider ways of reducing the number of broken clinic appointments in your own discipline. Would your methods vary with the social characteristics of the patient group?

4.5   THE PATIENT/CLIENT

When we consider the therapeutic interaction we have to consider the importance of the individual. No two patients or two therapy sessions are ever the same. This is partly what makes health care professions so interesting and varied, but too much variation can be very demanding. We will see in Chapter 7 how this can lead to professional stress.

4.5.1   Personality and Labelling

Our first impression about someone before we meet them may be affected if we already know something about them. Theories of social perception (see Box 4.6) describe how our assessment of a person is influenced by external factors.

Box 4.6   Social perception

Information that we have about an individual and object or an event is organised into a *schema*. The *schema* that we have about a person may lead us to interpret new information about that person. Look at chapters on perception in your introductory psychology text book for a discussion on top-down or bottom-up processing.

Asch (1946) suggested that we build up impressions of people based on general characteristics. These may be derived from our own social constructions of beliefs about characteristics of race, gender or age.

We are probably greatly influenced by first impressions. The *primacy effect* suggests that early information influences us more than later information. Using positive adjectives first in a description of a person leads to more favourable inferences than using the same adjectives last in the description.

> **Box 4.6   Social perception (*cont.*)**
>
> We are also influenced by surface impressions. Physically attractive
> people are judged to be more intelligent, competent, sociable and moral
> than less attractive people.

We use labels to help to make sense of all the information that we get
when we meet someone and this gives us consistency. When health professionals are coping with large numbers of people in one day it is easy to
reduce this complexity by labelling individuals as 'amputees' or 'hysterecto-
mies'. Labelling was shown to influence perceptions of normal behaviour by
Rosenhan's famous study on being sane in insane places (Rosenhan 1973).
Rosenhan and colleagues pretended to have 'heard voices' in order to gain
admission to mental hospitals. After admission and diagnosis as schizophrenics,
they stopped pretending, but were kept in hospital for up to seven weeks
before being discharged. They were treated as non-persons, were ignored
and had very little contact with the psychiatrists. Although practices will
have changed in the last 20 years, the point is that the researchers were
perceived as patients and therefore their behaviour (such as note taking)
was interpreted as symptomatic of their illness. In a follow up study, researchers warned the staff of another hospital that fake patients might try to
gain admission. Some patients were refused admission although, in fact,
there had been no fake patients.

Very often we describe someone who is difficult to cope with as being a
'difficult personality' or if an interaction goes badly there is a 'clash of personalities'. Personality is a difficult concept to pin down. It is used loosely in
everyday speech and it is used in different ways by different schools of
thought in psychology (see Box 4.7)

> **4.7   Personality**
>
> There are many definitions of personality, e.g.
>
> Characteristic patterns of behaviour, thought and emotion that deter-
> mine a person's adjustment to their environment (Atkinson *et al.* 1993)
>
> The **trait approach** suggests that we can describe a person's personal-
> ity profile in terms of personality dimensions such as sensitivity and
> conscientiousness, and that these will predict behaviour.
>
> The **social learning approach** suggests that our behaviour is influ-
> enced by the situation. We do not behave in the same way in all social
> situations. This approach suggests that we do not have stable and
> enduring characteristics, but that our public personality at least, differs
> according to the social context.

4.7   Personality (*cont.*)

The **psychodynamic approach** reflects the importance of unconscious motives (see Box 4.3 on Freud and psychoanalytic theory). There is a theory of personality development associated with this approach and changing personality involves addressing childhood conflicts.

Carl Rogers' **self theory** describes the importance of the perception of self. This is the way in which the individual views herself, the concept of 'I' or 'me'. Differences in the self concept reflect differences in behaviour and non-directive therapy addresses changes in the self concept.

We have already seen that patients in hospital wards (Chapter 3) may be perceived as 'difficult', 'good' or 'bad', and they can also be labelled in the context of therapy. Some patients may be seen as being more difficult than others but 'difficult patients' seem to have no typical personality characteristics. Health professionals quickly build up their prejudices and preferences based on experience. After a difficult session with a red-headed child it would be hard not to feel your heart sinking if the next patient was also red-headed.

Grove (1978) describes the characteristics of the 'hateful patient'. These fall into four categories. The 'dependent clingers' need repeated attention reassurance, explanation and affection. They need 'a firmly enforced schedule of appointments'. The second group, called 'entitled demanders', ask for excessive service but do not flatter or cooperate with the physician, and 'attempt to control the physician's behaviour. The third category involves 'manipulative help rejecters'. They believe that no treatment will help and are commonly known as 'crocks'. The 'self-destructive deniers' are very dependent, and frequently suicidal. They may 'even keep drinking even when told it will soon kill them'. The paper concludes by suggesting that even when the practitioner–patient relationship is good, a small number of patients will continue to be a problem. This is seen entirely from the doctor's perspective, and it seems unlikely that practitioners would be prepared to describe their patients in such terms today.

Activity 4.7

What does this account tell you about the author's view of the therapeutic relationship? Could you devise a description of the therapist, from the point of view of each of these patient groups? To what extent do you think that these stereotypes persist today?

4.5.2   Patient Expectations

Not only do therapist or doctors have different styles, but patients have different expectations and styles of verbal interaction. Studies of interactions with general practitioners have shown that patients may behave somewhere on a continuum between passive and active behaviour. Most seem to be passive and show minimal participation in the consultation (Tuckett *et al.* 1985)

Robinson and Whitfield (1987) divides patient contributions to the consultation into two types. Type 1 contributions include comments or questions that could, in principle, have been prepared before the consultation. Most people probably rehearse their symptoms internally and may have discussed them with others before coming to the consultation. Type 2 contributions are comments or enquiries that arise from information or advice from the doctor during the consultation. They suggest that failure to make Type 1 contributions could arise either because the patients have no further information to contribute or because they are unable to speak about it. This could be because they do not know the words or because they are too anxious. If people do not think that they are expected to make a contribution to the diagnostic process they would be unlikely to prepare beforehand. The view of the patient as a 'consumer' may lead the person to feel that they are getting advice or treatment from another rather than participating in a therapeutic situation.

The second type of contributions (Type 2) are questions that arise from the information given and their purpose is to seek further information, or confirmation of instructions or advice. There is a great deal of evidence (see review by Ley 1988) that there is poor recall of information during a consultation. People might be anxious and feel it is inappropriate to ask questions or are worried about taking up a busy doctor's time. Health professionals may be perceived by the patient as having more time and being more ready to answer questions.

Robinson and Whitfield (1985) assessed the effect of giving written instructions to patients to ask questions on the advice they were offered. Tape recordings of the consultations showed that it resulted in them making more comments and asking more questions. In post-consultation interviews they gave more complex and accurate accounts of the instructions and advice that they had been offered, compared with a control group who were given no instructions or who were told only to ask questions without checking their understanding.

The extent to which information is understood has been extensively investigated (Ley 1988). Most studies have found that there is very little understanding and there are a number of reasons that could explain this. As we have seen, many patients are reluctant to ask their doctor questions and this may be because patients have an 'over-deferential attitude towards doctors'. Most of the studies have looked at doctor–patient relationships, but similar principles apply to all therapeutic interactions.

The education and training of health professionals emphasizes social skills, and an empathetic and holistic approach should make it easier for patients to feel able to ask questions. There may also be times when a patient is waiting for a procedure to be carried out or is being monitored, and is accompanied by a health professional. On the other hand, some occasions, such as being in stirrups waiting for a gynaecology examination, are not the best time for a discussion. There may be other situations – while a dressing is being applied, while doing a series of exercises, or while working on feet, – which give an opportunity for more relaxed interaction. Interactions with health professionals may last longer than medical consultations, and are more likely to be longer with junior than with senior staff. In an experimental study (Foxwell and Alder 1993), we found that nurses were able to reduce the anxiety experienced by women having cervical smears by offering discussion and the opportunity to answer questions (Chapter 2). Compared with a control group who had a routine smear procedure, the intervention group had reduced anxiety scores after receiving the results of the test. The change in the nurses' approach was achieved after only one hour's briefing.

Activity 4.8

When do you think there would be an opportunity for patients to ask questions and for you to answer them? Make a list of the times in your own clinical practice or ask an experienced clinician. Make a second list of times when you think that it would be difficult. Compare these with a colleague.

4.5.3   Use of Language

Lee Whorf (1956) described a theory of linguistic relativity. He suggested that our thoughts follow our language ability. The more extensive our vocabulary the easier it is to think analytically and quickly. Specialists with a large medical vocabulary can think fast and may leave the patient behind. Clinicians or health professionals find it relatively easy to remember and recall specialist terms especially if they have written them down (and even been examined on them in the past). The same terms may be new and incomprehensible to the patient and the meaning of the word may differ. A subject in one study said that when she was told that a relative had carcinoma, her first reaction was relief that it wasn't cancer. Health professionals are highly trained and educated and there may be a danger that they do not attend to the vocabulary of their patients. Listening to the patient's own account can reveal a richness and colour often missing in textbooks. In one of our studies a woman said that after her hysterectomy operation she missed the 'turn of the wheel', meaning her menstrual cycle.

The use of abbreviations and acronyms may occur because it preserves a membership of an in-group of health professionals from which lay people are excluded. 'Medspeak' may be used because it is convenient and quick. It limits communication with patients, so protecting the health professional

from emotional reactions or demands from patients. It prevents patients from
detecting error and preserves a group identity among health professionals. It
has also been argued that it serves to exert power over the patient. The use
of jargon is probably unintentional and some specialized vocabulary is necessary. The other extreme is to oversimplify and to use baby talk to patients.

Activity 4.9

*Collect some examples of vernacular from your patients and col-
leagues, or from professionals in your discipline. Are there regional
differences?*

Even if information is given at the appropriate time and at the appropriate
level, there may still be differences in how much is understood. Many
studies (Ley 1988) suggest that very little is remembered accurately. Ley
and Spelman (1965), in a pioneering study, interviewed 47 patients after a
medical consultation at a medical out-patient clinic. Only 63% of medical
statements were recalled accurately and 56% of instructions were reported
inaccurately.

There may be differences between accuracy of recall and accuracy of
understanding. Imagine a patient reporting on a consultation to her relative
or friend. When she describes 'what the physiotherapist said', she is unlikely
to recount it in chronological order and as the conversation continues more
and more facts may be recalled. After a period of time some bits will be
forgotten. If she has not fully understood at the time, or been in pain, or
feeling anxious, then even less information may be recalled accurately. We
often do not know whether patients forget or whether they had never understood. Tuckett *et al.* (1985) criticize Ley's technique of questioning patients
to gather data. We would not necessarily regard all the statements made as
being equally important and so equal weighting may not be appropriate.
The timing of the post-consultation interview is also critical. Robinson and
Whitfield (1985) found that 28/80 patients made at least one error of omis-
sion immediately after the consultation, but two days later eight of these
then gave full and accurate accounts.

Activity 4.10

*Even leaflets or instructions on proprietary leaflets may be difficult
to read. Select a range of over the counter medicines and apply the
Flesch reading ease formula to the instructions (Flesch 1948). (This
can be done by typing into a word processing package with appropriate software.) The Flesch index counts the number of syllables
and the length of the sentences. Medical terminology often includes
long words and this may distort the index to some extent, but it
gives you a rough indication.*

Flesch Reading Ease = 206.84 – (0.8 × w + 1.02 × s)

where   *w = average number of syllables per 100 words*
                    s = average length of sentence in words

Scores
          >90 understood by > 90% of population
          70–90 understood by > 80% of population
          60–70 understood by > 75% of population
          50–60 understood by > 40% of population
          30–50 understood by > 24% of population
          <30 understood by < 5% of population

4.6 THERAPEUTIC COOPERATION
(or non-compliance, lack of cooperation or adherence)

After a consultation with a health professional, patients may behave in very different ways. Some will follow all the instructions to the letter, some will follow some of them for some of the time, and some will apparently ignore the instructions altogether. Patients may not collect prescriptions for medicine or may not attempt to exercise once they go home. Some patients may never return and drop out of treatment after the first consultation. This causes problems for health professionals, but it should be seen as part of the therapeutic process to understand the reasons why this non-compliance occurs.

Activity 4.11

In the preceding paragraph the term 'patient' was used. Substitute the word person, client or woman. Does it make any difference? Non-gender specific terms offered by my word processor are 'human being' or 'individual'. Would they have made sense?

The reasons for not attending a clinic may be very valid from the patient's point of view. He may not return because he has moved house, got better, got suddenly worse or has a general health problem. While this is likely to be known to the General Practitioner, the speech therapist may not know about a sudden accident or bereavement in the family, and be left wondering where she went wrong. There may be geographical or social barriers to attending the clinic or hospital and reduction in public transport may make it harder to attend specialist clinics. There are important demographic differences in clinic attendance and different locations or opening hours may solve some problems (Chapter 2). Some of these social factors may be outside health professionals' control. However, health professionals are more and more likely to have an input into planning health service provision and they probably have extensive knowledge of the practical problems of attending for treatment.

In the first classic textbook on health psychology (Stone *et al.* 1979), there is a major chapter on patient's problems in following recommendations of health experts (Kirscht and Rosenstock 1979, Ch. 8). They used the term 'adherence' whereas Ley (1988), Taylor (1986) and Pitts and Phillips (1992) talk about 'compliance'. Fiest and Brannon (1988) use the terms compliance and adherence interchangeably. In contrast, Harvey (1988), Burns (1991) and Carroll (1992) use the term adherence. Does it matter and is there a resolution? Are we making different assumptions when we use different terms? Friedman and DiMatteo (1989) attempt to resolve the issue by using the term 'therapeutic co-operation'. They base this on the assumption that the most effective approach in health care is when health professionals and patients work as a team. I think that the problem arises in the search for one term that will cover many different behaviour patterns. I might be very happy to comply with instructions to attend a clinic on Monday morning without wishing to re-negotiate the hospital routine. However, if there is only one bus a week from my village I might want an alternative. On the other hand, I may not wish to comply with a chemotherapy programme without feeling that I have had some say in the decision. A mother may not wish to cooperate with medical staff by taking analgesia in childbirth even though it may make the birth 'easier' for mother and staff.

Some authors prefer the term adherence rather than compliance because it emphasizes what people do rather than the kind of person that they are. The term compliance has been used more widely than adherence, and so it will be used here while acknowledging its limitations. It has also been used in studies of health professionals.

Compliance can be taken to mean behaviour against the will or behaviour that is subservient to others. This creates expectations that health professionals know best and suggests that there may be compliant personalities, or ways of behaving. It has been suggested that the term compliance should be abandoned in the discussion of control of diabetes, because it reflects an out-moded view of the care giver–receiver relationships, makes false assumptions about the nature of the regimen and gives the impression that compliance is a single construct (Shillitoe and Christie 1990). Ley (1988) suggests that compliance is the extent to which a person's behaviour (in terms of taking medication, following diets or executing lifestyle changes) coincides with medical or health advice. If a carefully thought out treatment programme or informed professional advice is not followed then health professionals may become despairing and disillusioned. Patients meanwhile may complain that they have been given inadequate information or advice. If they are dissatisfied with the interaction they are less likely to comply with the treatment or advice. It is very discouraging to health professionals when patients do not comply.

Could there be too much compliance? It is possible that someone might continue with treatment even thought they suffered pain or side effects if they though it important. If the relationship between the health professional and the patient (client) is very unequal and the health professional is perceived as dominant then the patient may feel that they should be obedient. Obedience is what we do when we are told rather than asked. Milgram (1965) devised a famous series of experiments that demonstrated the extent of people's obedience to authority (Box 4.8). If the subjects were told that they would have to accept responsibility for their actions or if there was someone who was present who was disobeying them, obedience was reduced. Milgram's experiments have been criticized as being culture-dependent but they illustrate the importance of social roles relative to personal beliefs (Abraham and Shanley 1992). Health professionals may also obey instructions because of their perception of their role (Box 4.9).

Box 4.8   Studies of Obedience

Laboratory studies of obedience carried out by Milgram and his colleagues in the 1960's have told us a lot about how people behave when they are in a subordinate role.

Subjects were recruited ostensibly to take part in an experiment on memory. They were told that they would be playing the role of teacher and the learner would be punished by receiving an electric shock every time they made an error in the task. The subjects were shown the 'learner' (who was an accomplice) strapped into a chair with an electrode attached to his wrist but they could not see him during the experiment.

The subject was seated in front of a shock generator which had a set of lever switches labelled with a voltage rating from 15 to 450 volts and groups labelled ranging from 'slight shock' to 'danger severe shock', The subject was instructed to move one level higher on the shock generator after each successive error on the memory test.

The accomplice did not in fact receive any shocks, but as he 'made errors' and supposedly received more shocks he began to complain loudly, kicked the wall and then (ominously) fell silent. If the subject showed signs of hesitating, the experimenter, who was present with the subject, exhorted him to continue. Milgram found that 65% of his subjects obeyed the instructions, continuing all the way up to 450 volts, and no one gave up until after 300 volts.

Many psychology textbooks show photographs from Milgram's experiments and there is a dramatic film that shows the agonised expressions on the subjects' faces as they take part (Milgram 1965).

Box 4.9   Obedience in Health Professionals

A much reported study by Hofling *et al.* (1966) was carried out in a
hospital setting. Nurses were given a bogus phone call from a Dr Smith
who asked them to get a drug called 'Aatroten' from the drug cabinet
and give it to a patient. The drug was marked with a maximum dose of
10 mg. The nurses' behaviour was observed and out of 22 nurses, 21
prepared the medication although the instructions had been given over
the phone, by an unknown doctor for an unlisted drug and for an
incorrect dose.

Some of the nurses may have attempted to check with others, but if
they did so they were excluded. In a replication Rank and Jacobson
(1977) repeated the experiment using the drug Valium. Only two out of
18 nurses were prepared to administer the medication without checking.
Ten prepared the drug but tried to recontact the doctor, pharmacist or
supervisor, and six tried to check the order.

Patients may report failure of communication as the reason for not following instructions. Ley (1988) summarizes the problems of non-compliance
with drug therapy as:

* not taking medicine
* taking too much
* incorrect intervals between doses
* incorrect duration
* taking other medicines in addition
* taking medicines with alcohol

If we substitute exercise or phonetic practice or any other health behaviour for pill taking, then we can see that there is plenty of opportunity for
advice to be disregarded. We are not likely to admit to professional staff that
we have not followed their expert advice, so measurement of compliance is
difficult. In research studies various ingenious ways have been devised to
measure compliance. These range from asking the clinician (gives an over-
estimate), asking the patient (gives low accuracy), counting pills left over
(gives total not the spacing), mechanical devices (e.g. measuring hand washing
using photo-electric cells), or urine assays to measure intakes. In spite of the
methodological problems, there is consistent evidence for low compliance
rates and it is estimated that this is about 50% (Ley 1988). Non-compliance
can be predicted on the basis of personal characteristics but no clear personality differences have been identified (DiMatteo and DiNicola 1982).

Social support may play a part in ensuring compliance. It will help if
family or friends remind the patient to take pills, to do exercises or to eat
more fibre, or check that they have carried out their therapy. Social support

makes it more likely that the patient will understand and follow medical advice. DiNicola and DiMatteo (1984) emphasize the quality of the communication (the instructional component) and the rapport with the professional (emotional component). Skills to improve both of these can be learned. Dickson *et al.* (1989) described the difficulties found in communicating with health professionals. Patients find it difficult to obtain information and find that information is insensitively presented; it is often unintelligible and health professionals are perceived as not listening. Physical symptoms are given more attention than psychological problems.

This lack of attention to communication skills in the psychosocial domain may have arisen from the predominance of the medical model of health and illness (see section 4.4.1). MacWhannell (1992) discusses the application of psychological research in communication in physiotherapy. Ley (1988) considers the quality of the communication to be most important. He estimates that if the instructions are understood then 67% will remember, 79% will be satisfied, and 68% will comply. He argues that if understanding is improved then compliance will be improved. However, it would not necessarily be desirable for compliance to be one hundred percent. If there are side effects, it is important that the patient does not continue to follow the instructions but stops taking the medication or carrying out the exercises.

One might think that the more severe the illness the more likely it would be that the patient would adhere to the instructions. However, absolute severity is not related to the degree of adherence, although the perceived severity is related. There is some evidence that if there are side effects there will be less adherence. In chronic conditions people become less reliable in taking medication as time goes on and the condition becomes more remote.

4.7 SUMMARY

There are common factors in all therapeutic relationships. The techniques often depend on the model of illness adopted. The traditional medical model classifies abnormal behaviour into syndromes that are given a label. The diagnosis often leads to a treatment. The psychodynamic model suggests that some illnesses may arise from repressed impulses and therapy tries to resolve inner conflicts. The behavioural model assumes that if a health behaviour has resulted from learning it can be unlearned. Behaviour therapy alters the environmental contingencies that are thought to control the behaviour. The cognitive model considers internal cognitive states and changes behaviour by changing inappropriate ways of perceiving and thinking. The sociocultural model considers health to be related to environmental factors, which may need to be changed in order to improve health.

The characteristics of therapists have been analysed in terms of styles. Non-verbal behaviour is very important in all therapeutic interactions, and is particularly important to health professionals who may have to break social rules. The patient or client is very important in the progress of the interaction but some patients may be labelled and expected to show certain characteristics. Patients also have different expectations of their therapists' behaviour and may not always understand the advice received. Language used by health professionals may differ greatly from the patients' vernacular.

Non-compliance means not following the advice of a health professional and may arise because of lack of understanding of instructions. Therapeutic co-operation or compliance can be increased by improving communication.

4.8   FURTHER READING

Rosenhan, D.L. (1973) On being sane in insane places. *Science,* 179, 250–258

This is a classic paper and is easy to read.

MacWhannell, D.E. (1992) Communication in physiotherapy practice. In *Physiotherapy: a Psychosocial Approach,* edited by S. French. Oxford: Butterworth-Heinemann

This chapter describes communication in the physiotherapy profession but the principles are relevant to all health professionals.

Burns, R.B. (1991) *Essential Psychology* 2nd edn. Dordecht: Kluwer Academic Publishers

A very comprehensive text. It includes discussion questions and although not glossy it is a useful alternative to a psychology undergraduate text.

Ley, P. (1988) *Communicating with Patients: Improving Communication, Satisfaction, and Compliance.* London: Croom Helm

This reviews much of the literature on communication, and draws extensively on health psychology research.

4.9   REFERENCES

Abraham, C. and Shanley, E. (1992) *Social Psychology for Nurses.* London: Edward Arnold

Alpert, J.J. (1964) Broken appointments. *Pediatrics,* **34**, 127–132

Argyle, M. (1972) *The Psychology of Interpersonal Behaviour.* Harmondsworth: Penguin

Asch, S.E. (1946) Forming impressions of personality. *Journal of Abnormal and Social Psychology,* **41**, 258–290

Atkinson, R.L., Atkinson, R.C., Smith, E.E. and Bem, D.J. (1993) *Introduction to Psychology,* 11th edn. San Diego: Harcourt Brace Jovanovich

Beck A.T. (1976) *Cognitive Therapy and the Emotional Disorders.* New York: International University Press

Ben-Sira, Z. (1976) The function of the professional's affective behaviour in client satisfaction: a revised approach to social interaction theory. *Journal of Health and Social Behavior,* **17**, 3–11

Burns, R.B. (1991) *Essential Psychology,* 2nd edn. Dordecht: Kluwer Academic Publishers

Carroll, D. (1992) *Health Psychology: Stress, Behaviour and Disease.* London: The Falmer Press

Cartwright, A. (1964) *Human Relations and Hospital Care.* London: Routledge and Kegan Paul

Darwin, C. (1872) *The Expression of the Emotions in Man and Animals.* London: John Murray (reprinted 1965, Chicago: Phoenix Books, University of Chicago Press)

Dickson, D.A., Hargie, O.D.W. and Morrow, N.C. (1989) *Communication Skills Training for Health Professionals.* London: Chapman and Hall

DiMatteo, M.R. and DiNicola, D.D. (1982) *Achieving Patient Compliance.* New York: Pergamon Press

Fiest, J. and Brannon, L. (1986) *Health Psychology: An Introduction to Behavior and Health.* Belmont CA: Wadsworth

Flesch, R. (1948) A new readability yardstick. *Journal of Applied Psychology* **32**, 221

Foxwell, M. and Alder, E. (1993) More information equates with less anxiety: reducing anxiety in cervical screening. *Professional Nurse,* **9**, 32–36

Friedman, H.S. and DiMatteo, M.R. (1989) *Health Psychology.* Englewood Cliffs, NJ: Prentice Hall

Grove, J. (1978) Taking care of the hateful patient. *New England Journal of Medicine,* **298**, 883–887

Hall, E.T. (1963) A system for the notation of proxemic behavior. *American Anthropologist,* 65, 1003. Quoted in Burns, R.B. (1991) *Essential Psychology.* Dordrecht: Kluwer Academic Publishers, p 226

Harvey, P. (1988) *Health Psychology.* London: Longman

Hofling, C.K., Brotzman, E., Darymple, S., Greaves, N. and Pierce, C. (1966) An experimental study in nurse–physician relationships. *Journal of Nervous and Mental Diseases,* **143**, 171–180

Kirscht, J.P. and Rosenstock, I.M. (1979) Patients' problems in following recommendations of health experts. In *Health Psychology – A*

Handbook edited by G.C. Stone, F. Cohen and N.E. Adler. San Francisco: Josey-Bass

Korsch, M.M. and Negrete, V.F. (1972) Doctor–patient communication. *Scientific American*, **227**, 66–74

Ley, P. (1988) *Communicating with Patients: Improving Communication, Satisfaction, and Compliance*. London: Croom Helm

Ley, P. and Spelman, M. (1965) Communication in an outpatient setting. *British Journal of Social and Clinical Psychology*, **4**, 114–116

MacWhannell, D.E. (1992) Communication in physiotherapy practice. In: *Physiotherapy: a Psychosocial Approach*, edited by S. French. Oxford: Butterworth-Heinemann

Mehrabian, A. (1969) *Tactics in Social Influence*. Englewood Cliffs, NJ: Prentice Hall

Milgram, S. (1963) Behavioral study of obedience. *Journal of Abnormal and Social Psychology*, **67**, 371–378

Milgram, S. (1965) *Obedience*. New York: University Film Library

Milgram, S. (1974) *Obedience to Authority: An Experimental View*. New York: Harper & Row

Pavlov, I.P. (1927) *Conditioned Reflexes*. Oxford: Oxford University Press

Pfeffer, N. and Woollett, A. (1988) *The Experience of Infertility*. London: Virago

Pitts, M. and Phillips, K. (1992) *The Psychology of Health An Introduction*. London: Routledge

Rank, S.G. and Jacobson, C.K. (1977) Hospital nurses compliance with medication overdose orders: a failure to replicate. *Journal of Health and Social Behaviour*, **18**, 188–193

Rosenhan, D.l. (1973) On being sane in insane places. *Science*, **179**, 250–258

Robinson, E.J. and Whitfield, M. (1985) Improving the efficiency of patients' comprehension monitoring: a way of increasing patients' participation in General Practice consultation. *Social Science and Medicine*, **21**, 915–919

Robinson, E.J. and Whitfield, M.J. (1987) Participation of patients during general practice consultations. *Psychology and Health*, **1**, 123–132

Shillitoe, R. and Christie, M (1990) Psychological approaches to the management of chronic illness: the example of Diabetes Mellitus. In: *Current Developments in Health Psychology*, edited by P. Bennett, J. Weinman and P. Spurgeon. Chur: Harwood Academic Publishers

Stone, G.C., Cohen, F. and Adler, N.E. (Eds) (1979) *Health Psychology – A Handbook*. San Francisco: Josey-Bass

Szasz, T.S. and Hollander, M.H. (1956) A contribution to the philosophy of medicine the basic models of the doctor–patient relationship. *Archives of Internal Medicine*, **9**, 585–592

Taylor, S. (1986) *Health Psychology*. New York: Random House

Tuckett, B., Boulton, M., Olson, C. and Williams, A. (1985) *Meetings Between Experts*. London: Tavistock

Whitcher, S.J. and Fisher, S. (1979) Multidimensional reaction to therapeutic touch in a hospital setting. *Journal of Personality and Social Psychology,* **37**, 87–96

Whorf, B.L. (1956) *Language, Thought and Reality: Selected Writings of Benjamin Lee Whorf,* edited by J. Carroll. New York: Technology Press, MIT.

5

Health Care Over the Lifespan

CONTENTS

5.1   INTRODUCTION

As we get older our bodies change and our health problems change. We also experience psychological and social changes. Health professionals work with many different age groups and some, of course, tend to specialise. Even if the client group is drawn from one particular age group, there will be other family members involved in their support and health. It is important to know something about psychological changes over the lifespan that may affect health. A child might be brought to a speech therapist for diagnosis, but the mother may be suffering from postnatal depression. A middle aged woman with back problems may be caring for an increasingly dependent mother.

Shakespeare described the seven ages of man as infancy, childhood, adolescence, young adulthood, middle age, old age and senility (Box 5.1). Erikson (1965) describes eight crises in his theory of life stages (Box 5.2). We can immediately see that these do not correspond to chronological age distributions. Four stages make up the first twenty years, and only three stages encompass the young adult to late adulthood in the remaining sixty years. Interestingly, Shakespeare describes a more even distribution, suggesting three stages before adulthood and three stages after adulthood. This was written in an age when life expectancy was much less. Most psychology texts give more emphasis to either the development of the child or to changes in the elderly. Berryman *et al.* (1991) devote twelve out of fourteen chapters to the years before middle age. All introductory texts give details about child development (e.g. Burns 1991, Chapter 3) and most also discuss ageing. The middle age tends to have less attention from psychologists, and yet it is where most of us are for longest.

Box 5.1   As you like it

At first the infant
Mewing and puking in the nurse's arms.
And then the whining schoolboy, with his satchel,
And shining morning face, creeping like a snail
Unwillingly to school. And then the lover,
Sighing like a furnace, with a woeful ballad
Made to his mistress' eyebrow. Then a soldier,
Full of strange oaths, and bearded like the pard,
Jealous in honour, sudden and quick in quarrel,
Seeking the bubble reputation
Even in the cannon's mouth. And the justice,
In fair round belly with good capon lin'd,
With eyes severe, and beard of formal cut,
Full of wise saws and modern instances;
And so he plays his part. The sixth age shifts
Into the lean and slipper'd pantaloon.

Box 5.1   As you like it (*cont.*)

With spectacles on nose and pouch on side,
His youthful hose well sav'd a world too wide
For his shrunk shank; and his manly voice,
Turning again to childish treble, pipes
And whistles in his sound. Last scene of all,
That ends this strange eventful history,
Is second childishness, and mere oblivion
Sans teeth, sans eyes, sans taste, sans everything.

William Shakespeare 1564–1616

Box 5.2   Major Life Stages (Erikson 1963)

	Stage	Psychosocial crisis
1.	birth to 2 years	trust versus mistrust
2.	second year	autonomy versus shame and doubt
3.	3–5 years	initiative versus guilt
4.	6 years to puberty	competence versus inferiority
5.	adolescence	identity versus role confusion
6.	early adulthood	intimacy versus isolation
7.	middle adulthood	generativity versus stagnation
8.	the ageing years	ego integrity versus despair

The relationship of psychological changes to health over the lifespan tends to have been studied in discrete areas. There are research areas devoted to the menopause, to adolescence, to early child development and to ageing. Health issues often provide an incentive to study psychological changes and sometimes the basic research informs the understanding of health. Paton and Brown (1991) point out that the psychological attributes and social and emotional health of the individual are not static; they are affected by illness, disability and hospitalization as well as the ageing process. Using a lifespan framework they relate health psychology to nursing. Their text provides a great deal of detail on the developmental stages of the individual. It also integrates development with health and illness, and it is a useful supplement for those who are ready to go further into the study of health psychology. Two other areas are relevant to this chapter. Research by social psychologists has provides much of the background material. Hayes (1993) gives a very clear introduction to the topic, and Abraham and Shanley (1992) have written a more academic and research-based text for nurses.

We will continue the approach of considering psychology in relation to health issues. We will ask if the chronological age or life stage matters to health; are there particular psychosocial-related health problems that are more likely at any one age, and are different therapeutic approaches needed at different ages. This chapter will consider the life span in four stages: infancy and childhood, adolescence, adulthood and old age. The psychological changes that affect health will be discussed.

Activity 5.1

If you could choose to prolong your life at one stage, which would you choose? Suggest a time now and then review it at the end of the chapter.

5.2   INFANCY AND CHILDHOOD

All health professionals who interact with children become aware of the importance of the child's previous history. Psychologists have tried to trace behaviour problems back in chronological time and a study of infancy may help us to understand behaviour in later childhood. The behaviour in the early months may help us to predict later behaviour and early experiences of medical care may be crucial. We will discuss the early influences, attachment and the infant in hospital in relation to health.

5.2.1   Pre-natal Influences

The first year of life is important, but psychological influences occur even before birth. The development of the baby doesn't happen in isolation and it is affected by the relationship with the mother and with other members of the family. If we go even further back we may find that this relationship has been influenced by the circumstances of the child's conception. The baby may have been planned or unplanned; it may be the first or the seventh; it may or may not be the desired sex. A growing number of children have been conceived as a result of modern reproductive technology. Adoptive parents may attribute psychological problems in their children to their perceived genetic background or the circumstances of the adoption itself. Parents who have been infertile for a number of years may be more anxious during pregnancy, and the procedure of artificial insemination by donor (DI) may itself disrupt the marital relationship (Alder 1984a). Of course many children who have been conceived by DI or IVF (*in vitro* fertilisation) have no health problems, but if they do, they may attribute them to the circumstances of their conception. If they (or their parents, grandparents, GP's or health visitors), think that this is important then this must be recognised as a real concern. Attribution theory (see Box 5.3) predicts that negative events are related to external causes.

Box 5.3   Attribution theory (Heider 1958)

People seek causes for their own, but especially other people's, behaviour

A **dispositional attribution** is one in which we explain someone's behaviour by the presence of a stable characteristic (she is an unpunctual person)
A **situational attribution** is when we attribute the behaviour to the situation (there must have been a lot of traffic)
If we are unsure we tend to make dispositional attributions and this is known as the **'fundamental attribution error'** (Jones and Harris (1967)).
We tend to attribute the cause of success to internal factors and attribute the causes of failure to external factors (Ross and Fletcher (1985)). We attribute failure in others to internal factors and failure in ourselves to external factors.

Feeding an infant takes up a great deal of time and attention from the mother and may cause the most concern and problems in the early months. Surprisingly few differences in infant behaviour have been found to be related to the method of feeding. In any case, it is not clear whether it is the feeding method *per se* or the mothers' relationship with the baby that would influence the behaviour of the infant. There may be differences in attitudes between those who choose to bottle feed and those who choose to breast feed. There are social class differences in breast feeding persistence, and there are, of course, hormonal differences (Alder 1984b, Alder and Bancroft 1988)

So far, no one has randomly assigned mothers into breast feeding and bottle feeding groups to test the suggestion that feeding method has long-lasting influences.

5.2.2   Attachment

The psychology of health of the infant is inextricably mixed with the health of the mother. Bowlby (1969,1973) suggested that babies form an emotional attachment to their primary caretaker and that there is a critical period in which this must occur for healthy psychological development. They suggested that increased risk of child abuse, greater incidence of non-organic failure to thrive and physical and behavioural delays resulted from a failure of attachment to the mother. There have been many challenges to Bowlby's position (Rutter 1972) and although it is not possible to do controlled studies, there are considerable problems of interpretation (Burns 1991, Chapter 10).

Activity 5.2

If you have access, visit a children's ward or out-patient clinic and observe the decor. What do you think it would have been like fifty years ago? Try and find someone over seventy (preferably a parent) who can tell you what it was like when their children were small.

The interaction between mothers and infants has been the subject of much psychological study. For thousands of years and in all cultures, artistic representations of mother and child in the form of pictures and sculptures have been found. Klaus and Kennell (1982) proposed that the first intimate contact of a baby with its mother was critical for the development of attachment between mother and child. This became known as 'maternal bonding'. Eye contact is particularly important and occurs with a few minutes of birth. Klaus and Kennell implied that early contact was crucial for maternal bonding. However, many mothers separated from their infants do develop normal relationships and early contact does not appear to be necessary or critical for healthy psychological development.

Infants become more responsive to their parents as they get older and parents report that they become more interesting and become 'people'. Responses are mutually reinforcing and carers interpret the outstretched arms and smiles of the baby as affection. Young infants up to four months will be relatively indiscriminate in their responses and may be easily cared for by health professionals. They will respond to familiar faces and may identify an individual nurse or recognise the parent. At about six months they may cry at an unfamiliar face and by the time they are mobile they may cry on separation and attempt to crawl after the departing parent. This causes distress to the parent and to the health professional who may wish to separate the child to carry out a medical procedure. As the child gets older the number of attachment figures increases, and the child may become more willing to accept an adult trusted by their parents.

5.2.3 Infants in Hospital

In an early study, Spitz (1945) found that babies in a foundling home showed a syndrome known as 'hospitalism'. They showed symptoms of depression that were attributed to the lack of a mother figure and the lack of perceptual stimulation. Douglas (1975) found a positive correlation between the number and length of hospital admissions and ratings of troublesomeness, poor reading, delinquency and unstable employment. On the other hand, Quinton and Rutter (1976) found no increase in problems in those who had been admitted for less than a week. A correlation tells us nothing about the causal relationship. The reasons for hopsitalization may also be the same as the reasons why reading was poor.

Clearly if there are other children in the family their needs are important too. Eiser (1990) found that their siblings may mature more rapidly and there may be greater flexibility in parental roles when there is another child in hospital. If the parents are denied the opportunity to care for their ill child then they may become de-skilled and lose their sense of self efficacy (see Chapter 2. 5.2). Attachment can pose problems if it is the mother of the baby who is ill. In this case it is unlikely that the child will stay in hospital with the mother unless she is breast feeding. In some psychiatric units, mothers suffering from severe postnatal mental illness are nursed successfully with their babies in specialised mother and baby units (Oates 1988, 1989). The attachment of the parent to the child is as important as the attachment of the child to the parent. Most hospitals now make it possible for the parent to stay in hospital overnight.

Box 5.4   Children's knowledge and understanding of health (Bibace and Walsh 1979)

Stage 1 under 7 years
Incomprehension. The child gives irrelevant answers or evades the question e.g.
Phenomenism. Illness is usually a sign or sound that the child has at some time associated with the illness

Contagion. Illness is usually a person or an object that is close to, but not necessarily touching the person. It can also be an activity that occurs before the illness

Stage 2:7–10 years
Contamination. The child cannot distinguish between mind and body, thus bad or immoral behaviour can cause illness as well as contact with germs e.g.
Internalisation. Illness is within the body and the cause comes from outside

Stage 3: approximately 11 years
Physiological. The child can now describe the functioning of internal organs and illness is often perceived as some malfunctioning part of the body
Psycho-physiological. An additional cause of illness is perceived, namely a psychological cause, feelings can now affect the functioning of the body

---

Activity 5.3

Ask some children of different ages some of these questions. Do the answers fit Bibace and Walsh's classification?

5.2.4   Concepts of Health and Illness

Children may see health and illness very differently from the way adults do. Very young children may play at being doctors and nurses, and toys can be easily nursed. More fathers now take part in early parenting, and one would hope that both boys and girls would play at caring for sick babies. Bibace and Walsh (1979) asked children aged between 3 and 13 years old questions about health and illness. The questions were about knowledge, e.g. 'what is a cold?'; about experience, e.g. 'were you ever sick?'; and attribution, e.g. 'how did he or she get better?'. The answers were analysed and divided into stages (Box 5.4). This revealed that there was a progression of understanding, and gradual awareness of causality. Children aged between 4 and 7 years thought that illness resulted from magic or from disobedience. Between the ages of 7 and 11 they accept the 'germ' theory of disease. The older children eventually understood the relationship between a behaviour (such as doing exercises or giving injections) and a change in health or even cure. Bibace and Walsh (1981) related the change in children's beliefs to Piaget's stages (Box 5.5). These findings were based on extended interviews with children and the questions were more about serious illnesses rather than everyday occurrences. There are alternative approaches to children's understanding of health and illness suggested by Eiser (1989). 'Script' theories suggest that children build up a set of expectations about events and their order. The theory of 'conceptual change' suggests that children move

Box 5.5 Cognitive Development. Piaget (1950)		
Stage	**Age**	**Characterization**
1. Sensorimotor stage	birth–2 years	differentiates self from objects recognizes self as agent of action realizes that things continue to exist even when no longer sensed
2. Pre-operational	2–7 years	learns to use language and to represent objects by images and words, egocentric, sees things from own point of view, classifies objects by a single feature e.g. sorts bricks by colour *or* shape

118 Psychology of Health

Box 5.5   Cognitive Development. Piaget (1950) (*cont.*)

Stage	Age	Characterization
3. Concrete operational	7–12 years	can think logically about objects and events, achieves conservation of number, mass, and weight, classifies objects according to several features
4. Formal operations	12 years	can think logically about and over abstract propositions and tests hypotheses systematically, becomes concerned with the hypothetical, the future and ideological problems

from an understanding of the human body in terms of wants and beliefs to a more biological understanding.

Eiser *et al.* (1983) showed that younger children were more likely to define being healthy in terms of activities such as eating the right food. Older children were more likely to describe health in terms of being fit or strong. Knowledge of these kinds of differences means that the health professional can adapt the information given to children according to their level of understanding. The relationship of understanding to the chronological age must not be taken too literally and it may be more useful to assess the kind of questions asked by the children.

Children may see illness and health as opposites, or as being two separate concepts. Healthy behaviour may mean not eating too many sweets, but breaking an arm following an accident is an illness. In a qualitative study, Bird and Podmore (1990) compared the responses of a group of five-year-old children and a group of nine-year-old children. They were asked about their understanding of health and about certain illnesses. Younger children were more positive about their own health and 28% of the five-year-old children expected always to be well compared with none of the nine-year-old children. Older children thought that heart attacks could be avoided. The authors concluded that access to knowledge about health was as important as stages in cognitive development in trying to understand children's concepts of health.

5.2.5   Therapy with Children

Stressful medical procedures may have to be carried out on children and they may cause as much anxiety and stress to the parent as they do to the child. There are a number of studies that have looked at interventions to prepare children for admissions to hospital and to reduce anxiety (Pruitt and Elliott 1990). These have been mostly carried out by nurses. The programmes have not always shown the expected reduction in anxiety or fear, but in many cases more information seems beneficial.

Nurses may be the most familiar health professionals to children, but many children will interact with occupational therapists, physiotherapists, podiatrists, speech therapists and dieticians. There is no reason to suppose that interventions that have been found to be successful in preparing children for admission to hospital would not work equally well in preparing children for out-patient clinic procedures. It would still be good to see these tested by research by health professionals other than nurses. French and Patterson (1992) argue that physiotherapists need to be aware of normal child development and the factors influencing anxiety that may impede assessment or treatment.

Therapists who work with children need play skills and children can often be uncooperative. Children may not wish to undress in front of strangers and there are constraints related to the Children's Act 1989 (Herbert 1993) in the UK.

Activity 5.4

Would wearing a uniform make it easier for children to identify and relate to different health professionals? Would there be any disadvantages to children if you wore uniforms?

5.3   ADOLESCENCE

As a patient, the adolescent may be regarded as neither adult nor child. The decision to admit someone to either a children's or an adult ward often depends on the chronological age. The ontological age or stage of physical maturity varies greatly in the teenage years and may bear little relation to the actual chronological age. A mature adolescent may be uncomfortable and self-conscious in a children's ward, but yet on an adult ward may feel ill at ease or frightened.

Adolescence is a stage in development that is accompanied by marked physical changes and very significant psychological and social changes. All of these affect health and we will also see how they interact. There are three psychological aspects of adolescence that are particularly relevant to health: cognitive development, the changing role with respect to adults and authority, and the importance of body image.

5.3.1   Cognitive Development

We have already seen (Box 5.1) that the concept of illness changes as children get older. Young adolescents explain illness in terms of physiological functioning and as the stage of cognitive development (Box 5.5) changes, they are able to understand illness even though they have not actually experienced it. The adolescent may also perceive that they have control over their health, i.e. an internal locus of control (see Chapter 2). At this stage they may be more able to accept promotion of health information. Bibace and Walsh (1979) suggest that towards late adolescence they become able to reason in a hypothetical and abstract way and deduce psychological causes. It is a further step to understand that psychological processes can be controllable. This may be a crucial stage in learning to cope with stress or in rehabilitation programmes (see Chapter 7). Another consequence of maturity is that the young person may appreciate the rôle of health care professionals because they are able to put themselves in their place. If the staff are young they may act as rôle models. In one study it was found that medical students were more likely to have had an illness in their childhood themselves, or to have had a severe illness in a close family member, compared with other students, such as lawyers.

The cognitive changes that are thought to occur during adolescence include moving from a concrete mode of thinking towards a 'formal operational' mode of thinking (Box 5.5). Moral development also changes as the young person wrestles with moral and ethical dilemmas. World issues may dominate and they may see issues in black and white terms. This often leads to conflicts with the older generation, and increasing cognitive sophistication may lead to more challenges and conflicts. Health professionals may well face searching questions about the meaning of medical procedures. It is very easy to underestimate the level of understanding of teenage patients, especially if they are being nursed in a children's ward.

5.3.2   Changing Roles

Adolescents can find it very difficult to cope with chronic illness. Adolescents are self-conscious enough about their bodies without the added burden of being different because of some disability or chronic illness. A young diabetic has to restrict food intake, someone with epilepsy may not drive a car, someone with asthma may not be able to take part in some sports, and some drug regimens prohibit alcohol. Disabled adolescents have particular problems. They may wish to go to ordinary school, to have relationships with the opposite sex and yet be anxious about these and have fears about future independence and employment prospects (Anderson and Clarke 1982).

Questioning authority can be a way of life in adolescence, and health professionals may be seen as representing the establishment. Paton and Brown (1991) discuss the problems that health professionals may have in communicating with adolescent patients. It may be difficult to avoid the role of 'parent'. On the other hand, identifying too closely may cause other problems. Young people are not only self-conscious about their bodies but also about appearing silly. They may mind very much about privacy and confidentiality is especially important.

5.3.3 Body Image

Puberty is the process of reaching sexual maturity. In girls it starts at about eleven years of age and menarche is about eighteen months later. Boys are about two years behind girls and growth differences are particularly marked in the early teenage years. Late-developing boys experience negative responses from others. They may feel inadequate, insecure and defensive and if they are treated like small boys they may behave like small boys too. This can set up a vicious circle and result in behaviour disorders. In contrast, early maturing girls are disadvantaged. They are considered less popular by their peers.

Behavioural disorders occur in a small minority, and some eating disorders (or distress) are commonest in late adolescence. Society promotes an image of thinness as being desirable. Women who attempt to reduce their weight and fail feel stigmatised and guilty. They may then comfort themselves by overeating thence leading to more guilt. Those that do succeed become trapped and some feel that they can never relax, or if they do then they also feel guilty. Many women's magazines devote many pages to new recipes and new foods, but also pictures of the latest fashions on skinny models. In addition to the articles in general women's magazines, there are magazines entirely devoted to the promotion of slimness. Most adolescent girls will diet at some time or another.

Overweight people are more likely to eat in response to emotional demands; some people may not be overweight but restrict their intake, and are known as *restrainers*. Dieting is a complex phenomenon and yet control of diet, whether for medical reasons (such as in renal failure or obesity), or for cosmetic reasons, can be understood in psychological terms. Psychological approaches to dieting are described by Lewis and Blair (1993).

Activity 5.5

Look at some of the magazines in the outpatient clinic waiting room. How many of them carry articles about losing weight? How many have articles about exercise and how many don't have recipes?

The adolescent years are generally healthy, although in late adolescence the accident rate rises. Some chronic illnesses become more problematic in adolescence during the growth spurt, and endocrine disorders may first become apparent.

5.3.4   Models

A number of models have been proposed to account for the specific behaviour problems of adolescence. The best known is probably the psychodynamic model (see Box 4.3) based on the theories of Sigmund Freud. Another perspective comes from biology and the hormonal changes that accompany puberty.

The choice of model may depend on the attributional style. The parent may attribute the child's adolescent problems to external factors such as the media or the influence of the peer group. They may attribute the cause of an accident to lack of co-ordination or the impetuosity of the young, or someone else's fault. In contrast, if a child is fulfilling parental expectations in sport or academic success, then the parents may attribute this to diet, upbringing or even parental example. Similarly, if receiving medical treatment, the uncooperative behaviour of an adolescent patient may be attributed to an 'adolescent phase'. Cooperation and progress towards recovery will be attributed to good nursing or good therapeutic skills. This is known as the fundamental attribution error (Box 5.3).

Adolescence is a social and cultural concept. In Western society the age of menarche is getting younger but the delay between physical maturity and adult status is getting longer. Education becomes progressively longer with increasing affluence and the individual may feel physically adult while being adolescent in education and status. The increase in health education at school may produce a very health conscious adolescent patient. Sex education has been given an impetus because of AIDS, and has increased the awareness of the physiology of reproduction and contraception, if not an understanding of sexuality. The vocabulary of today's sixteen-year old may be quite extensive and should make it easier for health professionals to discuss sexual matters.

Activity 5.6

How easily do you think today's teenagers discuss sex. Discuss the influence of television and health education with someone your own age and, if you can, with someone under eighteen.

5.4   ADULTHOOD

During adulthood there may be a watershed when the negative consequences of ageing become apparent. This realisation may not be inevitable and may occur at different ages for different people or indeed for men and women. Some individuals may see life as continually improving, but others may perceive losses such as changes in physical fitness. The ageism present in our society may perpetuate psychological changes because of the negative meaning attributed to the ageing process, and there are clear gender differences.

Activity 5.7

Shakespeare contrasts the roles of lover, the soldier, and the justice. (Box 5.1) We can see that little has changed, but would how would he have described the parts that women play? Rewrite a female version.

The ages between seventeen and forty are often described as early adulthood and, until relatively recently, would be regarded as the prime of life. Individuals and society emphasise growth and development on each birthday. Up to the later teenage years, birthdays are seen as a celebration, and as the beginning of more and more opportunities. In the UK, the eighteenth birthday is seen as being culturally important. Other important milestones may be passing the driving test, drinking alcohol in pubs, leaving school or voting.

There are important gender differences in the psychology of health in relation to age. The health of women in early adulthood is dominated by reproduction. Psychological issues related to sexuality are considered in Chapter 6.

5.4.1 Menstruation

The healthy female will spend the equivalent of six years of her life menstruating. Menarche may be seen as a positive milestone, but it is also surrounded by secrecy and shame (Ussher 1989). It may be thought of as a 'curse' or an illness, and concealment of menstruation is seen as being very important. Advertisements for tampons promote the idea that their use will mean that no one will know that the wearer is menstruating. There are also myths that during menstruation one should not wash one's hair or take a bath. Menstruation may be acutely embarrassing for a patient in hospital. The disposal of sanitary towels may be inconvenient and the insertion of tampons may be difficult for an immobile patient. Not only do women have to overcome their own feelings of shame, but health professionals must also acknowledge their own feelings. The sociological view of menstruation has been considered from the point of view of work and of sexual relationships (Laws 1992) but not from the point of view of care of the female patient.

It has been claimed that when groups of women live together their menstrual cycles tend to coincide. McClintock (1971) found that the menstrual cycles of women living in all-female colleges became increasingly synchronised and suggested that this may have been mediated by smell. Graham and McGrew (1992) studied menstrual cycles in female nurses and they found that the cycles of friends were more closely synchronised than those of randomly chosen pairs. The synchrony did not depend on the amount of time spent together, or the amount of time spent with men.

The Premenstrual Syndrome (PMS) has acquired the status of a medical diagnosis, although there is little agreement about definitions or aetiology (Graham and Bancroft 1993, Ussher 1989, Asso 1983). Recent studies have found little difference between PMS reporters and those who believe that they are asymptomatic (Ussher and Wilding 1992). Premenstrual research is a methodological minefield and there are problems of definition, subject recruitment, drop out and variation in hormone assays (Walker 1992). The tendency to use an ill–well distinction also goes against the concept of health as a continuum. The female world cannot be easily divided into PMS sufferers and the rest. Even those that do report changes may not do so on every cycle. However, there are undoubtedly perceived health-related changes in the premenstrual phase and it may be worth enquiring about menstrual phase.

There have been some suggestions that accident proneness increases at the time of menstruation. Dalton (1960) reported that over 50% of accident admissions to hospital were in the premenstrual or menstrual phase. An early study of post mortems in coroner's reports found that the majority of deaths took place in the last half of the cycle (McKinnon *et al.* 1959). These studies have been criticised (Ussher 1989) because they are correlational rather than causal and ignore the effect that stress may have had on the menstrual cycle. The menstrual cycle has also been linked with the illness behaviour of mothers with young children. In a frequently quoted study, mothers were found to take their children to the doctor much more often in their premenstrual and menstrual phases (Tuch 1975). The children were also rated as being less ill by doctors.

These studies have not been replicated. We do not know whether the mothers were negatively affected by their cyclical hormones and asking for help because of their low mood or increased neuroticism, or whether they had negative images of menstruation and lacked confidence in their own judgement at the time. Of course they could have been *more* perceptive to changes in their child's health.

5.4.2 Marriage

During adulthood most people will form a relationship with the opposite sex, and most formalize the relationship by getting married. Marriage is still very popular even though the divorce rate is also high and the age of marriage is getting later (Social trends 1994). The institution of marriage has received much attention from sociologists and feminists, but does it have any bearing on health?

There is considerable evidence that men benefit from marriage in terms of physical and mental health (Argyle 1987, Hafner 1986), and of course there are all the benefits of having unpaid housekeepers. This may be a false perception because Britain also has one of the highest rates of married women in paid employment. However, for women, being married can have disadvantages. They are more likely than single women, to suffer from depression (Hafner 1986). Women have higher rates of depression than men overall, but if we consider those that are single, widowed or divorced, women have lower rates of depression than men. However women with affective psychosis (a very severe form of depression) were more likely to have borne children (Gater *et al.* 1989). This may be because of a biological trigger or because of psychosocial changes associated with childbearing. In a study of women in mid-life, Hoeffer (1987) found that never married women were healthier, less lonely and more positive about life than widows.

Marriage can be a danger to health. There is a risk of violence within the family. We are more likely to be murdered, beaten or physically abused by our mother, father, or siblings than by a random stranger. Blaxter (1987) found that men living with a spouse had lower illness scores than men living alone, but for women there was no difference. McIntyre (1986) reported that married men between the age of 30 and 70 had better health than single men but there was no consistent pattern for women. Social support could be one reason for the protective effect of marriage and we will return to the relationship between marriage and stress in Chapter 7.

Activity 5.8

List the reasons why the age of first marriage is getting later. Why do some couples marry only when they are planning or expecting children?

The research into the formation of close bonds is fascinating and it appears that the pattern of courtship may lay the basis for the later demands of the marriage (Box 5.6). Couples with high levels of conflict in courtship may have conflicts in marriage, particularly if the conflicts are about the nature of the relationship, rather than who does what. Predicting the success of marriage is fraught with difficulties. The ability to deal with conflict and effective communication are probably the most important (Duck 1986, Chapter 4, and Tysoe 1992).

Box 5.6   Courtship and marriage Huston *et al.* (19

In this study four different pathways that l̶ ntified
They asked 50 couples who had been
affectionate activities, leisure activiti
chores.

Box 5.6   Courtship and marriage Huston *et al.* (1981) (*cont.*)

1. *Accelerated–arrested* begins with a high level of confidence in the probability of marriage, but slows down towards the end of courtship
2. *Accelerated* starts off more slowly but proceeds smoothly and directly
3. *Intermediate* evolves quite slowly and gradually with most problems at the last stage
4. *Prolonged* is slow and uncertain with many problems

Those in the intermediate group were most independent of one another and showed less affection. Those in the accelerated group showed close affiliation and high levels of liking. They were not necessarily more cohesive when it came to activities and time shared with other people.

As we have seen, our health is inextricably confounded by our current mood state and marital dissatisfaction can certainly make people very unhappy. Can it be avoided? In an extraordinary intervention study (Markman *et al.* 1988), couples who went on a 'marital distress prevention' programme before they got married showed significantly more marital and sexual satisfaction and less intense problems three years later than those who had not attended (Box 5.7.). They found that the programme prevented a decline rather than increased levels of satisfaction. This supports the concept of working to maintain a relationship.

Box 5.7   Cognitive behavioural marital distress programme

The programme designed by Markham *et al.* (1988) consisted of training groups of couples who were about to get married. Forty-two couples who were planning marriage were randomly allocated into two groups.

One group followed a training programme which consisted of:
Communication skill training. Couples were shown active listening and expressive speaking skills
Problem-solving training. They were taught how to monitor their own and their partner's behaviours and how to make specific requests for behavioural change in addition to skills such as brainstorming and contracting as problem-solving techniques
Clarification   arital expectations. Couples were encouraged to discuss   their expectations about themselves, their partne   tionships
Se   *ationship enhancement.* Here the focus
                              lems and ways to prevent problems

---

Box 5.7 Cognitive behavioural marital distress programme (*cont.*)

At 8–10 weeks they were assessed and there were no differences between the intervention group and the control group. At 18 months the intervention group reported higher levels of satisfaction, and at three years they showed higher levels of marital and sexual satisfaction and less intense problems.

5.4.3   Divorce

If marriage is good for health (at least for men), then what about divorce? There are many statistics that show that men suffer more severely than women from loss of their spouses by bereavement or breakdown of marriage. Bloom *et al.* (1978) found that the period of divorce or separation from wife and family is particularly stressful for men and they are more likely to suffer from a range of health problems.

Divorce or separation are just the outward signs of marital disharmony. This means that many people who are being treated or who have interactions with health care professionals may be having marital problems. It is difficult to be sure about retrospective surveys. The couples that are divorced may be more likely to recall rows in early marriage than those who are celebrating their 25th wedding anniversary.

Health professionals may find that therapy is being disrupted by marital problems. This may be a relatively minor disruption like missing an appointment because the father has been kept late at work, or a major problem if the wife has been physically abused. A marital separation may be followed by depression and withdrawal, and would certainly impede recovery from illness or surgery. Health professionals may not be able to do much on their own other than being sensitive and sympathetic, but there may be counselling services offered by voluntary groups or the health service. Tysoe (1992) describes in a very amusing way how psychology has contributed to our understanding of love and marriage and gives insight to the development and maintenance of relationships.

5.4.4   Being Single

The single state has received far less attention from researches than the married state apart from research on widowhood and divorce. Government statistics show that in 1991 26% of all households consist of one single person. Although 45% of adults over 20 years of age are married, 14% were single in 1991 (Social Trends 1994). When we look at the age distribution, the figures are even more striking, especially for women. Being single may be perceived as abnormal, and the word 'spinster' seems faintly derogatory.

Activity 5.9

Think of words used to describe unmarried adult women. Now think of the male equivalent. Do they have different associations? Why?

Society perpetuates negative images of single women, whether it is the widow who is ignored socially or the divorcee who may be considered threatening (Llewelyn and Osborne 1990). Women may lack confidence in their ability to live by themselves or even to do things by themselves. Women who have lived on their own have to learn to rely on their own resources, not only in the practical sense but also in maintaining their own self esteem. They do not have as much feedback from other people compared with those in a stable marital relationship or living with their parents. The maintenance of our identity comes from others and our feelings of self worth may be closely linked to the emotional support received in a relationship. Being single and independent may be advantageous to some women, and it may be easier to avoid emotional and sexual complications. Relationships can distract from work and careers and being single may be advantageous in giving freedom to pursue career opportunities. Gigy (1980) found that single women placed more value on personal growth and assertion than a comparable married group, but overall there were very few differences between them.

If a single or widowed woman is ill then there may be practical problems. Women often earn less than men or they may not have had employment that has generous sick pay arrangements. The absence of a partner at home may make convalescence difficult. However, a woman who has been used to being at home on her own may be better off than a married woman who finds herself widowed after fifty years. If she has been working she may have a network of colleagues who will support her if she is ill. Many health professionals will have had experience of caring for a retired or ill colleague. (See Chapter 7)

5.4.5 Pregnancy

For most women (and their partners), their first encounter with routine medical care will be during pregnancy, and they will come into contact with a wide variety of health professionals. At the antenatal clinics or in hospital, they will meet nurses, midwives, health visitors, physiotherapists, and dieticians. If there are specific health problems with the baby, they may meet podiatrists and speech therapists. Many pregnant women will be screened in pregnancy, and foetal screening will bring them into contact with radiographers and possibly genetic counsellors. Pregnancy is probably the most significant change in a woman's life and will affect her psychological and physical health in the future. Life will never be the same again. Erikson's model suggests that in early adulthood the individual is struggling to reconcile needs for independence and needs for intimate relationships (Box 5.2). Parenthood may occur when these conflicts are still in balance. The changes during pregnancy and the first postnatal year have been well documented (Kumar and Brockington 1988, Oates 1989, Holden 1991). The life events of childbirth, caring for a new member of the family and change in the work role may all act as stressors. They may also be accompanied by a change in financial circumstances and moving house. All these life events come at a time when the mother is recovering from the physical effects of childbirth.

In terms of reproductive life events, pregnancy may be equally problematic for fathers. The expectant father may be a figure of fun, but many men become closely involved with the progress of the pregnancy. Young men tend to have had less experience of babies than young women, and are less likely to have been to classes on parenthood at school than women. In a study of fathers, Lewis (1986) found that few fathers accompanied their wives to the antenatal clinic or attended parentcraft classes.

Even though family sizes are often small, and more women are in employment, having children is still significant in economic, psychological and health terms. Most women become mothers in early adulthood and will carry the role of mother for the rest of their lives. Mothers have been given a central role in psychology (Phoenix *et al.* 1991) and have been regarded as being important for the psychological development and for the physical health of the child. Health educational programmes may be targeted directly at the mother in order to improve the health of the next generation, for example, aiming to improve diet. Mothers are expected to comply with health behaviour patterns expected in pregnancy such as restricting their intake of alcohol and eating healthily. They are expected to attend antenatal clinics and when the baby is born, to take it for check ups, feed it appropriately and to teach it healthy habits. Marshall (1991) discusses the construction of motherhood as seen by childcare manuals, and finds that they emphasize the importance of the mother for the normal development of the child. This implies that if the child's behaviour is not normal, the mother is to blame.

5.4.6 Postnatal Depression

In the first ten days after birth a new mother may experience a greater range of emotions than at any other time of her life. She may be ecstatically happy, worried and anxious; feel loved and esteemed and tearful and confused; she may be excited and terribly tired. The first three days are sometimes known as the pinks and about the fourth or fifth day she may experience the blues. The blues are short episodes of emotional ups and downs, and are experienced by the majority of first-time mothers. They should not be confused with postnatal depression that is a 'morbid and persistent depressed mood, usually commencing six to twelve weeks after delivery' (Cox 1989, p 840).

Postnatal depression probably occurs in about 9–13% of women (O'Hara and Zekoski 1988), and the more severe post partum psychosis occurs in about 2 in 1000 deliveries (Kumar 1989). One in ten mothers encountered by health professionals may be depressed and others may be distressed. In the first few days after delivery they may be emotional and not necessarily receptive to the attentions of health professionals whether they be physiotherapists or dieticians.

Health visitors can play an important role in recognising and treating postnatal depression and other health professionals can alert GPs or health visitors to investigate a distressed mother further (Cox 1986, Holden 1991). Most mothers cope well and do not get depressed but most of them are also likely to feel very tired. The reasons for depression at this time are not fully understood. Hormones have been suggested, but there is little direct evidence. There are significant changes in sexuality in the first year after delivery. Although there may be direct effects of changes in hormones on vaginal pain (Alder and Bancroft 1988), we do not know to what extent they also affect interest and enjoyment (Alder 1989).

5.5   MID AGE

Erikson's view of mid age is one of conflict between *generativity* (guiding the next generation) and *stagnation* (concern with own needs). Middle age will be associated with different patterns of health and illness. The assessment of a middle aged patient may have to include their relationship with their own increasingly ageing parents, as well as their dependent teenage children.

Bond and Coleman (1990) suggest that there has recently been a social reconstruction of middle age, attempting to establish an ever increasing distance between the middle years (mid 30's to late 60's) and 'geriatric' old age.

5.5.1   Mid-life Transition

An important transition studied by many psychologists is that of changing from being a young adult to a mid-aged adult. Levinson *et al.* (1978) in their study of forty men aged between 37 and 41 identified a period of uncertainty, anxiety and change that became known as the mid-life crisis. Half of the men saw mid-life as a last chance to achieve goals but others saw mid-life as a dead end and life as pointless. They also became aware of changing physical strength and vigour.

The years between maturity and the beginning of old age may be regarded as the prime of life. If chronic illness or death occurs at this stage it will be seen as unexpected and cruel. We use phrases such as 'struck down' or 'cruel blow'. Illness may also be seen as being a failure of medical care or at the least 'unfair'.

Activity 5.10

These phrases reflect a physical model of ill health. Look at Chapter 1 for discussion of models. Can you think of phrases that might reflect other models?

As people enter mid-age they may increasingly focus on preventive health measures as the spectre of an unhealthy old age becomes more apparent. People aged 45 to 55 may have parents who are retired and at risk of ill health. The time perspective of the young adult may be limited to the demands of their jobs, marriage and bringing up families. In mid-age, people may begin to make plans for retirement. This may be seen as the end rather than the beginning. At this time there may be an intense interest in health shown by joining clubs or fitness programmes. This could be regarded as a successful outcome of health education programmes or as reflecting a fear of growing old in our ageist society.

5.5.2   Ageing and Physical Appearance

Bond and Coleman (1990) give a fascinating account of images of ageing. They point out that there is a traditional symbolic equation between youth, beauty and goodness. A stereotypically attractive physical appearance is a source of power for women but is bound to wane eventually. In contrast, men's power depends on wealth and occupation. This has been described as the double standard of ageing. The Association of Graceful Ageing, Health and Moral Attractiveness developed in the 1920's illustrates the anxieties that are reflected in the belief that a healthy middle age will somehow postpone the ageing process.

It is not surprising then, that physically attractive people are judged more positively. There are noticeable changes in physical appearance with increasing age, such as greying hair and loss of skin elasticity. In an ageist society these become negative attributes and generate a vast cosmetic industry. Men seem to be different, and greying hair and cragginess of features may suggest increasing maturity and competence. Physical attractiveness bears little relationship to health in reality. Those who are physically attractive may be assumed to be healthy even though they are not.

Activity 5.11

Describe the physical appearance of a high status middle aged male. Now re-read your description as if it were a female. Is there any difference?

5.5.3   Changes in Sensory Abilities

Sensory abilities progressively decline in adulthood. Changes to the lens of the eye reduce visual ability. Older people may not only be dependent on glasses for reading but also require higher levels of illumination for reading. Information leaflets and instructions on medicines may be in very small print and a patient admitted to hospital may not be able to carry her reading glasses with her. There is also progressive loss of hearing and the patient may require a higher volume on the television or radio.

There is little decline in psychomotor skills during mid-age and knowledge, confidence and maturity acquired through years of experience are still valued by society. In spite of stereotypes all is not gloom and doom for half the population (and more than half the population cared for by health professionals).

5.5.4 Menopause

The menopause is part of normal development and is defined in medical terms as having occurred when twelve months have elapsed since the last menstrual period. The average age is fifty-one years, yet the menopause is often thought to be a problem of the forties. This is because the years leading up to the menopause, (described as the peri-menopause), may be characterised by hot flushes and night sweats. These can be very distressing and may lead to feelings of low self esteem. Psychosocial changes also happen at this time of life, and the peri-menopause may be a time when children leave home, parents become ill or dependent and marriages become stale. They can also be years in which the fear of pregnancy and the need for contraception is past, finances become easier and children no longer need to be supported. Hunter (1990) describes the negative attitudes that prevail about the menopause, and suggests some positive approaches.

During the peri-menopause, periods become irregular and as fewer cycles are ovulatory, fertility declines rapidly. Loss of oestrogen production by the corpus luteum means that there may be symptoms of oestrogen deficiency. Low oestrogen levels have been associated with hot flushes and night sweats, although many women will have few symptoms or not be distressed by them even though their oestrogen levels are falling. Hormone replacement therapy is very effective in reducing vasomotor symptoms and vaginal dryness, and it reduces the risk of osteoporosis. Loss of mobility can make an old person dependent and lead to social isolation, so anything that reduces the risk of hip or wrist fractures will have psychosocial benefits. Not everyone is at risk of osteoporosis or has menopausal symptoms, and some women will not wish to put up with the monthly bleeds induced by most forms of HRT.

5.6 OLD AGE

The elderly population make up a high proportion of those seeking help from health professionals. Every health professional, whether an occupational therapist, or a speech therapist will find themselves trying to understand the psychology of old age. It can be depressing, and Western society can take little pride in its treatment of the old. The lack of understanding and tolerance is not new. Kafka (1916) describes the reactions of a family to a young man who has changed overnight into an insect. Their initial concern and tolerance degenerates into rejection and neglect.

'Later life', 'old age', and 'the third age' are all terms used to describe the precise chronological age of 60 onwards. In contrast to the importance of the number of years and months since birth in the infant, the length of the life span becomes increasingly irrelevant to physical and psychological health. One geriatrician advises medical students to ignore the date of birth in the geriatric patient. If the date of birth is taken to be significant it can lead to inappropriate expectations of the individual. Commenting that an elderly person is wonderful for her age implies that we have low expectations for that age.

Activity 5.12

Consider the implications of an older person revealing her age and the response of a younger person who says "But you don't look it".

5.6.1   Psychosocial changes

The psychosocial changes that accompany old age have been well documented (Bond and Coleman 1990, Paton and Brown 1991). The high incidence of illness in this age group means that the elderly will make up an increasing proportion of the health professionals' practice. Elderly people may expect their physical health to be poor. They may think of loss of mobility, poor foot health, or poor digestion as part of growing old and so be reluctant to seek help. An elderly person's illness behaviour may be different (see Chapter 2) and they may not attend to symptoms, or may feel that there is no point in seeking treatment. Depression, which may or may not be related to bereavement, is common in old age.

Activity 5.13

Look at the poem in Box 5.8. What does it tell you about old age? Can children empathise with old age better than adults?

Box 5.8   Images of old age
The lonely scarecrow It's cold and windy, Rainy and stormy, And I am bored. I don't have any friends Or family.

Box 5.8   Images of old age (*cont.*)

Nothing to do,
Nobody to talk to.
My head is stuck in one position,
I can't move a limb.
Children laugh at me,
The birds ignore me,
They fly away from me,
They even take my straw and hay.
The farmer passes by without a word
I am tired,
And cramped.
I wish I could move about.

Lucy, aged nine

5.6.2   Dying and Bereavement

Elderly people may be more ready to accept death than the young, and are more likely to have thought about dying and made some preparations. Very elderly people will have lost many friends and relatives and death may become familiar. A famous study of dying patients was carried out by an American physician called Elizabeth Kubler-Ross. She challenged the taboos of discussing dying and identified the needs of dying patients. Kubler-Ross (1969) described five stages of dying.

Denial is often the patient's first reaction to being told the news; learning that life will not continue as thought can be a severe shock. This may be followed by *anger;* the patient begins to look for a scapegoat and may resent others, including health professionals. Even elderly people may become bitter and resentful as they near the end of their lives. *Bargaining* may take place in which the patient promises to be good or very compliant in return for more time to live. If death seems unavoidable the patient may become very *depressed* and withdraw from all social contact and even refuse to cooperate with treatment. They may be mourning their own death in anticipation. The final stage in Kubler-Ross's theory is that of *acceptance*. The patient becomes resigned and may make farewells. Subsequent studies have found that these are not chronological stages and that many patients may move from one to another or miss out a stage altogether. Patients may also be very anxious, about either the nature of their dying or uncontrolled pain.

Bereavement is the term for significant loss, and is followed by an emotional response called the 'grief reaction'. Parkes (1986) described stages of the grief reaction of widows to the death of their husbands, during the first year of bereavement:

Denial
There may be feelings of numbness and unreality, and the loss may seem like a bad dream. The person may cry uncontrollably or feel that they should not do so. Mourning is the cultural expression of grief and there are differences across cultures.

Yearning
The bereaved person tries to reassure the lost person, perhaps by clinging on to clothing or letters.

Despair
This may be intense and lead to prolonged depression. The widows felt that they would not be able to cope and that life without their spouses was not worth living.

Recovery
Gradual acceptance of the bereaved state, although 'you never get over it'.

As in Kubler-Ross's study of dying patients, these stages are not fixed or even necessary, but they are recognisable. Anniversaries become important times and may re-awaken the grieving process.

5.6.3 Loss of Sensory Abilities

The changes in sensory ability increase and it may become harder to compensate for loss. Changes in visual ability may restrict mobility or ease of reading. Loss of hearing may make conversation difficult to follow, or the volume on the television may need to be turned up higher than other family members wish. Higher thresholds of smell mean that body odour may be undetected. Many of these changes make it less likely that the elderly person will be socially active. When the individual withdraws and loses practice in these skills this may be taken as further evidence of psychosocial decline, and lead to further withdrawal. This situation could contribute to a decline in self efficacy that may become more and more evident. Old people may experience increasing difficulty in moving around; they may become dependent and suffer further reductions in self esteem and self confidence. The less mobile an elderly person becomes the less use the senses are given. This may lead to clumsiness and embarrassment by dropping things or bumping into objects. The health professional can break this cycle.

A decline in visual acuity, dark adaptation and narrowing of the visual field can all reduce mobility. Elderly people find it hard to distinguish objects in low levels of illumination and cope less well with glare. Colour discrimination especially blue/green is reduced so that identifying pills by colour could be a problem.

The ability to perceive depth also declines and elderly people frequently trip or fall down stairs. The reduction of the ability to hear high frequency sounds means that speech may be less easily understood and conversation difficult to follow. Loss of taste sensitivity may be accompanied by a loss of interest in food. The importance of eating in social interactions means that another opportunity may be lost. Similarly, loss of sense of smell will alter the perception of food and malnutrition may lead to mental confusion. Loss of memory and a decline in the rate of learning may be the most obvious difficulties in caring for very old people. The implications of changes in mental performance for therapy with elderly people are discussed by Simpson (1992).

There are many positive aspects of therapy with elderly people. Bond and Coleman (1990) point out that many old people are well adjusted but 'because of our lack of imagination we do not appreciate their achievement'. Most old people under 80 years of age are not patients. The better the reported health the less likely there is to be intellectual decline (Perlmutter and Nyquist 1990).

If time is taken to listen to a patient in old age, there is a wealth of fascinating personal history to rival any soap opera. While the present very elderly population may reminisce about the Second World War, from the young-old a perceptive listener can elicit accounts of music in the 50's, life before television, or sex before the pill.

Activity 5.14

Review the losses experienced by the very old. Medical research may lead to a reduction in the rate of these losses. The same research may lead to ways of prolonging life. To what extent do you think that such research should be supported?

If the length and quality of life could be prolonged, would you set an upper limit? What are the implications of extending life expectancy by ten or twenty years?

5.7   SUMMARY

There are psychological changes over the lifespan that affect health. The early experience of attachment and childhood illness experiences may influence health in later life. During adolescence we come to understand the relationship of behaviour to health. In adulthood, reproductive issues play an important part in determining health and health behaviour, especially for women. Changes in midage have been studied in terms of life events and life crises. In old age there are physical changes, but elderly people are not necessarily ill.

5.8 FURTHER READING

Bond, J. and Coleman, P. (eds) (1990) *Ageing in society: An Introduction to Social Gerontology*. London: Sage

This draws together psychology and sociology, and is less negative than many books on ageing. A good source book.

Berryman, J.C., Hargreaves, D., Herbert, M. and Taylor, A. (1991) *Developmental Psychology and You*. Leicester: The British Psychological Society

A very readable and informative book – a successor to *Psychology and You*.

Llewelyn, S and Osborne, K. (1990) *Women's Lives* London: Routledge

The authors consider women's psychology from a developmental perspective and draw on their experience as clinical psychologists.

Tysoe, M. (1992) *Love Isn't Quite Enough. The Psychology of Male–Female Relationships* London: Fontana

This book will make you laugh. It also describes up-to-date psychological research in a readable format.

5.9 REFERENCES

Abraham, C. and Shanley, E. (1992) *Social Psychology for Nurses*. London: Edward Arnold

Alder, E. (1984a) Psychological aspects of AID. In: *Psychological Aspects of Genetic Counselling,* edited by A. Emery and I. Pullen. London: Academic Press

Alder, E.M. (1984b) Postpartum changes in mood and sexuality and some implications of care. In: *Maternal and Infant Health Care* edited by M. Houston. Recent Advances in Nursing series Edinburgh: Churchill-Livingstone

Alder, EM. and Bancroft, J.(1988) The relationship between breastfeeding persistence, sexuality and mood in postpartum women. *Psychological Medicine, **18**,* 389–396

Alder, E.M. (1989) Sexual behaviour in pregnancy, after childbirth and during breast feeding. In: *Psychological aspects of Obstetrics and Gynaecology,* edited by M. Oates. Bailliere's Clinical obstetrics and gynae cology, **3–4**, 805–821

Anderson, E.M. and Clarke, L. (1982) *Disability in Adolescence*. London: Methuen

Argyle, M. (1987) *The Psychology of Happiness*. London: Methuen

Asso, D. (1983) *The Real Menstrual Cycle*. Chichester: Wiley

Berryman, J.C., Hargreaves, D., Herbert, M. and Taylor, A. (1991) *Developmental Psychology and You*. Leicester: The British Psychological Society

Bibace, R. and Walsh, M. (1979) Developmental stages in children's conceptions of illness. In: *Health Psychology,* edited by G Stone *et al.* San Francisco: Jossey-Bass

Bibace, R. and Walsh, M.E. (1981) Children's conceptions of illness. In: *Children's Conceptions of Health, Illness, and Bodily Functions,* edited by R. Bibace and M.E. Walsh. San Francisco: Josey-Bass

Bird, J.E. and Podmore, V.N. (1990) Children's understanding of health and illness. *Psychology and Health,* **4**, 175–185

Blaxter S. (1987) Self-reported health. In: *The Health and Life Style Survey,* edited by B.D. Cox. London: Health Promotion Trust

Bloom, B., Asher, S.J., White ,S.W., (1978) Marital disruption as a stressor: a review and analysis. *Psychological Bulletin,* **85**, 867–894

Bond, J. and Coleman, P. (eds) (1990) *Ageing in society An Introduction to Social Gerontology*. London: Sage

Bowlby, J. (1969) *Attachment and Loss, V1, Attachment*. London: Hogarth

Bowlby, J. (1973) *Attachment and Loss, V2, Separation, Anxiety and Anger*. London: Hogarth

Burns, R.B. (1991) *Essential Psychology,* 2nd edn. London: Kluwer Academic Publishers

Cox, J.L. (1986) *Postnatal Depression. A Guide for Health Professionals*. Edinburgh: Churchill Livingstone

Cox, J.L. (1989) Postnatal depression: a serious and neglected phenomenon. *Psychological Aspects of Obstetrics and Gynaecology* (ed.) M. Oates, Bailliere's Clinical obstetrics and gynaecology, **3**, 839–855

Dalton, K. (1960) Menstruation and accidents. *British Medical Journal,* **ii**, 1425–1426

Douglas, J.W.B. (1975) Early hospital admissions and later disturbances of behaviour and learning. *Developmental Medicine and Child Neurology,* **17**, 456–480

Duck, S. (1986) *Human Relationships. An Introduction to Social Psychology*. London: Sage Publications

Eiser, C. (1989) Children's concepts of illness: towards an alternative to the "stage" approach. *Psychology and Health,* **3**, 93–101

Eiser, C. (1990) *Chronic Diseases in Childhood. An Introduction to Psychological Theory and Research*. Cambridge: Cambridge University Press

Eiser, C., Patterson, D. and Eiser, J.R. (1983) Children's knowledge of health and illness: implications for health education, *Child: Care, Health and Development,* **9**, 285–292

Erikson, E. (1965) *Childhood and Society.* Harmondsworth: Penguin and Hogarth Press

French, S. and Patterson, M. (1992) Psychological development of the child. In: *Physiotherapy: A Psychosocial Approach,* edited by S. French. Oxford: Butterworth-Heinmann

Gater, R.A., Dean, C. and Morris, J. (1989) The contribution of childbearing to the sex difference in first admission rates for affective psychosis. *Psychological Medicine,* **19**, 719–724

Gigy, L.L. (1980) Self concept of single women. *Psychology of Women Quarterly,* 5, 321–340

Graham, C. and Bancroft, J. (1993) Women, mood and the Menstrual cycle In: *The Health Psychology of Women,* edited by C. A. Niven and D. Carroll. Chur: Harwood Academic Publishers

Graham, C.A. and McGrew, W.C. (1992) Social factors and menstrual synchrony in a population of nurses. In: *Menstrual Health in Women,* edited by A.J. Dan and L.L. Lewis. University of Illinois

Hafner, R.J. (1986) *Marriage and Mental Illness.* New York: Guilford Press

Hayes, N. (1993) *Principles of Social Psychology.* Hove (UK): Lawrence Erlbaum Associates

Heider, F. (1958) *The Psychology of Interpersonal Relations.* New York: Wiley

Herbert, M. (1993) *Working with Children and the Children Act.* Leicester: BPS Books

Hoeffer, R.B. (1987) Predictors of life outlook of older single women. *Research in Nursing and Health,* **10**, 111–117

Holden, J. (1991) Postnatal depression: its nature, effects and identification using the Edinburgh Postnatal depression scale. *Birth,* **18**, 211–221

Hunter, M. (1990) *Your Menopause.* London: Pandora

Huston, T.L., Surra, C., Fitzgerald, N. and Cate, R. (1981) From courtship to marriage: mate selection as an interpersonal process. In: *Personal Relationships. 2. Developing Personal Relationships,* edited by S.W. Duck and R.W. Gilmour. London: Academic Press

Jones, G.J.O. and Harris, V.A. (1967) The attribution of attitudes. *Journal of Experimental Social Psychology,* **3**, 1–24

Kafka, F. (1916) Metamorphosis. In: *Metamorphosis and Other Stories,* translated by W and E Muir, 1961. Harmondsworth: Penguin Books

Klaus, M. and Kennell, J. (1982) *Parent Infant Bonding.* St Louis, CV: Mosby

Kubler-Ross, E. (1969) *On Death and Dying.* New York: Tavistock

Kumar, R.F. (1989) Postpartum psychosis. In: *Psychological Aspects of Obstetrics and Gynaecology* (ed.) M. Oates. Bailliere's Clinical Obstetrics and Gynaecology, **3–4**, 823–838

Kumar, R. and Brockington, I.F. (1988) *Motherhood and Mental Illness. 2. Causes and Consequences.* London: Wright

Laws, S. (1992) 'It's just the monthlies, she'll get over it'. Menstrual problems and men's attitudes. *Journal of Reproductive and Infant Psychology,* **10**, 117–128

Levinson, D.J., Darrow, C.B., Klein F.B., Levinson, M.H. and McKee, B. (1978) *The Seasons of a Man's Life*. New York: Knopf

Lewis, C. (1986) *Becoming a Father*. Milton Keynes: Open University Press

Lewis, V.J. and Blair, A.J. (1993) Women, food and body image. In: The *Health Psychology of Women*, edited by C. Niven and D. Carroll. Chur: Harwood Academic Publishers

Llewelyn, S. and Osborne, K. (1990) *Women's Lives*. London: Routledge

MacIntyre, S. (1986) The patterning of health by social position in contemporary Britain: directions for sociological research. *Social Science and Medicine*, **23**, 393–415

Markman, H.J., Floyd, F.J., Stanley, S.M. and Storaasli, R.D. (1988) Prevention of marital distress: a longitudinal investigation. *Journal of Consulting and Clinical Psychology*, **56**, 210–217

Marshall, H. (1991) The Social Construction of Motherhood: an analysis of child care and Parenting Manuals. In: *Motherhood, meanings, practices and ideologies* edited by A. Phoenix, A. Woollett and E. Lloyd. London: Sage

McClintock, M.K. (1971) Menstrual synchrony and suppression. *Nature* 229, 244–245

McKinnon, I., McKinnon, P., and Thomson, P. (1959) Lethal hazards of the luteal phase of the menstrual cycle. *British Medical Journal*, i, 1015–1017

O'Hara, M.W. and Zekoski, E.M. (1988) Post partum depression: a comprehensive review. In: *Motherhood and Mental Illness. 2.* edited by R. Kumar and I.F. Brockington. London: Wright

Oates, M. (1988) The development of an integrated community-orientated service for severe postnatal mental illness. In: *Motherhood and Mental Illness. 2.* edited by R. Kumar and I.F. Brockington. London: Wright

Oates, M. (1989) Management of major mental illness in pregnancy and the puerperium. In: *Psychological Aspects of Obstetrics and Gynaecology* (ed.) M. Oates. Bailliere's Clinical Obstetrics and Gynaecology, **3–4**, 905–920

Piaget, J. (1950) *The Growth of Intelligence*. London: Routledge

Parkes, C.M. (1986) *Bereavement; Studies of Grief in Adult Life,* 2nd edn. Harmondsworth: Penguin

Paton, D. And Brown, R. (1991) *Lifespan Health Psychology Nursing Problems and Interventions*. London: Harper Collins

Perlmutter, M. and Nyquist, N.L. (1990) Relationships between self-reported physical and mental health and intelligence performance across adulthood. *Journal of Gerontology*, **45**, 145–155

Phoenix, A., Woollett, A. and Lloyd, E. (1991) (Eds.) *Motherhood, Meanings Practices and Ideologies*. London: Sage

Pruitt, S.D. and Elliott, C.H. (1990) Paediatric Problems. In: *Stress and Medical Procedures,* edited by M. Johnston and L. Wallace. Oxford: Oxford University Press

Quinton, D. and Rutter, M. (1976) Early hospital admissions and later disturbances of behavior: an attempted replication of Douglas' findings. *Developmental Medicine and Child Neurology,* **18**, 447–459

Ross, N. and Fletcher, G.J.O. (1985) Attribution and Social Perception. In: *Handbook of Social Psychology,* edited by G. Lindzey and E. Aronson V2. 2nd edn. New York: Academic Press

Rutter, M. (1972) *Maternal Deprivation Reassessed.* Harmondsworth: Penguin

Simpson, J.M. (1992) Growing older: changes in mental performance. In: *Physiotherapy: A Psychosocial Approach,* edited by S. French. Oxford: Butterworth-Heinmann

Social Trends 24 (1994) London: HMSO

Spitz, R.A. (1945) Hospitalism. In: *The Psychoanalytic Study of the Child,* edited by O. Fenickel. *et al.* New York: IUP

Tuch, R. (1975) The relationship between a mother's menstrual status and her response to illness in her child. *Psychosomatic Medicine,* 37, 388–394

Tysoe, M. (1992) *Love Isn't Quite Enough. The Psychology of Male–Female Relationships.* London: Fontana

Ussher, J.M. (1989) *The Psychology of the Female Body.* London: Routledge

Ussher, J.M. and Wilding, J.M. (1992) Interactions between stress and performance during the menstrual cycle in relation to the premenstrual syndrome. *Journal of Reproductive and Infant Psychology,* **10**, 83–01

Walker, A. (1992) Premenstrual syndrome and ovarian hormones: a review. *Journal of Reproductive and Infant Psychology,* **10**, 67–82

6

Health and Reproduction

CONTENTS

6.1 INTRODUCTION

Reproductive issues affect all of us throughout our lives. They also feature prominently in the patterns and norms of our society. Imagine a daily newspaper in which all references to sex, birth or parenting were removed. Psychological issues relating to sexuality, pregnancy and birth are of intrinsic interest to all of us, but they also have special relevance to health professionals.

Reproductive issues are relevant to us all when we become patients, both men and women. Our psychological and physical health may be affected by the stage of reproductive career or sexual relationships. Our state of health may be the consequence of previous reproductive events. Reproductive changes over the lifespan particularly affect women, and from puberty onwards, biological changes, social changes, and psychological changes have powerful effects. We will consider just some of the influences of reproduction on health that are relevant to care by health professionals.

Box 6.1 Reproductive events in women's lives

Biological event	Psychosocial event
Puberty	Adolescent rôle change
Menstrual cycles	
Sexual interest and arousal	Contraceptive behaviour
Hormonal contraception	Stable relationships
	Decision to have children
Infertility	
Pregnancy	
Childbirth	Transition to parenthood
Lactation	Breast feeding
	Postnatal depression
Sterilization	Decision to have no more children
Premenstrual syndrome	
Physical changes with ageing	
Irregular menstrual cycles	Children leave home
Menopause	The climacteric or change of life
Ageing	Change in rôle

Activity 6.1

If you are female: To what extent do you think that your own experience fits into the events in Box 6.1? Discuss with a colleague how you would adapt it. Has anything been left out?

If you are male: Does this fit with your knowledge of women? Could you make up your own version of the list of events in column 1. Would column 2 be very different?

6.2   SEX AND GENDER

When considering the influence of reproductive events it seems obvious to distinguish between those of us that are men and those of us that are women. This distinction is very simple and we need also to have an understanding of the concept of gender. *Gender identity* is the awareness that we have of our membership of one particular sex. *Gender designation* is the gender assigned by others to an individual and may not be the same as gender identity which is the individual's perception of themselves. These two aspects may have different relationships to the psychology of health.

The biological differences between the sexes are usually obvious, but of course, the similarities are greater than the differences. *Biological sex* is determined by sex chromosomes that determine the embryonic development of the testes and ovaries. Sexual differentiation at puberty is regulated by sex hormones secreted mainly by the ovaries or testes. At birth the baby is designated as a boy or girl on the external evidence of genitalia. This designation will not only determine the individual's own perceptions of self, but it will determine the reactions of other people.

Gender also refers to expectations of appropriate male or female behaviour and these vary across cultures (Oakley 1974). We may think of women as being understanding, warm, and cooperative and men as being confident, competent and self reliant. These are not necessarily opposite characteristics and are not necessarily mutually exclusive. I would like my daughters to have all of these characteristics (and my husband to have them too)! Bem (1974) showed that people can have both 'masculine' and 'feminine' characteristics, and described such people as being *androgynous*. Androgynous people may be more adaptable and more able to cope with different demands made on them by modern society. Women in traditional roles may be disadvantaged in coping with competition in the work place and power struggles. Horner (1970) described the 'fear of success', which is experienced by many women. Success may threaten their self concept of femininity.

In the past the profession of nursing has been associated with the traditional feminine behavioural characteristics of caring, altruism and obedience. More recently the emphasis in the health professions has been on independent decision making. The number of men entering the nursing profession is increasing and there are also changes in the sex ratios of other health professions. The profession of physiotherapy lies between the traditional male role of the doctor and the traditionally female role of the nurse

(Sim 1986). Physiotherapists, whether male or female, are expected both to cure and to care. A Swedish study found that the proportion of men entering courses in physiotherapy increased from three per cent before 1962 to 25% in 1987. Similar increases were noted in nursing, but at the same time in medicine the proportion of male students decreased (Bergman and Markland 1989). In a study in Australia, physiotherapy students who enrolled in 1976 were compared with those enrolling in 1986 (Westbrook and Nordholm 1987). In 1976, ten out of 74 students (14%) were male, compared with 58 out of 173 (34%) in 1986. There were no changes in androgyny scores in women over the ten years, suggesting that female physiotherapy students had not decreased in 'femininity' or increased in 'masculinity'.

Health may be perceived differently in the two sexes, and may also be perceived differently by the two sexes. Broverman *et al.* (1970) asked psychologists, psychiatrists and social workers to describe the characteristics of three people; a healthy woman, a healthy man and a healthy person. The healthy *person* was described in masculine terms, similar to terms used to describe the *healthy man*. We know that we make many attribution errors when we know the sex of a person. Symptoms taken seriously when presented by a man may be dismissed when presented by a woman.

Activity 6.2

What is the gender ratio in your profession or institution? Is it changing or likely to change? Could this be related to changing traditional gender roles?

6.3 SEX AND ADOLESCENCE

The years between childhood and adulthood are described in our society as adolescence (see Chapter 5). It is a time of changing role and changing body image, and many adolescents appear moody and difficult. Sexuality in adolescent patients is frequently ignored. Douglas (1993) discusses the problems of nursing older children. She describes behaviour problems of drug abuse, anorexia nervosa; emotional problems of anxiety and depression, and mental illness in adolescents of schizophrenia and disintegrative psychoses, but she does not discuss sexuality or sexual problems.

The concern about the transmission of the human immunodeficiency virus (HIV) by unprotected sexual intercourse, has focused attention on the sexual behaviour of young people. Abraham *et al.* (1991) in a study of over 1000 Scottish teenagers found that health professionals were an important source of informal advice and information about HIV. Discussion of the risks of unprotected sexual activity outside stable relationships may lead health professionals into discussions about normal sexual activity, sexual problems and sexual morality.

Activity 6.3

How many of these problems of adolescents discussed by Douglas (1993) do think could be complicated by changes in sexuality? Why do you think sexuality in adolescent patients is often not discussed?

6.3.1   Premarital Sex

There is probably a greater acceptance of premarital sex today. This may be partly because of a declining influence of the 'double standard'. At one time it was considered more acceptable for boys to be sexually active than for girls. Wellings (1994) reported the results of a large survey of interviews with over 18 thousand people aged 16 to 59. They had a 65 % response rate and the study gave a picture of sexual activity in Britain in 1990. The median age for loss of virginity in women was 21 for those born in the 1930's but 17 for those born between 1966 and 1975. First intercourse took place at a younger age in men but the difference between men and women is getting less. There was one year's difference between the sexes for those born before 1966, but for those born after 1966 the median age at first intercourse was the same.

6.3.2   Masturbation

Masturbation may still be associated with guilt, although it is now less of a taboo subject. At one time it was regarded as a vice and Kellogg (of corn-flakes fame) suggested that adolescents should be discouraged from mastur-bating by placing a spiked ring around the penis (Marshall 1992). It was thought that masturbation could lead to insanity, and even though this may sound ridiculous, some of this thinking may persist today. Masters and Johnson (1966) in their very influential book on human sexuality reported that all of their sample of over 3000 men thought that 'excessive' masturbation could lead to a mental disorder. However, they didn't believe that their own levels of masturbation were dangerous! Most adolescent boys masturbate, and yet the subject may cause them and their carers embarrassment. Even modern textbooks frequently ignore sexuality and the practice of masturbation by adolescent patients, even though it must be a common practice in adoles-cent wards.

In women the subject is even more taboo. The Kinsey data of the 1940's suggests that 40% of women have masturbated to orgasm at some time. Ban-croft (1989) suggests that the number of women masturbating has probably increased slightly since then, and women now masturbate at an earlier age.

6.3.3   Teenage Pregnancies

The teenage mother may confront the health professional with particular demands. If she is very young, (under fifteen years old), her nutritional needs and physical development are different; she may lack financial and social support; and she may have little appreciation of the demands of parenting. Her pregnancy challenges the idea of childhood innocence and may arouse moral judgements. However, there is little evidence that adolescents make poor mothers. In the USA less than half of teenage pregnancies are terminated and most teenagers keep their babies rather than having them adopted or fostered, although fewer are now getting married (Jorgensen 1993). The outcome of adolescent pregnancy may depend much on economic conditions. Many adverse health consequences result from poor antenatal care and low social class, rather than the biological age of the mother. Very young adolescents are more likely to suffer from pregnancy complications, and to have premature births. Horowitz *et al.* (1991) followed up 180 black pregnant 13–18-year-old women first studied in 1967–1969, and found most of their children did not become teenage parents. Those that did were more likely to have had mothers who were chronically depressed.

6.3.4   Sexual Preferences

Although it is becoming more acceptable for gay young people to define and recognise themselves as gay, many adolescents will experience conflict about recognizing their sexual identity. Many gay young men will 'come out' in the late teenage years, but some will not recognise their orientation until adulthood and sometimes not even until after marrying and having children. Limits to the legal age of consent may inhibit acknowledgement of sexual preference. An adolescent patient may be unsure of his sexual identity and so may his carer. It is a very difficult area in which to carry out research and assessing sexual identity in children and adolescents is fraught with problems (Savin-Williams and Rodriguez 1993). We do not know how many people pass though a 'homosexual phase'. Lesbian, gay and bisexual adolescents may feel devalued and victimized, and this will have a negative effect on their self esteem.

6.4   MENSTRUAL CYCLES AND MENSTRUATION

6.4.1   The Menstrual Cycle

The menstrual cycle is a major influence on health and in caring for women it may be important to know the stage of their menstrual cycles (Box 6.2) Menstruation has mystic associations and menstruating women may be regarded as unclean (Ussher 1989). Women themselves may not perceive menstruation negatively. They may think that having regular bleeds is a sign of good health, and a reassurance they are not pregnant.

Box 6.2   The menstrual cycle

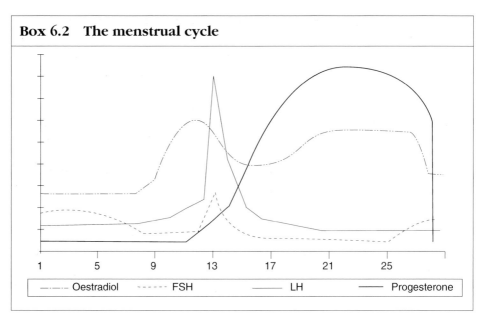

—·—·— Oestradiol	------ FSH	——— LH	——— Progesterone

Changes in menstruation may be an indication of ill health and gynaecologists take detailed menstrual histories. The subjective rating of menstrual periods may not be directly related to health. Women are not very good at estimating menstrual blood loss (Fraser *et al.* 1984), yet heavy menstrual bleeding (menorrhagia), is often a reason for hysterectomy. Granleese (1990) found that women who were poor at measuring their menstrual loss were no different in personality from those who were accurate. Some women who complain of excessive blood loss are found not to have objective blood loss. They are not neurotic, but may be responding to total fluid loss. What actually prompts complaint is the personal experience of the woman who suffers embarrassing flooding or has a continual need to change sanitary towels or tampons. Menstrual pain may be made worse by stress, but it undoubtedly has a physiological basis. It can be treated with prostaglandin inhibitors but psychological treatment can also help. Relaxation and exercise have been shown to reduce pain and discomfort (Gannon 1989).

6.4.2   Premenstrual Syndrome

Within the normal cycle there may be positive and negative changes in mood and physical symptoms. The premenstrual phase has received most attention, but these changes do not only take place during the few days before menstrual bleeding. It is interesting that so much attention has been given to negative aspects of the menstrual cycle, when there are also reports of more energy, self confidence and positive mood at other times of the cycle (Asso 1992).

The premenstrual syndrome (PMS) or premenstrual tension is difficult to diagnose and to define, yet many women complain about it. It is generally described as feeling miserable and irritable in the few days before the period, and then the symptoms disappear when bleeding starts. Fluid retention and feelings of breast tenderness are also reported. There is much variation between women and some months will be better than others even for the same woman. This makes it difficult to assess premenstrual changes and even harder to relate them to social or hormonal factors. There could be different causes of PMS in different women. Some women might be simply more sensitive to hormone changes, and others might be prone to stress-related changes.

There has been much debate about whether PMS is a biological phenomenon or whether it results from social conditioning (Graham and Bancroft 1993). As we saw in Chapter 2 there are different models of health and illness. If the biological view is taken then the woman may ask her doctor for help and may be given hormone treatment or, in cases of severe PMS, even have her ovaries and uterus removed. Alternatively, a social model of health might suggest that the ill effects arise because of negative expectations and that education and changes in society's attitudes towards women would help.

A biological explanation would predict that PMS sufferers would differ in some endocrinological way from non-sufferers, but Walker (1992) reviewed the evidence and found no consistent differences. It is possible to influence the reporting of symptoms by changing women's expectations of the time of menstruation and this suggests a psychosocial phenomenon (Ruble 1977). A feminist perspective suggests that men exert social pressure on women to keep silent about problems with menstruation (Laws 1990).

Activity 6.4

What do you think that women believe about the relationship between moods, premenstrual syndrome and their menstrual cycle? Ask some women about their beliefs.

6.5   REPRODUCTION AND FERTILITY

6.5.1   Contraception

The majority of people in contact with health professionals will be sexually active but relatively few women will be pregnant. We know there is a connection between sexual intercourse and pregnancy even though there is poor correlation of behaviour and outcome! If most young couples are sexually active, and most of them are not infertile, lactating or pregnant, we can assume that they are using contraception. Contraceptive behaviour is therefore widely practised, and it is now an accepted part of our Western culture, although there may be religious and cultural influences on choice of methods of contraception. Contraceptive advice and supplies are widely accessible and contraceptive methods are safe, reliable and relatively inexpensive.

Oral contraceptives are the first choice of contraception in the early years of reproductive life. There has been a fall in the popularity of oral contraceptives and a rise in the use of condoms between 1976 and 1988 (Social Trends 1990). In the 1990 sexual survey on Britain (Wellings 1994) it was found that young people were more likely to report that they had used contraception at the time of first intercourse than older people. Why are some methods more popular than others? As we have seen in much of health psychology, there have been attempts to explain this by the use of models (Alder 1993).

Two models have been suggested. The *contraceptive career* model suggests that the choice of contraception depends on the circumstances at the time and this change with age, the stage of relationship of the couple and their plans for parenting. The model of contraceptive career and the decision model are described in Box 6.3. Whitely and Schofield (1986) considered contraceptive users and non-users in a comprehensive meta analysis of 134 studies of the use of contraception by adolescents. They found strong sup-

---

Box 6.3   Models of Contraceptive Choice

1. Lindemann (1977) described a *contraceptive career* consisting of three stages. In the first **'natural stage'** sexual intercourse is relatively rare and unplanned and the woman does not perceive herself as a sexual being; she neither uses contraception nor takes responsibility for it.

In the second **'peer prescription'** stage there is more frequent sexual activity and a moderate acceptance of sexuality. At this stage she may seek information from intimate women friends but not from outside agencies.

In the **'expert'** stage she has incorporated sexuality into her self concept and so is more willing to use contraception that requires pre-planning, and to seek contraceptive advice. There is little empirical evidence for the career model, although it does have some intuitive validity.

2. The *decision* model suggests that people weigh up the costs and benefits of the expected outcomes and work out the likelihood of the outcomes. They then select the one that gives them most benefits and fewest costs. If the expected benefits are greater than the expected costs, then they will use contraception.

port for the contraceptive career model for women but not for men. Sexual self-acceptance was a major variable for both men and women. Other important variables were frequency of intercourse, age, self esteem and rejection of traditional sex roles.

The *decision* model suggests that the decision is made on a costs/benefit analysis. The decision model also received good support for women in Whitely and Schofield's study. The perceived risk of pregnancy (not surprisingly) was highly associated with contraceptive use. The more positive women felt about the benefits of contraception and its perceived importance, the more likely it was that they would use contraception. Contraceptive use by young women depends on how psycho-sexually mature they are. The decision will also depend on the amount and quality of information that they have (related to their career stage) and their perceived social norms (how acceptable contraceptive behaviour is). The third factor is the stage that a relationship has reached; contraception is more likely to be used if there is a stable sexual relationship.

The oral contraceptive pill has become the gold standard for pregnancy prevention, against which other methods may be compared. Its ease of use, reliability, lack of side effects and availability has undoubtedly raised the general expectations of contraceptive methods. If the woman is ill then she may think that she should stop taking the pill, but then she would lose its protection. Sickness, diarrhoea and the use of antibiotics can also reduce the protection of the oral contraceptive pill.

6.5.2   Safe Sex and Condom Use

The use of condoms has been encouraged to stop the spread of human immunodeficiency virus (HIV) infection. Wellings (1994) reported that condom use rose steeply in the 1980's. Sonerstein *et al.* (1989) compared the behaviour of a sample of 17–19-year-old men interviewed in 1979 with a sample interviewed in 1988. They found that condom use increased from 20% in 1979 to 50% in 1988 at first intercourse, and from 21% to 58% for the most recent occasion of intercourse. The number using no method at all also fell.

'Safe sex' has become an acceptable term for sexual behaviour which includes condom use. Early AIDS campaigns attempted to increase the use of condoms by giving information about AIDS and the transmission of the HIV virus, and about behaviours that increased the risks of infection and safe sex. Although knowledge has increased, heterosexual behaviour does not seem to have changed greatly. In Australia one campaign tried to increase the level of fear in the hope that people would take fewer risks. In this campaign, as we saw in the UK campaigns, although knowledge increased, there was little effect on behaviour. These findings don't support the health belief model and suggest that condom use is very complex.

6.6   REPRODUCTIVE STRATEGIES

Couples may consider if and when to have children long before they get married. The decision to start a family may also influence the decision to get married. The timing of the pregnancy, spacing of births, the number of children and the gender balance may all influence reproductive strategies and hence the choice of contraceptive method.

6.6.1   Whether to have Children

A few married couples prefer to remain childless, but a larger proportion chooses to delay parenting. Most couples are expected to want to have children and they may feel pressurized by family and friends. Woollett *et al.* (1991), in a study of Asian women living in London, found that most women expected to become mothers. Some wanted to have their first child soon after marriage and to have a second child soon after the first. These women tended not to have used contraception before the birth of the first child and were interested in limiting family size only when they had two or three children. Others wanted to delay the birth of the first child for two or three years until their marriages or finances were well established. Half of the 32 women interviewed had given birth within 15 months of marriage. The women balanced the benefits of spending only a few years caring for young children by having them close together, against reducing the effort by having them more widely spaced out.

6.6.2   When to have Children

There has been a trend for later motherhood, and many women have children in their late thirties. There is controversy surrounding the practice of offering post-menopausal women the opportunity to have children by IVF. We have an idea that there is a 'right' time to have children and we may be prejudiced against older mothers (Berryman 1991).

6.6.3   How Many Children

The increase in the use of permanent methods of contraception has undoubtedly reduced family size in the last few decades. The oral contraceptive pill is the most frequently used method during the childbearing years and there has been little change in the past fifteen years. It is now an accepted part of Western culture that the number of children is a matter for choice, at least in non-Catholic countries. The oral contraceptive pill is often used before the birth of the first child, and then to space the second (Hunt and Allendale 1990). Couples may assume that they will be able to control their fertility. The expectations of being able to rely on contraception may have contributed to the recent rise in the popularity of sterilization. Sterilization operations are now taking place at a younger age and at lower levels of parity, suggesting that the reproductive strategy of the future is to limit family size. Some couples will choose to have only one child, and may be considered selfish. There may be prejudice against only children, although there is little evidence to support this popular view (Laybourn 1994).

Activity 6.5

From the point of view of your own profession or discipline consider the advantages and disadvantages of a woman having children close together or spaced apart by two years or more. What are the psychological advantages and disadvantages? Are the advantages and disadvantages different for men?

6.7   INFERTILITY

About 10% to 15% of couples have infertility problems and childlessness can occur in couples who have never had children (primary infertility), and in those who have already had children (secondary infertility). The inability to have children can arise because women miscarry or have stillbirths. Many causes lie within the reproductive system of the woman, but male factors account for about a quarter of couples with subfertility. In about another quarter the infertility problem will be unexplained, although this depends on the length of time of investigation, and the extent to which the couple are prepared to undergo investigations.

Young couples who do not have children and who have been married for a number of years, are expected to have children. Their families and friends may well begin to ask them about their family plans. They may assume that they are childless by choice and to isolate them for being selfish. Campbell (1985) suggests that in our society, parenthood is perceived as having status. For women it is a natural expression of their femininity and for men a duty. This view may be changing, as couples come to expect to be able to make choices and women feel able to choose alternative careers.

For those that want children, but are unable to have them, grief can be very intense. Their pattern of grief may resemble that described for bereavement (Kubler-Ross 1969). Their initial reaction to the diagnosis may be shock and disbelief and the couple should be told together and given time to absorb the information and a chance to return to ask questions later. Denial may result in rejection of the clinic's findings and a renewed search for medical advice. Some couples get caught up in a series of medical investigations that may become more and more invasive (see Chapter 3 for discussion of stressful medical procedures). Some couples become obsessed with monitoring their basal temperature, frequency and timing of sexual intercourse so that their sexual relationships suffer (Bell and Alder 1994). Their anger may be directed at themselves, perhaps for a previous termination, venereal disease, or premarital promiscuity. It may also be directed at their employers for an undefined environmental cause or to health professionals for not being able to diagnose and treat. Women in particular may feel distressed and they may grieve for children that they have never had. The grief may be for loss of immortality when they feel unable to leave something of themselves for the future; it could be for loss of role or status; or for a positive desire for motherhood. Both men and women can have a very intense longing for children, and this has been recognized in folklore.

Activity 6.6

Discuss the kinds of reasons that couples might give to explain their lack of children to themselves, to their immediate family and to others. Analyse these in terms of attribution (see Chapter 2).

Activity 6.7

Look at typical fairy tales for young children and identify those that refer to a longing for children, e.g. Tom Thumb, The Gingerbread Man, The Sleeping Beauty. What are they telling us about having children, and what do they mean to the young children that listen to them?

It seems unlikely that there is infertility of 'psychogenic' origin, but psychological factors have been considered to have an effect. Sexual problems associated with conditions such as diabetes may well reduce the chances of conception, as will excessive use of alcohol, or drug abuse. Most couples with unexplained infertility eventually conceive and stress appears unrelated to the chances of conception. It is more likely that there are subtle endocrinological differences, which reduce the chances of conception or implantation.

Modern reproductive technology has increased the opportunities for treatment for infertile couples and advances are constantly being made. Artificial insemination by donor (DI) can be used in couples where the man is infertile but the woman ovulates normally. Semen from an anonymous donor is inseminated into the vagina of the fertile woman. If she conceives she will have a child who carries half of her genes and half of those of the donor. The pregnancy proceeds normally, and the couple need not tell anyone that the conception did not occur in the usual way. There is much controversy about the implications for the children. In a study carried out ten years ago, we found that out of 20 couples receiving DI, seven wives and ten husbands would never tell a child that it was conceived by DI (Alder 1984).

Since the birth of the first 'test tube baby' in 1978, *in vitro* fertilization (IVF) has been used throughout the world. The procedure carries a low success rate but it may be the only way in which women who have damaged fallopian tubes can bear children. There are, of course, implications that are far reaching. Surrogate mothers can carry embryos resulting from donated eggs and sperm for women who cannot maintain a pregnancy. There is controversy and debate about the moral and ethical issues, and advances in reproductive endocrinology have even made it possible for post-menopausal women to bear children.

Activity 6.8

What are your views on the implications of 60-year-old women having children? How would your colleagues react to caring for a pregnant 60-year-old in your profession? Would there be any special psychological care that older mothers might need? Contrast this with the teenage mothers discussed in Section 6.3.3.

6.7.1   Sterilization

Once a couple decides that their family is complete, they are faced with the problem of choosing a contraceptive method that they may have to continue using for another twenty years or more. Some women remain fertile into their forties and if they miss a period this may mean that they are pregnant. Health professionals need to be alert to the possibility of pregnancy in older women.

Many women will have chosen laparoscopic sterilization when their families are complete and will effectively forget about contraception. The procedure involves tying, cutting, or more often clipping, the Fallopian tubes that transport the eggs from the ovary to the uterus. The method became popular in the 1970s because it was a simple and effective surgical procedure, involved one post-operative check, no provision of supplies, few side effects and had a low failure rate. From the woman's point of view the operation could be done on a day care basis, left only two small scars and was safe. However, sterilization operations are effectively irreversible and so the decision to be sterilized means the couple need to be very sure that they will not want more children. It is very difficult to repair Fallopian tubes successfully, but very few women regret that they have had the operation. In a retrospective study of over 500 patients only 2% complained about physical problems (Lawson *et al.* 1979). Prospective studies report low rates of regret of around 5% (e.g. Cooper *et al.* 1982). Lambers *et al.* (1984) identified the factors associated with regret following sterilization as being: lack of freedom of choice in the decision-making process; a belief that the sterilization operation would solve other problems; an inability to cope with loss of fertility, and a strong adherence to a sex role identity that was linked to reproductive capacity. There is some evidence that young women may be more likely to regret sterilization, but this is closely tied to the increased risk of marital breakdown associated with both early marriages and later regret. In our retrospective study six women expressed some regret. These consisted of two whose housing conditions had improved, one whose marriage had broken down, one because of a perceived loss of femininity, one who wanted more children, and one because of menstrual problems that began after she had stopped taking the oral contraceptive pill (Alder *et al.* 1981).

Vasectomy in men involves cutting or heat sealing the vas deferens that carries the sperm to the penis for ejaculation. It is a simpler and safer operation than female sterilization and has a lower failure rate. Some men are reluctant to undergo an operation on their genitals. Others do not want to end their fertility prematurely, as they may be potentially capable of fathering children into their sixties. The decision to be sterilized needs to be carefully considered and counselling will help the couple decide which partner should undergo the operation.

6.8   PREGNANCY AND CHILDBIRTH

The majority of women become pregnant and give birth. A pregnant woman or a mother of a young baby is in no sense ill (see Chapter 2 for discussions of definitions of illness), but she experiences considerable biological and psychological changes. Awareness of these changes may help to understand the reasons for illness behaviour in pregnant women or in mothers of young children. Health professionals are particularly aware of the way in which biological and psychological factors work together, because they are interacting with people who have or have had a health problem but are not necessarily ill.

When a woman becomes pregnant she also comes into contact with the medical profession and health professionals, perhaps for the first time. Admission to maternity hospital may be her first admission to hospital and her experience may influence her attitudes and beliefs about hospitals and medical care. It may be the first time that she meets dieticians and physiotherapists as well as nursing and midwifery staff.

6.8.1   Changes in Sexuality

A woman who is pregnant experiences both physical and psychological changes. These begin in pregnancy when there are physical changes in muscle tone, size and shape of the body, and sometimes overwhelming fatigue. The woman may give up work, change her role in her family, and feel that her body image has changed. Childbirth itself is physically stressful and may involve analgesia and an episiotomy. It is often a very emotional experience for both partners. Stitches at the episiotomy site (a cut made in the vagina at delivery to avoid tearing) may cause pain and discomfort with sexual intercourse after the baby is born. The vagina may feel dry and the breasts become enlarged and heavy. The psychological effects on sexual behaviour include changes in mood, almost certainly fatigue, and the unpredictable and irresistible demands of the baby. Of course there are positive aspects too. Both partners may feel reassured about their gender role; they may feel more 'feminine' or more 'masculine'. There is a high status attached to becoming a parent and they may feel more mature and confident.

There are interesting psychological changes that take place during the transition to parenthood, including changes in sexuality in its broadest sense. Studies that have assessed changes in sexual activity during pregnancy have mostly found a gradual decline over successive months. This is followed by a slow return to pre-pregnancy levels over the first postnatal year. Many reasons have been suggested for this pattern such as fatigue, changes in body image, perineal pain, mood state, breast feeding or hormones (Alder 1994). Robson *et al.* (1981), in a prospective study of middle-class women in London, found little change in sexual activity during pregnancy until the third trimester. Those reporting little or no pleasure from sex before pregnancy were much more likely to have stopped having intercourse in the first trimester. Only 40% said that they found sex enjoyable in the third trimester and only 26% had orgasm.

6.8.2   Changes in Mood

The transition to parenthood can be seen as a developmental crisis and there are emotional changes during pregnancy as well as social changes and relationship with their own parents will change. Parenthood is rated as one of the most important aspects of life. Although there are costs in terms of increased risk to mental and physical health, having children also brings satisfaction and a sense of meaning to life for many couples.

Health professionals may be more aware of problems of adjustment during pregnancy and following childbirth. In the first postnatal year the mother has to adjust to the demands of a young baby, maybe the loss of her job and changes in family dynamics. She will establish a different relationship with her partner and with her mother. She may give up work and change her perceived status. She may also miss the social contacts, the structure and routine of work, and may feel isolated from former colleagues. Even her own mother is likely to be at work during the day. Changes in body image as she increases in size may reawaken fears of being fat and she may wonder if she will ever be the same again.

It has been suggested (Cox 1989) that between 9% and 13% of mothers suffer from a prolonged postnatal depression in the first postnatal year (see Chapter 5). The consequences of pregnancy and childbirth can thus be far reaching.

6.8.3   Breast Feeding

It may be important to know if a mother of a young baby is breast feeding for a variety of reasons related to health, and to understand the psychological state of a new mother. Breast feeding is an important influence on post-natal sexuality, mood and sleep. Not only are hormonal profiles in breast-feeding women different from those in bottle-feeding women but there may also be psychological differences between those who persist in breast feeding for several months, those who never attempt breast feeding and those who begin breast feeding in hospital, but discontinue when they go home. The relationship between breast feeding and sexuality has been investigated in a number of studies (Alder *et al.* 1986, Alder and Bancroft 1988), but it is a very complex issue (Alder 1989).

One of the difficulties in comparing groups of bottle feeders with breast feeders is that within a group of bottle feeders there may be different reasons for giving up breast feeding. Some women give up breast feeding in order to resume an active sex life because they are more sexually interested. Others may be inhibited about their bodies and dislike physical contact.

6.8.4   Fatigue

Mothers of new babies get very tired and some babies may continue to wake for night feeds for many months. In our study of 25 primiparous women, (Alder and Bancroft 1983), nineteen babies were breast fed exclusively for at least six months and nine of these still woke for night feeds at six months. These babies were fed more frequently than the babies who did not wake in the night. The mothers of these babies that woke in the night also took longer to resume sexual intercourse. This could be because the couples who wanted to have sex might have encouraged their babies to sleep through the night (e.g. by topping them up with an extra feed in the evening). Alternatively, those couples whose babies slept through the night might have been less tired and would have had more opportunity to be sexually active than those with waking babies.

Activity 6.9

Talk to a couple who have had children. Ask them what was the worst and what was the best thing about the first few weeks after their baby was born. Did the father differ from the mother?

6.8.5   Miscarriage and Abortion

About 20% of pregnancies end in miscarriage before twenty weeks, but this may be an underestimate because some miscarriages will occur too early to be recognised. Friedman and Gath (1989) followed up women one month after they had had a miscarriage and found that nearly half of them could be rated as suffering from psychiatric disturbance. This was measured on a standardized psychiatric diagnostic interview that gives an incidence of psychiatric disturbance in the normal population of about 12%. Similar levels were reported in a small study in Ireland (Jackman *et al.* 1991). Loss from early miscarriage may not be recognised, especially if the couples have not told their family and friends that they are expecting a baby. Their grief remains hidden and unspoken. It may be falsely assumed that if they have not experienced the baby kicking that they do not feel that the baby is real. The practice of ultrasound scanning may make it more likely that the mother is aware that her foetus is a baby.

Miscarriage may be regarded as a gynaecological event rather than a pregnancy, and women can be helped by health professionals who recognize that it is a significant event. Partners may also be distressed and men often find it difficult to discuss their emotional feelings. The grief may be similar to that experienced by a woman who has been diagnosed as infertile; she may feel the loss of an image of herself as a pregnant woman and as a parent, and may feel that she may never be able to bear children and feel guilt and anger (Hunter 1994).

6.9   MENOPAUSE

The menopause means literally 'the last period'. However, women don't know that it is their last period until a year later. If twelve months have passed with no periods then they know that they are through the menopause. All is not yet over, however, and the term 'climacteric' or 'perimenopause' is used to describe the years either side of the menopause. Many women have several years of irregular periods, and Studd *et al.* (1977) suggest that the climacteric may begin some ten years before the menopause, and end some ten years after. This would be an exceptionally long time for any one woman, but the climacteric can take place at any time between the ages of 40 and 60. (Box 6.4)

Box 6.4   Definitions of the Menopause

Menopause the permanent cessation of menstruation resulting from loss of ovarian follicular activity

Climacteric the period immediately prior to the menopause and at least the first year after the menopause. Gradual reduction in frequency of ovulation and reduction of oestrogen produced by the ovaries

Pre-menopausal regular menstruation

Peri-menopausal irregular menstruation

> **Box 6.4　Definitions of the Menopause (*cont.*)**
>
> **Post-menopausal** no menstruation for at least twelve months
>
> **Change of life** biological and psychological changes
>
> **Premature menopause** menopause before age 40
>
> **Surgical menopause** results from removal of both ovaries (oophorectomy)

The menopause has been held responsible for the increase in psychological problems in mid age, but the evidence for a causal relationship is weak. There are recognized physical changes that result from the loss of production of oestrogen (see Chapter 5). Climacteric symptoms have been described in a number of ways. Most studies (e.g. Greene 1984, Hunter 1990) distinguish vasomotor symptoms of hot flushes, night sweats and vaginal dryness from psychological symptoms such as increased depression, irritability, or low libido. There is little association between menopausal status and psychological symptoms. Greene (1984) reviewed 14 studies of menopausal women and concluded that only vasomotor symptoms were associated with the time of the menopause. The experience of hot flushes and night sweats are the most distressing complaints during the peri-menopause.

Stress may be related to the symptoms reported in the menopause. Women may be particularly susceptible to stress experienced during the climacteric. Psychiatric problems may be more common in the years before the actual menopause, and family and sociocultural factors may be more important than changes in hormones (Ballinger 1990). Coleman (1993) suggests that there may be a relationship between physical changes and depression in post-menopausal women. There are negative effects of certain diseases that begin in mid age such as diabetes mellitus, and weight gain and urinary incontinence can add to women's problems.

Models of health and illness described in Chapter 2 can also be applied to symptoms described in the menopause.

Biomedical model

The menopause is seen as a hormone deficiency disease. Vasomotor symptoms occur because of a decline in the levels of oestrogen produced by the ovary. These symptoms respond well to oestrogen therapy and a number of well-controlled studies have shown the benefits of oestrogen therapy (e.g. Dennerstein *et al.* 1979). This is in spite of studies that find no relationship between absolute levels of oestrogen and symptoms (Alder *et al.* 1992). Clearly the relationship is complex and although all women go through the menopause not all women experience hot flushes or night sweats.

Cultural model

Just as in the example of negative stereotypes of menstruation, society may take a negative view of the menopause (Greer 1992). In some societies ageing is associated with increased status and wisdom and there may be an increase in freedom when women are no longer seen as sexual. In these societies the menopause is seen positively, and there are fewer emotional problems (Gannon 1989). Women may see the menopause as a loss of femininity or as an end to the demands of childbearing. On the other hand the menopause is an unavoidable sign of the passing of time and the increasing approach of old age. If the middle aged woman is also caring for elderly parents then she may be painfully aware of the problems of old age.

Mayan Indians in rural Mexico experience loss of oestrogen production in the same way as Western women, although it occurs at a relatively early age (usually between 41 and 54). In a study of 54 women it was found that they did not report hot flushes or night sweats, nor did they suffer from osteoporosis (Martin *et al.* 1993). The interviewer was a Mayan nurse's aide and fluent in Spanish and Mayan. From their hormone levels, about 80% would be expected to have hot flushes but not one of the 54 women reported hot flushes. This suggests a strong cultural component

Psychosocial model

Stressful life events may be associated with psychological and physical symptoms in the climacteric. Greene and Cooke (1980) assessed menopausal symptoms using a standardized scale and found that life stress contributed far more to menopausal symptoms than the menopausal status. Children leaving home may be a cause of grief, but there may be just as many problems if they don't leave home and remain dependent. Being in paid employment outside the home is protective against depression for women. Several studies have found that previous depression and negative images of the menopause influence depression and psychological symptoms during the menopause (Hunter 1995).

Treatment of vasomotor symptoms by replacing oestrogen can be very effective, but the evidence for its success in treating psychological problems such as depression is less good. Behavioural techniques such as relaxation, exercise or joining a self-help group have all been advised (Hunter 1990).

6.10   SEXUALITY IN LATER LIFE

Sexuality in later life is another taboo subject. Sexuality may not only be assumed to have been left at the hospital door, but sexual activity may be thought to belong exclusively to the young. Old people are sexual people although their level of sexual activity and interest in sex may be less, and sexual activity and interest varies greatly between individuals. For many it is the lack of opportunity rather than desire that changes. Sexual expression is important for self esteem. Although there may be a popular stereotype that being old is not sexy, sexual activity continued into old age can reaffirm sexual identity. As we have seen (Chapter 5), the majority of the elderly population are likely to be widows or women on their own. For today's elderly widows, sexuality may only be acceptable in the context of marriage and they may acutely miss their physical relationships with their spouse.

There are physical and psychological effects of normal ageing that may influence interest and feelings (Bancroft 1989). In an interesting article written for nurses, Roberts (1989) describes the changes in sexuality in later life. This article had line drawings of sexuality in elderly people that some readers disliked (Andrews 1989).

In men the rate of arousal slows and the penis becomes less sensitive, needing more stimulation to become erect. The angle of erection of the penis lowers, the volume of the ejaculate reduces, and the length of time before another erection can occur following ejaculation lengthens. In women the rate of arousal also slows, and the number of orgasms tends to decrease. The vulva, vagina and breasts may become less sensitive. In post-menopausal women the lining of the vagina becomes thinner and there is less lubrication. In both sexes there can be psychosocial influences on sexual activity. These may include lack of privacy, poor health, poor self image, boredom and performance anxiety.

Activity 6.10

Look at the drawings in Roberts (1989). Do you think they are appropriate? Would some members of your profession object to them in your professional journal. If so, why?

6.11   SEXUALITY DISABILITY AND ILLNESS

6.11.1   Sexuality and Disability

The emotional consequences of being disabled may be worse than the physical difficulties of coping with toilets or managing a wheelchair. Not having anyone to take to a restaurant or cinema may be harder to cope with than difficulties in gaining access to them. Disabled people may feel excluded from the world of sex that seems so important in our society. Defining disability is itself far from simple (French 1992). Images presented by charities in order to raise funds may be calculated to arouse pity but may also be demeaning. There is pressure to present more positive images such as a visually impaired person using a computer rather than a stick. Another step we have yet to take may be to present disabled people as sexual people. Independence is often regarded as a goal by health professionals, but not acknowledging a need for help may be just as damaging. In sexual relationships, and in order to be sexually active, disabled people may need help. The concept of normality in the context of sexual activity may be inappropriate. French (1992) argues that the process of normalization is often at the expense of the disabled person's needs and rights.

The role of sexuality for a disabled person will depend on the time of life that it occurred. The disability may have been present at birth or early childhood before they became sexually aware. They may not have had social experiences that led to the formation of sexual relationships and knowledge of their own and others' bodies. Caring for a young person who is disabled, e.g. with cerebral palsy or spina bifida, will involve much handling by health professionals. They try to maintain an asexual approach to their therapy, but young bodies sometimes respond anyway. At the same time the young person will be aware of television, video and music that is overtly sexual and this may cause confusion and conflicts. Disabled adolescents may be treated as children by their parents as they cope with their dependency needs, but this may be denying the young people's sexuality.

A person who is disabled in adulthood may have had a full and satisfying sexual life that has been disrupted. They may become depressed and suffer loss of self image and role in their relationship. There may be direct effects of the disability on sexual performance and interest. They may no longer be able to conceive or carry a pregnancy to term.

In residential homes there may be dilemmas for health professional staff if they are asked to aid sexual activity. The disabled person may need help with positioning in order to have sexual intercourse and yet sexual activity is usually regarded as a very private activity. Similar dilemmas were expressed in caring for elderly people who are sexually active by Roberts (1989). There are now counsellors who specialize in sexual counselling for the disabled.

6.11.2   Sexuality and Illness

Illness can affect a person's sexuality and yet it may be difficult to discuss. The effects can occur as a result of the physical effects of the illness; because of the psychological effects of having the illness on the individual's self esteem, sexual behaviour and relationships; and the effects of particular treatment such as drug therapy (Bancroft 1989). This almost implies that most people cared for by health professionals experience some change in their sexuality, and this may be near the truth. The effects of disease on sexual functioning may be neural or hormonal, and it is often difficult to separate psychological and physical causes and effects (see discussion in Bancroft 1989, Chapter 11).

Physical effects of illness

Diabetes mellitus is caused by insufficient production of insulin and there are degenerative effects in small blood vessels. About a third of men with diabetes experience erectile problems and in some cases these are associated with other vascular or neurological damage. People with renal damage also experience sexual problems which are related to specific effects of renal failure.

Multiple sclerosis is most common in young men and in addition to anxiety and depression experienced by MS sufferers, there may be neural effects on genital sensations and responses in both men and women.

Psychological effects

Diabetic men with erectile impotence often report loss of sexual interest, and erectile failure can lead to performance anxiety thereby increasing the risk of further difficulties in sustaining an erection.

There is often a decline in sexual activity following a heart attack, probably because of pain of exertion, fear of raising blood pressure or the fear of another heart attack.

Renal patients on dialysis may impose demands on the partner and uncertainty about the prognosis will cause anxiety.

Effects of treatment

Hypertensive drugs appear to increase the risk of erectile impotence and ejaculatory failure in men (Bulpitt *et al.* 1976), but there are different effects with different drugs. Compliance with long-term drug therapy may be severely reduced if one of the side effects is loss of libido or sexual functioning.

Psychotropic drugs are widely prescribed and anti-depressants may have negative effects on sexuality in both men and women. Not only will this affect compliance but the treatment may be counter-productive. Sexual activity and interest may be very important to the individuals' self image and to relationships.

6.12 SUMMARY

Reproductive issues affect us all our lives. They are part of society and affect our health. Sexuality in adolescent patients is often ignored but is very important. The relationship of menstrual cycles to health and mood changes is complex. Most sexually active couples use contraception and psychological models have been suggested to explain contraceptive behaviour including safe sex. Decisions about reproduction will influence choice of contraceptive method.

There has been much research into the psychology of pregnancy and childbirth, and both feeding and fatigue may affect care by health professionals. Problems related to the menopause could be psychosocial and/or hormonal. Sexuality persists into later life and disabled people are also sexual people.

6.13 FURTHER READING

Bancroft, J. (1989) *Human Sexuality and its Problems,* 2nd edn. Edinburgh: Churchill Livingstone

This is a detailed and readable book that discusses many aspects of sexuality. It discusses sexuality in a medical context.

Bradford, N. (1990) *The Well Woman's Self Help Directory.* London: Sidgwick and Jackson

A guide to women's health written for the lay person, but full of sensible advice and references.

Hunter, M. (1994) *Counselling in Obstetrics and Gynaecology.* Leicester: BPS Books

One of a series of books about counselling. It makes extensive use of clinical material.

Roberts, A. (1989) Systems of Life no 172 Senior systems, 37: Sexuality in later life. *Nursing Times,* **85**, 65–68

This should be read by everyone caring for elderly people in residential care.

6.14 REFERENCES

Abraham, S.C.S., Sheeran, P., Abrams, W.D.J., Spears R. and Marks, D.(1991) Young people learning about AIDS: a study of beliefs and information sources: *Health Education Research Theory and Practice,* **6**, 19–27

Alder, E.M. (1984) Psychological aspects of AIDS. In: *Psychological Aspects of Genetic Counselling,* edited by A. Emery and I. Pullen. London: Academic Press

Alder, E.M. (1989) Sexual behaviour in pregnancy, after childbirth and during breast-feeding. *Psychological Aspects of Obstetrics and Gynaecology* edited by M. Oates. Bailliere's Clinical Obstetrics and Gynaecology, **3**, 805–821

Alder, E.M. (1993) Contraception In *The Health psychology of women* edited by Niven, C.A. and Carroll, D. Chur: Harwood Academic Publishers

Alder, E.M. (1994) Postnatal sexuality. In: *The Psychology and Biology of Female Sexuality,* edited by P. Choi and P. Nicolson. London: Harvester Wheatsheaf

Alder, E.M., and Bancroft, J. (1983) Sexual behaviour of lactating women: a preliminary communication. *Journal of Reproductive and Infant Psychology,* 1, 47–52

Alder, E.M., Cook A., Gray J., Tyrer G., Wainer P. and Bancroft J. (1981). The effects of sterilisation: a comparison of sterilised women with the wives of vasectomised men. *Contraception, **23**,* 45–54 (1992)

Alder, E.M., Cook, A., Davidson, D., West, C. and Bancroft, J. (1986) Hormones, mood and sexuality in lactating women. *British Journal of Psychiatry,* **148**, 74–79

Alder, E.M., Bancroft, J., Livingstone, J., (1992) Estradiol implants, and reported symptoms. *Journal of Psychosomatic Obstetrics and Gynaecology,* **13**, 223–235

Alder, E.M., and Bancroft, J. (1988) The relationship between breastfeeding persistence, sexuality and mood in post partum women. *Psychological Medicine,* **18**, 389–396

Andrews, J. (1989) Anti-ageists unite. *Nursing Times,* **85**, 22

Asso, D. (1992) A reappraisal of the normal menstrual cycle. *Journal of Reproductive and Infant Psychology,* **10**, 103–110

Bancroft, J. (1989) *Human Sexuality and its Problems,* 2nd edn. Edinburgh: Churchill Livingstone

Ballinger, C.B. (1990) Psychiatric aspects of the menopause. *British Journal of Psychiatry,* **156**, 773–787

Bell, J.S. and Alder, E. (1994) Psychological aspects of infertility. In: *Male Infertility,* 2nd ed. Edited by T.M. Hargreaves. London: Springer-Verlag

Bem, S. (1974) The measurement of psychological androgyny. *Journal of Clinical and Consulting Psychology,* **42**, 155–162

Bergman, B. and Marklund, S. (1989) Masculinisation and professionalisation of the physiotherapy profession: a study of Swedish physiotherapists. *Physiotherapy Practice,* **5**, 55–64

Berryman, J. (1991) Perspectives on later motherhood. In: *Motherhood, Meanings Practices and Ideologies,* edited by A. Phoenix, A. Woollett and E. Lloyd. London: Sage

Broverman, I.K., Broverman, D.M. Clarkson, F.E., Rosenkranz, P. and Vogel, S.R. (1970) Sex role stereotypes and clinical judgements of mental health. *Journal of Consulting and Clinical Psychology,* **34**, 1–7

Bulpitt, C.J., Dollery, C.T., Carne, S. (1976) Change in symptoms of hypertensive patients after referral to hospital clinics. *British Medical Journal,* **3**, 485–490

Campbell, E. (1985) *The Childless Marriage. An Exploratory Study of Who Do Not Want Children*. London: Tavistock Publications

Coleman, P.M. (1993) Depression during the female climacteric period. *Journal of Advanced Nursing,* **18**, 1540–1546

Cooper, P. Gath, D., Rose, N. and Fieldsend, R. (1982) Psychological sequalae to elective sterilization: a prospective study. *British Medical Journal,* **284**, 461–4

Cox, J.L. (1989) Postnatal depression: a serious and neglected phenomenon. *Psychological Aspects of Obstetrics and Gynaecology,* edited by M. Oates, Bailliere's Clinical obstetrics and gynaecology **3**, 839–855

Dennerstein, L., Burrows, G.D., Hyman, C. and Sharpe, K. (1979) Hormone therapy and affect. *Maturitas,* **1**, 247–259

Douglas, J. (1993) *Psychology and Nursing Children*. Leicester: BPS Books

Fraser, I.S., McCarron, G., Markham, R. (1984) A preliminary study of factors influencing perception of menstrual blood loss volume. *American Journal of Obstetrics and Gynecology,* **149**, 788–793

French, S. (1992) Defining disability—its implications for physiotherapy practice. In: *Physiotherapy: A Psychosocial Approach,* edited by S. French. Oxford: Butterworth Heinemann

Freidman, T. and Gath D. (1989) Infertility and assisted reproduction. *Clinical Obstetrics and Gynaecology,* **3**, 805–821

Freidman, T. and Gath, D. (1989) The psychiatric consequences of spontaneous abortion. *British Journal of Psychiatry,* **155**, 810–813

Gannon, L. (1989) Dysmenorrhoea, premenstrual syndrome and the menopause. In: *The Practice of Behavioural Medicine,* edited by S. Pearce and J. Wardle. Oxford: BPS Books/OUP

Graham, C. and Bancroft, J. (1993) Women, mood and the menstrual cycle. In: *The Health Psychology of Women,* edited by C.A. Niven and D. Carroll. Chur: Harwood Academic Publishers

Granleese, J. (1990) Personality, sexual behaviour and menstrual symptoms: their relevance to clinically presenting with menorrhagia. *Personality and Individual Differences,* **11**, 379–390

Greene, J.G. (1984) *The Social and Psychological Origins of the Climacteric Syndrome*. London: Gower

Greene, J.G. and Cooke, D.J. (1980) Life stress and symptoms at the climacterium. *British Journal of Psychiatry,* **136**, 486–491

Greer, G (1992) *The Change* London: Haimish Hamilton.

Horner, M. (1970) Femininity and successful achievement: a basic inconsistency. In: *Femininity and Conflict,* edited by J. Barwick. Belmont California: Brook and Cole

Horowitz, S.M., Klerman, L.V., Kuo, H.S. and Jeckel, J.F. (1991) Intergenerational transmission of school age parenthood. *Family Planning Perspectives,* **23**, 168–177

Hunt, K. and Allendale, E. (1990) Predicting contraceptive usage among women in West of Scotland. *Journal of Biosocial Science,* **22**, 405–421

Hunter, M. (1990) *Your Menopause*. London: Pandora

Hunter, M. (1994) *Counselling in Obstetrics and Gynaecology*. Leicester: BPS Books

Hunter, M. (1995) Gynecology. In: *Health Psychology. Processes and Applications,* 2nd edn. Edited by A. Broome and S. Llewleyn. London: Chapman and Hall

Jackman, C., McGee, H.M. and Turner, M. (1991) The experience and psychological impact of early miscarriage. *The Irish Journal of Psychology,* **12**, 108–120

Jorgensen, S.R. (1993) Adolescent Pregnancy and Parenting. In: *Adolescent Sexuality,* edited by T.P. Gullota, G.R. Adams, R. Montemayor. Newbury Park, California: Sage

Kubler-Ross, E. (1969) *On Death and Dying*. New York: Macmillan Inc.

Lambers, K.J., Trimbos-Kemper, G.C.M. and van Hall, E.V. (1984) Regret and reversal of sterilization. In: *Psychology and Gynaecological Problems,* edited by A. Broome and L. Wallace. London: Chapman and Hall

Laws, S. (1990) *Issues of Blood: The Politics of Menstruation*. London: Macmillan

Lawson, S., Cole, R.A., and Templeton, A.A. (1979) The effects of laparascopic sterilization by diathermy or silastic bands on post operative pain, menstrual symptoms and sexuality. *British Journal of Obstetrics and Gynaecology,* **86**, 659–663

Laybourn, A. (1994) *The Only Child*. London: HMSO

Lindemann, C. (1977) Factors affecting the use of contraceptive in the nonmarital context. In: *Progress in Sexology,* edited by R. Gemme and C.C. Wheeler. New York: Plenum

Marshall, P. (1992) *Now I Know Why Tigers Eat Their Young*. Vancouver: Whitecap Books

Martin, M., Block, J.E., Sanchez, S.D., Arnaud C.D., Beyene Y. (1993) Menopause without symptoms: the endocrinology of menopause among rural Mayan Indians. *American Journal of Obstetrics and Gynecology,* **168**, 1839–1845

Masters, W.H. and Johnson, V.E. (1966) *Human Sexual Response*. Boston: Little Brown and Co.

Oakley, A. (1974) *Housewife*. Allen Lane

Roberts, A. (1989) Systems of Life no 172. Senior systems, 37: sexuality in later life. *Nursing Times,* **85**, 65–68

Robson, K.M., Brant, H.A., Kumar, R. (1981) Maternal sexuality during first pregnancy and after childbirth. *British Journal of Obstetrics and Gynaecology,* **88**, 882–889

Ruble, D.N. (1977) Premenstrual symptoms: a reinterpretation. *Science,* **197**, 291–292

Savin-Williams, R.C. and Rodriguez, R.G. (1993) A Developmental, Clinical Perspective on Lesbian, Gay Male and Bisexual Youths. *In Adolescent*

Sexuality, edited by T.P. Gullota, G.R. Adams and R. Montemayor. Newbury Park: Sage

Sim, J. (1986) Physiotherapy: a professional profile. *Physiotherapy Practice,* **1**, 14–22

Social Trends 20 (1990) London: HMSO

Sonerstein, F.L., Pleck, J.H., Ku, L.C. (1989) Sexual activity, condom use and AIDs awareness among adolescent males. *Family Planning Perspectives,* **21**, 152–158

Studd, J., Chakravarti, S. and Oram, D. (1977) The climacteric. In: *Clinics in Obstetrics and Gynecology,* edited by R. Greenblatt and J.W.W. Studd. Philadelphia: WB Saunders and Co.

Ussher, J.M. (1989) *The Psychology of the Female Body.* London: Routledge

Walker, A (1992) Premenstrual symptoms and ovarian hormones; A review. *Journal of Reproductive and Infant Psychology,* **10**, 67–82,

Wellings, K. (1994) *Sexual Behaviour in Britain.* Harmondsworth: Penguin

Westbrook, M.T. and Nordholm, L.A. (1987) Changes in the characteristics of physiotherapy students in New South Wales over the decade 1976–1986 *The Australian Journal of Physiotherapy,* **33**, 101–109

Whitely, B.E. and Schofield, J.W. (1986) A meta analysis of research on adolescent contraceptive use: Population and environment. *Behavioral and Social Issues,* **8**, 173–203

Woollett, A., Dosanjh-Matawala, N., and Hadlow, J. (1991) The attitudes to contraception of Asian women in East London. *The British Journal of Family Planning,* **17**, 72–77

7

Stress, Health and Illness

CONTENTS

7.1 INTRODUCTION TO STRESS

We have become increasingly aware of the effects of stress on health, even though physical health has improved markedly in the last century. We may regard living in an industrialized society in the twentieth century as being very stressful. Yet a hundred years ago there must have been a great deal of stress that came from chronic poor health, worries about housing, accident rates, high infant mortality and the threat of violence. However there is no doubt that even though we may have the physical comforts of warmth, housing and food, life events can cause much disruption and distress.

We now know more about helping people to cope with change and about managing the effects of stress. Stress is related to changes in health and the changes in morbidity discussed in Chapter 1 may be related in part to stress.

Illness itself can also have stressful consequences and medical treatments themselves may be stressful. Health professionals as individuals are vulnerable to stress and there have been a number of studies that have looked at the causes and prevention of occupational stress. Psychobiological concepts are closely related to our understanding of stress and its relation to illness and health care.

Activity 7.1

List as many stress-related symptoms that you can think of that you might recognize in your own profession, under the following headings:
physical
emotional
behavioural
cognitive
see Bond (1988) for examples in nursing.

7.1.1 Definitions of Stress

The term 'stress' is often used as a general term, meaning disagreeable stimuli. It can have at least three meanings in the context of health. These meanings tend to be confused, and stress is thought to precede a great variety of life's problems or ill health (Wilkinson 1992).

The terms *stress, stressor,* and *strain* all have precise meanings in mechanical engineering and can be distinguished in physiology. Their distinction in health psychology may lead to a mechanistic model of health (see Chapter 1), but it can be useful to try and sort out some of the conflicting views about stress and health.

Stressors

The term '*stress*' can be used to mean the stimuli that produce physiological behavioural and psychological responses to stress. These might be described as *stressors*. These are events that happen to a person that threaten or disturb, and may be further divided.

Disasters These may be only brief in time but may have long-lasting effects. The sinking of the Marchioness in London in 1989 was a very brief event, but it was followed by lasting psychological disturbance. Fifty-one people who were attending a birthday party died when the pleasure cruiser was hit by a 1500 ton dredger. Eighty survived, and a study of 27 survivors found significant psychological distress. The event was sudden: one moment they were celebrating with friends and minutes later they were in the river which was cold and dark. Many lost their friends and suffered days of uncertainty before bodies were recovered (Thompson *et al.* 1994.)

> **Activity 7.2**
>
> *Discuss any recent disaster. Look out for reports in the newspapers. Was any psychological help offered to the survivors or relatives?*

Personal stressors tend to be acute but have long-lasting effects.

Life events (Chapter 2) may be very disruptive, but they may be infrequent. Some events will be predictable and those that are uncontrollable are seen as most stressful.

Background stressors are chronic and may include some of the environmental factors discussed in Chapter 1.

Many of these are minor stressors or hassles that may occur daily and have less severe impact but are nonetheless very irritating. Kanner *et al.* (1981) found a significant correlation between hassles and negative affect and psychological symptoms. The scores on their hassles scale predicted more variance in psychological symptoms than life events alone.

Strain

The term 'stress' can also be taken to mean the *strain*, or the physiological response to an event or stimulus. Hans Selye, a Canadian physiologist published an influential book on stress (Selye 1956). He suggested that stress was a non-specific response that could occur as a result of many different stimuli. His description of a 'General Adaptation Syndrome' suggested that different phases of the stress response were related to different diseases. However, the model was derived from the results of animal experiments and so cognitive and emotional factors were probably underestimated. Stressors that produce the experience of stress tend to be emotional. Having a painful injection is not the same as having a vaginal examination, although both could be considered stressful.

Distress is commonly used to mean negative effects of strain. Selye (1974) distinguished between distress (from Greek *dys* meaning poor) and eustress (from Greek *eu* meaning good). Spector (1990) recommends totally abandoning the word stress.

Stress as an interaction

Stress can also be regarded as an interaction between the stimulus and the individual. Lazarus (1966) considered the meaning of the event. The same event may not be seen by everyone as equally stressful.

When someone first reacts to an event, they may see it as either positive or negative. This is the primary appraisal. A hysterectomy operation may be seen as potentially painful, or as the beginning of relief from heavy menstrual periods. Thereafter a secondary appraisal leads to consideration of what can be done about it. Some patients will be confident that they are prepared for the operation and will be able to cope with the pain. This confidence is related to the concept of self efficacy (see Chapter 2, Section 2.6.2).

As the stressful event gets underway, there may be a reappraisal. The event may be seen as having been better (or worse) than had been expected, or it may be followed by relief that it is over. Cox (1978) describes stress as being a failure to cope, i.e. an imbalance between existing resources and perceived demand. Examinations will be stressful if the student is ill prepared or if the questions are difficult to answer. If the examinations include questions that had been anticipated and are straightforward, what had been seen as a stressful event may be reappraised as an enjoyable experience. (Of course, if the examination turned out to be worse than had been expected it will then be seen as a very negative and stressful experience). The stressful experience can be resolved by increasing the students' resources (more tutorial help, more time spent studying) or varying the demands (e.g. by choosing a different course).

Some stress is desirable. We have seen that some people who are described as hardy (Kobasa 1982) enjoy stress, but they might describe it as stimulation. We also get bored. The need for stimulation has been suggested as a drive in motivational terms and most animals will explore a new environment. Early animal experiments showed that monkeys would perform tasks that allowed them to open a window to look out on the outside world. The opportunity to receive stimulation acted as a reinforcer. Hebb (1966) suggested that individuals have an optimum level of stimulation and that we have ways of maintaining this. We strive to obtain a balance between boredom and over-stimulation.

Zuckerman *et al.* (1978) devised a sensation seeking scale (SSS). High scorers would tend to agree with statements like 'I would like to try new foods that I have never tasted before', and 'I can't stand watching a movie that I've seen before'. High scorers tend to be extrovert and independent and to value change and stimulation, but they are also more likely to smoke. We often put ourselves in situations of stress and enjoy being stressed, even paying money to do it. However, one difference between watching a horror video and being in a real life situation may be the degree of control. The television can be turned off and you can close your eyes. We may also, at an unconscious level, recognize that it is fiction not reality, although we are receiving stressful stimuli.

7.1.2   Management of Stress

Coping is an important concept in health psychology. Lazarus and Folkman (1984) proposed that coping with stress could be either *problem centred* or *emotion centred.* In a problem-centred approach efforts are directed at managing or alleviating the stressful situation. If it is emotion centred he tries to control the reaction to the stress.

> **Activity 7.3**
>
> *A student is behind with his coursework. What can he do?*
> *Compare an emotion-centred approach with problem-centred approach.*

The best solution might be a combination of both approaches. Emotion-centred problem solving can be used to maintain hope and keep up spirits. This might be important in coping with bereavement or coping with high levels of stress such as war or life-threatening situations. Problem-solving approaches may be appropriate for moderate levels of stress that are potentially long term but capable of change, e.g. work situations or chronic illness.

Coping strategies

Antonovsky (1979) describes three components of coping strategies:

Rationality
The accurate objective assessment of the stressful situation. It is difficult to see how there can be an objective assessment of a stressor. However there may be some agreement on the relative stressfulness of an event.

Flexibility
There are usually a number of different possible ways of dealing with a stressful situation and the ability to consider a range is a useful coping strategy.

Farsightedness
This means thinking through the consequences. This is often helped by discussing the problem with someone else.

Individuals develop their own coping styles. Defence mechanisms, based on Freudian theories of the unconscious (see Chapter 4) can be very effective.

Monitors and blunters

As we saw in Chapter 3, when patients are anticipating surgery they may seek out information (*monitors*) or deny the stressfulness of the situation (*blunters*). These strategies may also be used by people in work. They may choose to ignore conflict going on around them. Think how much time is spent on discussing conflicts in relationships at work. Can they be explained by categorising individual patterns of behaviour?

Many programmes for managing stress have been proposed and stress management may become a routine part of professional support. If support is lacking, one appropriate coping mechanism is to become detached. A certain amount of detachment can be useful, and health professionals may be encouraged not to become involved emotionally with patients. If this detachment becomes excessive it can lead to automation which in turn can lead to dehumanization. At this stage the patient is no longer a person and becomes a medical problem.

7.1.3 Social Support

The degree of stress may be related to the perceived social support e.g. 'A good friend is the best medicine'.

Social support has been defined as the presence of others, or the resources provided by them before and during and following a stressful event (Ganster and Victor 1988). Social support has been shown to have a beneficial effect on mental health. Leppin and Schwarzer 1990 (in Schmidt *et al.* 1990) reviewed a large number of studies. They concluded that it was not always clear how the social support had its effect. It could have been the *actual* social support received, which is often measured in terms of the number of contacts with others. It could also have been the *perceived* social support, which is whether the individual felt that they were getting the attention that they should.

Social support may have either a specific effect on health or a general effect, possibly by affecting mood. Caspi (1987) measured hassles, social support and mood. Mood scores were less affected by the previous day's hassles if the subjects had more perceived social support. This suggests that minor stresses will be more easily borne if the person feels they are emotionally supported. It is interesting to observe how much better people feel when they have talked about their worry and received reassurance or sympathy. This is the basis of much of non-directive counselling. The question of whether social support has an effect on physical health is complex. It has been suggested that social support might provide a buffer against the effects of stress. Ganster and Victor (1988) review a large number of studies and suggest that there might be a number of mechanisms that explain the buffering effect. Social support may change the behaviour of people. People on their own may adopt different eating patterns from people living in families. An elderly person may be more likely to put on the heating if there is someone else to share it. They may take more care over their health and appearance for the sake of the other family members. Social support probably boosts self esteem, and we see ourselves through the responses of others; their perception of our health will affect our self perception.

Cobb (1976) suggests that social support reduces perceived stress because the person feels loved and cared for, esteemed and valued. If they feel that they are part of a network, there will be feelings of mutual obligation. The need to be needed should not be underestimated. Social support may reduce the stress response and so have a positive physiological effect. This protective effect of social support is sometimes described as buffering.

7.1.4   Self Help Groups

Support may be given by families and friends, but many people also get support from groups. The groups may be specifically set up to provide support. A self help group is a group of people who feel that they have a common personal problem, typically concerned with a medical, social or behavioural condition. Self help implies self run, but the groups may range from informal local groups to members formally affiliated to a national organization. Self help groups are characterized by having face-to-face interactions, and they are often spontaneous in origin. They may arise from a magazine article, an interested health professional or a shared stressful experience. Their essence is that there is personal involvement and the membership is active. The activities may include social meetings to share problems and information about the condition and its management, fund raising and exerting political pressure. Often members start from a position of powerlessness and may have to struggle against prejudice and stigma.

The reasons for the popularity of self help groups are both sociological and psychological. By using volunteers, self help groups provide an inexpensive service, and may make up for inadequate state provision. They may be particularly appropriate for chronic illnesses that need management rather than treatment. The psychological benefits come from establishing a group identity, reducing social isolation, receiving positive reinforcement for social interactions, and for maintaining self esteem in the presence of uncritical and accepting others. The subjective experience of members of self help groups is that they are very beneficial and they have become recognised and valued by health professionals (Gartner and Reissman 1977).

One theory of their success is the helper theory. By helping and supporting another the individual gains help himself. Rabinowitz and Zimmerlin (1976) found that the main effects of a school health education programme on anti-smoking in children, was to reduce the smoking behaviour of the teachers! Being part of a self help group increases self esteem (I must be well if I can help others). Being able to give, as well as take, increases the sense of equality. Those who are being helped and other people that know about the activities of the groups will give social approval.

Another possibility is that it is being involved in an activity that is impor-tant. This is based on the theory of consumer involvement. Here, active participation is stressed and of course this is also true of counselling. Active learning is known to be more effective than passive learning and in an active self help group there will be active involvement by members. Taking part in a group may also distract from one's own problems, especially if there are others who are seen to be worse off.

Self help groups may have difficulties and may not last indefinitely. They may be seen to be a challenge to the professionalization of medicine, and cause divisions between laymen and professionals. There can be problems of discretion and confidentiality. Some groups will only admit those who have actually experienced the problem but others accept those who have relatives or a special interest. They may become a focus for anger and frus-tration and this may be enhanced not diffused. By their very nature they may not last long. Often they may be formed in a moment of crisis, and not survive once the crisis has passed. The membership may become increas-ingly elderly or progressively more ill, and this may deter new members. For some members the need becomes less as they adjust to the health problem. There may be considerable practical problems, although many health authorities provide premises and even limited funds. Health professionals may be the point of referral and can put patients with similar problems in touch with each other. Health professionals can be involved with support groups but there is always a danger that if the health professional becomes too intrusive, the nature of the self help is lost. Health professionals may be most useful as facilitators, and as a line of communication between formal health and social services.

Activity 7.4

Find out about self help groups in your professional area. Do you know any patients or professionals that take part? Have any friends or relatives joined such a group? How would you find out? There may be reference books in your library, e.g. The Well Woman's Self Help Directory *has addresses (Bradford 1990).*

7.2   MODELS OF STRESS AND ILLNESS

We expect people who are stressed to be more likely to become ill, just as we expect those who are chronically ill to feel under stress. Being 'run down', 'under the weather', and having 'low resistance' are all expressions that indicate that we associate stress with illness.

There are a number of different ways of looking at the relationship between stress and illness. First we will look at the effect of stress on health, and then the effects of illness on stress.

7.2.1   Stress and Illness

Four models have been suggested to link stress and health or illness (Figure 7.1).

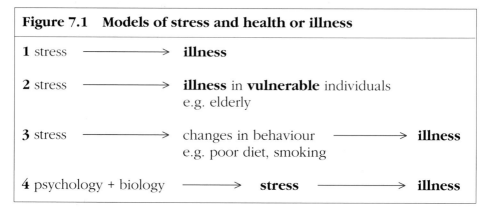

Figure 7.1   Models of stress and health or illness

1 stress ⟶ **illness**

2 stress ⟶ **illness** in **vulnerable** individuals
e.g. elderly

3 stress ⟶ changes in behaviour ⟶ **illness**
e.g. poor diet, smoking

4 psychology + biology ⟶ **stress** ⟶ **illness**

Stress causes illness directly

The study of the effect of stress on the immune system (Box 7.1) has become known as psycho-immunology or human behavioural immunology, and has been studied by health psychologists and psycho-biologists. Health professionals usually have more knowledge of physiology than many psychologists, and more knowledge of psychology than many medical practitioners, so they may have a particular interest in the relationship between health, psychology and the immune system. The relationship between health and the immune system has had recent attention from research into the progress of AIDS-related diseases.

Box 7.1   The Immune System

The body's defence mechanisms against disease include behaviour such as coughing and sneezing, but a second line of defence is provided by the immune system. White blood cells called phagocytes engulf bacteria that are then digested. These are non-specific and act generally against a wide range of infections. There is also a specific immune response. Certain lymphocytes recognise protein molecules called antigens, and respond by producing antibodies. Viruses have a protein layer that acts

Box 7.1   The Immune System (*cont.*)

as an antigen: when the specific antibodies come into contact with the antigen they combine like a lock and key and the virus becomes harmless. The antibodies are produced by B lymphocytes are released as free molecules. Other cells called killer T cells form antibodies on their surfaces. Some cells develop as memory T cells and memory B cells. After the first wave of infection some of the B cells and T cells remain in the body as memory cells, and will respond if there is a subsequent invasion. This is the basis of immunization procedures.

Cells that are infected with a virus produce interferon, a protein that passes to other cells, protecting them from infection. Production of interferon for humans may allow treatment of viral infections.

The human immunodeficiency virus (HIV) acts on the T cells and AIDS (acquired immunodeficiency syndrome) may then develop. Some psychosocial factors are thought to influence the immune function in those infected with the HIV virus (O' Leary 1990), but the results are conflicting.

Changes in the immune system have been found in depressed patients compared with non-depressed patients, but it is difficult to control for other behaviour patterns. People who are depressed may smoke and drink more and exercise less. They may show changes in sleep patterns (early morning waking is a diagnostic criterion for depressive disorders). Some individuals may be stress-prone. They see life's hassles as more intense and are then more likely to become ill (Levy and Heiden 1991).

The effect on the immune system could be mediated through the central nervous system or the endocrine system and all three systems are inter-related. The immune system controls the production of lymphocytes and antibodies. The lymphocytes include T helper cells, T killer cells and T suppressor cells which all influence antibody production. Thus any influences on lymphocyte production will affect the response to illness. One interesting study found evidence for an observable effect on lymphocyte production. Bartrop *et al.* (1977) assessed 26 spouses at two and six weeks after bereavement. Lymphocyte production was significantly depressed compared with matched controls. Kiecolt-Glaser *et al.* (1987) found that divorced women, and those rating their marital quality as poor, had reduced lymphocyte functioning. It is difficult to take physiological measurements at times of stress but one very predictable time of stress in normal, healthy adults is when they take academic examinations. Studies of medical students showed that there was a decrease in the number of T cells and NK cell activity before and during major exams.

Evans and Edgerton (1991) measured 52 minor life events from daily diaries kept by a hundred clerical workers. They also rated their physical health
and mood state. They compared the four days before the onset of a cold
with the previous three days in the same week. The scores of 'uplifts' were
significantly fewer and there was a trend for fewer hassles in the four days
preceding the cold. The most important hassles were those which concerned
not meeting self expectations or failures of intentions. The most important
significant uplifts were having close interactions with spouse or partner – so
maybe sex *is* good for health! However, in a recent replication Stone *et al.*
(1993) assessed 79 mid-aged men and followed them up for twelve weeks.
They used the same methodology but found no differences in the ratings of
desirable events (uplifts), or undesirable events in days preceding illness.
They suggest that this may have been because of difficulties in defining
illness. We know that individuals vary in their illness behaviour which could
include scoring symptoms in a research study. The links are not clear but it
seems likely that if someone is feeling low than their behaviour will change,
and if there is mild infection then they may feel low, so the interactions are
complex.

Stress is related to illness in vulnerable individuals

We have already seen that there is a relation between health and socioeco-
nomic factors (Chapter 2). The evidence for a relationship between psychological vulnerability factors and physical illness is less convincing. We may
find that a group that has an identifiable illness is different from a control
group on a number of psychological measures. This may be a result of the
diagnosis rather than a factor causing the illness. Someone who has been
given a diagnosis may subsequently perceive himself as 'ill'. A better approach is to screen a population and look for characteristics of those who
reach the diagnostic criteria. These studies have produced few significant
results. Waal Manning *et al.* (1986) found that raised blood pressure levels
were not associated with neuroticism, anxiety or depression in a sample of
over 1000 people in New Zealand. They did not find a relationship with
anger although this had been reported in earlier studies.

Greer and Morris (1975) assessed 160 consecutive patients admitted for
breast tumour biopsies. Forty per cent turned out to be malignant. Five years
later they assessed the survival rate of these patients, and found that those
that had shown either 'denial' or 'a fighting spirit' had a better survival rate
than those who showed 'stoic acceptance' or 'helpless/hopelessness'. Factors such as extroversion, depression and stressful life events were not significantly related to the progress of the breast cancer. However, it may depend on the stage that the diagnosis is made and the stage of the disease. It
is likely that we have many potential cancers in our bodies and these are
dealt with by the immune system. Early cancers are therefore more likely to
be affected by psychological factors influencing the immune system. Derogatis

et al. (1979) found that survivors after one year had higher ratings of hostility or anger. These findings suggest that coming to terms with an illness or acceptance may not necessarily be beneficial. However, we do not know whether there is an underlying characteristic that influences both the attitude and the illness, or a direct effect of the attitude on the progress of the illness.

Stress leads to a change in behaviour that leads to illness

A stressful event may disrupt lifestyle, but most behavioural risk factors are long term and therefore more likely to be associated with chronic stress. Weight control is a good example of this model. When an individual is feeling stressed he may eat more high-calorie foods such as chocolate (which can be very comforting). This may disturb the sympathetic nervous system or endocrine system and have a direct physiological effect. Alcohol consumption rises with perceived stress and this is directly related to elevated blood pressure levels. Blood pressure falls if alcohol intake is reduced (Potter and Beevers 1984).

Stress management programmes that give relaxation training have been shown to be effective in reducing systolic and diastolic blood pressure levels. The effect of the relaxation programmes could come from the relaxation itself, but it was noted that groups receiving the relaxation programmes also showed other changes in general health and life satisfaction. The illness itself may cause changes in behaviour and so may result in the reduction of stress. After a heart attack or diagnosis of hypertension the patient may be advised by friends and family to take it easy and to avoid stress. He will then enter the sick role (see Chapter 3).

Could the results of the studies of those who are diagnosed as hypertensive help others to avoid problems? Stress management is an obvious example, but it might be more effective to target those at risk rather that attempt mass programmes of stress management. Health behaviour is not specific and diet, exercise and avoiding excessive alcohol and smoking will reduce the risk of a number of associated diseases.

7.2.2   Psychology, Biology, and Stress

Psychological factors in genetically predisposed individuals may lead to stress which causes illness.

Evidence for a relationship between stress and physical illness comes from changes in the menstrual cycle. A number of studies report negative changes in the premenstrual week, and in particular they have found increases in fluid retention, breast tenderness and irritability. It is difficult to do research into Premenstrual Syndrome (PMS), partly because there are considerable problems of definition and measurement, but also because not all menstrual cycles are equally symptomatic (see Chapter 5). In a study of premenstrual changes, 138 student nurses kept diaries of their general health (Slade 1984).

Both male and female students kept diaries and the purpose of the study was kept hidden from them. Complete data were obtained from 118 subjects and the symptoms were related to the time of onset of menstruation. There were peaks in scores for pain and water retention in the premenstrual and menstrual phases but not for concentration, behavioural changes or negative affect. They suggest that PMS sufferers may attribute negative symptoms to hormonal changes and they may see them as being under external control. We do not know whether biological changes cause stress which then causes symptoms, or whether they act directly on the central nervous system. This is not to say that the time in the menstrual cycle is irrelevant, and it might be worth noting. Even though we do not understand the mechanism, if the woman herself perceives a change, this could influence her illness behaviour.

Chronic fatigue syndrome may be diagnosed in a patient with no identifiable organic disease who persistently complains of fatigue. In a follow-up study Sharp *et al.* (1992) found that many sufferers believed that their illness had been caused by an infection and that stress had played a part. Coping with symptoms often included limiting exercise, avoiding certain foods, and doing anything to avoid 'stress'. Two-thirds scored above the threshold for diagnosing depression on the Hospital Anxiety and Depression scale (Zigmond and Snaith 1983). Both PMS and chronic fatigue syndrome are complex issues and may be a result of a combination of biological and psychological factors.

7.2.3   Stress and Coronary Heart Disease

Certain people may be at more risk of heart disease than others because of the way in which they behave. The image of the fast-living, ambitious executive is associated with having a stressful, if successful, lifestyle. Two cardiologists in the USA, Freidman and Rosenmann, observed that many of their cardiac patients were competitive and aggressive. They postulated that some people could be described as Type A. They were characterised as being highly competitive, ambitious, impatient, and aggressive (Box 7.2). Type B people are those who do not show these characteristics.

Box 7.2   Type A Behaviour Pattern

Do you:
  Eat quickly
  Feel guilty when you are relaxing or on holiday
  Try to do more and more activities in less time
  Insist on winning games rather than just having fun
  Feel irritated when others are late

Box 7.2   Type A Behaviour Pattern (*cont.*)

Feel dissatisfied with your current level of performance
Feel rushed and under pressure
Prompt or early for appointments
Eat walk and talk quickly
Tend to dominate group discussions
Find it difficult to surrender control or to share power
Easily become angry?

Are you:
Self critical
Competitive
In a hurry?

Type B people are characterized by the absence of the above. They relax more readily, are less ambitious and pace themselves.

Freidman and Rosenmann tested their hypotheses in a major study (The Western Collaborative Group study) in which they assessed and followed up over 3000 men (aged 39–59) for eight and a half years. Those that had been described as Type A were twice as likely than Type B to have a heart attack (Rosenmann *et al.* 1975). In another large study in California, both men and women were assessed, and Type A assessment again predicted heart attacks (Haynes *et al.* 1980). Attempts to relate Type A, which is a behaviour pattern, to the physiology of cardiac disease have produced conflicting results (Ray 1991), and the relationship may not be as clear as was suggested at one time. When factors such as cholesterol levels, blood pressure and body weight were controlled, these results were not replicated in another study of men at risk (called MRFIT – Multiple Risk Factor Intervention trial, Shekelle *et al.* 1985). The differences may be in the measurement of Type A, or in the selection of people who were at high risk into the study. Type A is more usefully seen as a general behaviour pattern rather than a personality trait, and can be modified.

Stress may precede a heart attack, but surviving a heart attack may increase perception of stress. We have considered change as generating stress responses and there may be considerable life changes for a patient following a heart attack. Type A individuals may attribute their heart attack to their lifestyle and be prepared to change it. They may well have the encouragement of their families and be able to take part in rehabilitation programmes or stress management courses. For the Type B individual who has had a heart attack it may not be so easy for him to see how to change his lifestyle and reduce the risk of further attacks.

7.2.4   Stress and Skin Disorders

These four models of stress and illness can be well illustrated by looking at skin problems. Skin diseases were thought to be related to personality and there are clinical reports of a high incidence of psychiatric problems in skin clinics (James 1989).

The first model suggests that physiological stress in the form of changes in blood flow or skin conductivity has direct effects on skin condition. The second model suggests that if the skin is vulnerable, e.g. there is an inflammation, then the behaviour of scratching will make it worse. The eventual skin problem could be related to the behaviour. In the third model the problem is directly related to the behaviour of scratching. Eczema can cause severe itching that makes the sufferer want to scratch. If he does it will make it worse directly, but if he doesn't he may feel frustrated leading to physiological stress that could also make it worse. Finally some individuals may be more prone to the problem and to react badly to it, thereby becoming more stressed.

It is possible that skin problems such as eczema and psoriasis are caused by stress, but stress may also result from the condition rather than being the cause. There is a need for controlled studies of relaxation or stress management to investigate the relationship between psychology and skin condition. Podiatrists and physiotherapists will be particularly aware of changes in skin condition.

Activity 7.5

Consider these four models in explaining lower back pain, headaches, or irritable mood spells.

7.3   STRESS AND HEALTH PROFESSIONALS

Stress is regarded as a major problem in the caring professions. It is important because of the suffering experienced by many people working in the health care sector. Stress could also affect the care of the patients. It may be difficult to continue to maintain technical competence under stress, and even harder to maintain a positive relationship with a patient. Many health care professionals are women, and stress at work has an effect on their families.

7.3.1   Occupational Stress

Physicians are more likely to have heart attacks, diabetes or strokes and to commit suicide than other professional groups. Pharmacists are more likely to commit suicide than other professionals but nurses have the same rate of suicide as in the general population. It may be that working with people who have social or health-related problems is itself stressful. McGrath *et al.* (1989) found that teachers and social workers perceived contact with clients and students to be more stressful than nurses did with patients. Patient contact may be stressful but this may be balanced by positive feedback. Much research has been carried out into stress in the nursing profession, (e.g. Chapter 6 in Sutherland and Cooper 1990), but we know less about stress in other health professionals. Stress in the health care professions seems to come from administrative and organizational factors. Van der Gaag (1988) surveyed 160 district speech therapists and found that 80% said that they had been under increased stress recently, as a result of recent changes in management. Increase in the number of referrals, pay levels and career structure were major factors. Conflicts at work can have physical and psychological ill effects, but if the conflicts can be resolved then there may be increased creativity and productivity as a result (Edelmann 1993).

Some second year speech therapy students identified workload, wide variety of patients, poor pay and career structure, and lack of working space as causes of stress. When asked to discuss more acute and personal stressors they included abuse by clients, being given responsibility too early, reluctant clients and the possibility of an emergency.

A number of reasons have been suggested to account for the high morbidity in the health professions:

Selection bias

Perhaps because of selection into the professions, people who themselves have had health problems may be particularly interested in health. High rates of suicide, alcohol abuse and marital problems could be related to personal factors. Allen (1988) interviewed over 600 doctors and found that most had been good at science at school and wanted to fulfil the aims and aspirations of others. Sixty per cent of the sample decided to become doctors before the age of fifteen. Paris and Frank (1983) found that, after excluding those medical students that had a medical parent, medical students were more likely than law students to have had a serious illness in the family. One mechanism proposed by Johnson (1991) is that medical students may be making reparation for emotional neglect by giving care and attention to others that was not received as a child. About 14% of medical students have medical parents. Gerber (1983) found that medical fathers spend an average of 4 minutes per day with their children compared to an average of 20 minutes spent by working men. The length of time spent does not necessarily reflect the quality of the relationship.

Working conditions

Occupational stress has received a great deal of attention and clearly there are economic benefits in reducing stress. Working in health care is unlike working in industry or commerce, but some of the management skills that have been developed outside health care can be applied across employment (Sutherland and Cooper 1990). The practice of regular staff appraisal or career reviews is becoming more common. There may be particular aspects of the work that are stressful such as isolation, irregular hours and awareness of death. A large number of studies have found that the profession of nursing is stressful (Llewelyn 1989, Bond 1988), and nurses may find coping with dying and the suffering of relatives particularly stressful. Third-year nursing students identified shift work (impacting on their social life?), death and dying, technology and relationships with other staff as the main sources of stress in hospital placements. In a small study of 50 physiotherapists working in Scotland, Mottram and Flin (1988) found that 79% found that being too busy was stressful, but then 28% thought that having too little to do was stressful.

Career development

The health care professions have different career structures and these have certainly changed in the last ten years or so as they have moved to graduate education. There is now a change from the monopoly of employment by the NHS to the introduction of Trusts in the UK. The increase in alternative medicine means that there is now a greater diversity of career pathways. Career stress has been identified by Sutherland and Cooper (1990) as having four components. Job insecurity, over promotion, under promotion and thwarted ambition.

Stress management

Health professionals may have poor coping strategies, and be unable to adjust to rapid change. Stress management principles apply across all professional groups but health professionals may cope in more specific ways. Support groups within a working team can be very effective. They reduce absenteeism and make the individual feel loved and cared for. A sense of humour can be very helpful and 'in-jokes' play a useful part in forming a group identity within a team. However unfunny the jokes may seem to an outsider at the Christmas party, they play an important part in group cohesion. Organising limited time in high stress areas such as paediatric intensive care is a pragmatic approach to coping with stress.

Access to medical services

There may be more recorded illness among health professionals because they have more ready access to medical services. They may be more aware of early signs of ill health, although they may also deny being ill, which they see as a sign of weakness.

Emotional demands

Emotional stress can be very difficult to cope with. One area of medicine that does not concern illness and is non-life-threatening is the investigation and treatment of infertility. The experience of infertility is very distressing (Alder 1984), and the procedures that are used to investigate the problem and even some treatments, can cause much emotional distress (Alder and Templeton 1985). Caring for patients who are infertile can also be distressing for nurses. Treatment by *in vitro* fertilization (IVF) probably carries a 20% chance of success and so the staff know that the majority of couples are going to be disappointed. Anderson *et al.* (1989) looked at stress in nurses involved in an IVF programme. The main cause of stress was knowing that the chance of conceiving was low and the nurses found it hard to cope with the women's loss. Studies of professional stress (Bond 1988) show that stress is most likely to be caused by the emotional aspects of caring such as demanding and unreasonable patient behaviour, illnesses that are difficult to treat, and expectations that expressed emotions should be denied. If we add to this specific stimuli such as suppurating wounds, screaming, blood and vomit, it isn't surprising that health care is stressful.

Activity 7.6

In your own profession or discipline which of the categories discussed above do you think contributes most to levels of stress (assuming that there is stress in your profession)? If you have not yet had clinical experience, ask a senior professional.

7.3.2   Burnout

The concept of burnout has been popular in the health professional literature. Maslach (1981) described burnout as having three components: emotional exhaustion, depersonalization of the client or patient, and a reduced sense of job satisfaction.

The concept is derived from Maslow's theory of hierarchy of needs (Box 7.3, Maslow 1943), which attempts to integrate biological and psychosocial needs. It continues to be popular in the nursing and health care professions but receives less attention in recent social psychology texts, e.g. Abraham and Shanley (1992). In his theory, needs are organized into a hierarchy, with a broad base of biological needs culminating in a peak of intellectual needs. Although Maslow did not regard the hierarchy as rigid, the lower layer of needs have to be satisfied before the next layer can be addressed. The hierarchy is a very general statement and may not apply to individuals, and may not apply across different age groups, genders or races. Needs at lower levels can be ignored if the higher one becomes more important. Rock climbers may not eat or drink for hours while they concentrate on difficult climbs, and Marie Curie was so absorbed in her research that she forgot to eat.

Box 7.3   Maslow's hierarchy of needs

A the *physiological* level the dominant motives are those needed to sustain life, and these must be met before the next layer can be realised. These may dominate the care of an acutely ill patient.

Safety needs include the need for security. Consistency of care and familiar routine becomes important. The removal of fear and anxiety is important for recovery.

Patients also want to feel that they *belong* and to receive affection and friendship. Closeness of relatives is important and social needs may include time spent talking to the staff and other patients.

Self esteem includes personal needs for self respect and self confidence and also recognition by others of their importance and respect. At this level it may be difficult to satisfy needs because they may be dependent on the individual's personal history and status in society. As the hierarchy progresses, it becomes harder to satisfy these needs.

The concept of *self actualization* or self realization is important in Maslow's theory. He suggests that individuals may feel a sense of achievement whether it is managing a clinic, or passing an exam. The sense of achievement will vary among individuals but essentially involves a feeling of creativity. It is the most difficult of the concepts to interpret. He suggests that we each have a need to become what we are capable of or to find fulfilment. Self actualization involves certain ways of behaving and thinking (Rathus and Nevid 1989).

Finally, at the peak of the hierarchy is the *acquisition of knowledge and understanding*. At this point intellectual and aesthetic needs become important.

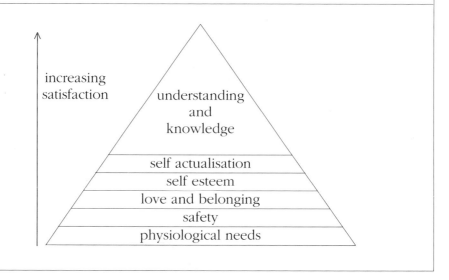

If the hierarchy is taken too literally then the higher needs may be ignored while the lower needs are being attended to. This may be distressing to some individuals. For instance they may want their spiritual needs addressed before physical needs. The theory has intuitive appeal but is essentially untestable; however, it does attempt to link biological and psychological needs, and their interaction has a bearing on individual differences in stress responses.

The perception of love is based on expressed support from others and this could be found in the working team. If teams are constantly broken up, there is less chance of providing feedback and support. Women seem to be more dependent on emotional support than men. Their self esteem is maintained by relationships at work with patients and colleagues and also the status of the profession.

Schuster *et al.* (1984) found that 160 active members of the American Physical Therapy Association (53%) said that they were currently experiencing symptoms of 'burnout'.

Symptoms of burnout are:
* *Distancing*
  This is shown by excessive use of impersonal terms, e.g. 'the coronary', the use of medical jargon and acronyms, and flippant jokes.

* *Withdrawing*
  The nurse may spend more time in the linen room or sluice; the podiatrist may spend more and more time making up plaster casts rather than interacting with patients.

* *Absenteeism*
  This may increase and there may be more minor illnesses. Chronic illness may be more frequent in high-stress occupations. Studies on traffic controllers find higher hypertension rates in those working at busy airports.

* *Survivor guilt*
  The health professional is surrounded by illness, disability and death and may suffer from survivor guilt. She may experience grief but feel unable to show it.

The concept of burnout is very wide ranging and it is not surprising that surveys of health professionals find these behaviour patterns. The concept is descriptive rather than explanatory, and many psychologists prefer to concentrate on coping strategies, rather than symptoms of lack of coping. In addition, there may be very stressful units in which staff have long hours and heavy demands but do not report a high level of burnout. These units may operate management practices which protect staff from feelings of dissatisfaction. Some individuals may have particularly adaptive coping mechanisms.

Niven (1989, Chapter 9) describes an organizational model that considers individual factors of health care professionals themselves, social factors, including social support, and the work setting (Box 7.4). He discusses the importance of theories of organizational change and how they could apply to health care settings.

Box 7.4   Stress, an organizational model (Niven 1989)

1. Individual factors, e.g.
Realistic expectations. Personal goals may be too ambitious and expectations of rapid changes in health may be unrealistic.
Rewards. Learning theory (Chapter 2) suggests that immediate reinforcement leads to effective learning and positive aspects of work need to be continually stressed to reward effective care.
Problem solving. Skills in problem identification and solution can be learned and professional training programmes can be offered.

2. Social factors, e.g.
Degree of contact. Scores on the Maslach Burnout scale were related positively to the amount of time spent in contact with patients.
Control. Emotional exhaustion in nurses was found to relate to the perception of control over discussions of doctors and administrators.
Role ambiguity. The expectations that others have of the role of the health professional may differ from the individuals' perceptions of her role.
Attribution, the medical model lends itself to a person-centred attribution, i.e. it is something about patient that caused problems not the organization.
Social support. Coping can involve distancing and avoiding others, or sharing problems and frustrations with sympathetic listeners

3. Work setting, e.g.
Overload. Sharing responsibility reduces stress
Taking a break, Time off is necessary, but one symptom of 'burnout' may be a reluctance to let go, and a tendency to regard oneself as indefensible.
Staff development. For many health professionals, continuing education is part of their professional code. There is no doubt that in a changing health care world there is a need for opportunities to keep up to date, but also to have time to take a longer look at the effects of change, rather than being reactive to events.

Activity 7.7

List stimuli causing stress and compare with the symptoms that you listed in activity 7.1 Identify links. Are particular stimuli likely to result in particular symptoms?

Activity 7.8

List coping mechanisms
Make up a three column table of stimuli (from activity 7.1) symp-
toms (from activity 7.2), and now add coping mechanisms

7.3.3 Detection of Stress

Stress (the response) is linked to health, and it is important to recognize stress-related symptoms not only in patients but also in health professionals themselves.

Stress-related symptoms may be difficult to distinguish from those of organic origin and it is important to realise that they are rarely independent. If it is assumed that life changes lead to stress, then we need to measure these changes. Holmes and Rahe (1967) developed a schedule of recent events to measure life change, described in Chapter 2 and these have been used in a number of large-scale studies (Box 2.2). This measurement depends on recall, so usually a carefully constructed interview is needed to establish the timing of events. People may only remember events that are significant to them and forget others. (Try and recall where you spent your summer holidays two years ago.) The total score is a summation of the number of life change units and does not include meaning. An extended personal interview may establish not only whether the event has occurred but also its emotional impact. The death of an elderly relative may be very distressing for some but for others it may represent a relief and regaining of freedom. Assessment of an individual's 'stress' needs to take into account whether the stress is internal, e.g. fear of failure, or external, e.g. threat of job loss. We may not have a realistic perception of the prognosis of an illness, but if we believe that there is a poor prognosis we may become very stressed.

Open-ended questions in questionnaires or interviews can be used to elicit reports of stressful events and have the advantage that they can be closely related to the health profession. The disadvantage is that coding and analysis can be difficult and time-consuming. Firth and Morrison (1986) analysed stressful events reported by medical students, and were able to establish high levels of reliability between coders. Dealing with death and relationships with senior doctors were important areas of concern.

7.4 SUMMARY

Different concepts of stress have been applied in relation to health. There are individual differences in managing stress and in the adoption of coping strategies.

Social support can act as a buffer to reduce the effects of stressful life events. Self help groups may be facilitated by health professionals and contribute to coping with specific health problems.

Models have been suggested to link health or illness and stress. Stress may cause illness directly by acting on the immune system. It may lead to illness only in vulnerable individuals; it may lead to a change in behaviour or lifestyle; and there may be biological factors that cause changes in health.

Stress and coronary heart disease have been closely linked in a number of studies in which Type A behaviour increased the risk of heart attack, although the assessment of Type A is difficult.

Stress is a major problem in the health professions and can be accounted for by: selection of vulnerable individuals into the profession; poor working conditions and lack of career development; lack of stress management skills; and ready access to medical services increasing illness behaviour. Maslow's theory of hierarchy of needs has been used to explain the phenomenon of burnout.

7.5   FURTHER READING

Bond, M. (1988) *Stress and Self Awareness: A Guide for Nurses*. London: Heinmann

This well-written book gives exercises and draws on experience of running groups.

Llewelyn, S.P. (1989) Caring: the cost to nurses and relatives. In: *Health Psychology: Processes and Applications,* Edited by A. Broome London: Chapman and Hall

A chapter in a useful book that looks at applications of psychological theory to behavioural medicine.

Mottram, E. and Flin, R.H. (1988) Stress in newly qualified physiotherapists. *Physiotherapy,* **74**, 607–612

An example of research on stress in health professions.

Sutherland, V.J. and Cooper, C.L. (1990) *Understanding Stress: A Psychological Perspective for Health Professionals*. London: Chapman and Hall

Discusses theory as well as management.

7.6 REFERENCES

Abraham, C. and Shanley, E. (1992) *Social Psychology for Nurses.* London: Edward Arnold

Alder, E.M. (1984) Psychological aspects of AIDS. In: *Psychological Aspects of Genetic Counselling,* edited by A. Emery and I. Pullen. London: Academic Press

Alder, E.M. and Templeton, A.A. (1985) Patient reaction to IVF treatment. *The Lancet,* 1 no. 8421, 168

Allen, I. (1988) *Doctors and their Careers.* London: Policy Studies Institute

Anderson, S., Nero, F., Rodin, J., Diamond, M. and Decherney, A. (1989) Coping patterns of *in vitro* fertilization nurse coordinators: strategies for combating low outcome expectance. *Psychology and Health,* **3**, 221–232

Antonovsky, A. (1979) *Health, Stress and Coping.* San Francisco: Jossey-Bass

Bartrop, R.W., Lazarus, L., Luckhurst, E., Kiloh, L.G., and Penny, R. (1977) Depressed lymphocyte function after bereavement. *Lancet,* **1**, 834–836

Bond, M. (1988) *Stress and Self Awareness: A Guide for Nurses.* London: Heinmann

Bradford, N. (1990) *The Well Woman's Self Help Directory.* London: Sedgewick & Jackson

Caspi A., Bolger, N. and Eckenrode J. (1987) Linking person and context in the daily stress process. *Journal of Personality and Social Psychology,* **52**, 184–195

Cobb, S. (1976) Social support as a moderator of life stress. *Psychosomatic Medicine,* **38**, 300–314

Cox, T. (1978) *Stress.* London: Macmillan

Derogatis, L.R., Abeloff, M.D. and Melisataros, N. (1979) Psychological coping mechanisms and survival time in metastatic breast cancer. *Journal of the American Medical Association,* **242**, 1504–1508

Edelmann, R.J. (1993) *Interpersonal Conflicts at Work.* Leicester: BPS Books

Evans, P.D. and Edgerton, N. (1991) Life events and mood as predictors of the common cold. *British Journal of Medical Psychology,* **64**, 35–44

Firth, J. and Morrison, L. (1986) What stresses health professionals? *British Journal of Clinical Psychology,* **25**, 309–310

Ganster, D.C. and Victor, B. (1988) The impact of social support on mental and physical health. *British Journal of Medical Psychology,* **61**, 17–36

Gartner, A. and Riessman, F. (1977) Self help in the Human Services. London: Jossey-Bass Publishers

Gerber, L.A. (1983) *Married to their Careers. Career and Family Dilemmas in Doctors' Lives.* New York: Tavistock

Greer, S. and Morris, T. (1975) Psychological attributes of women who develop breast cancer: a controlled study. *Journal of Psychosomatic Research,* **19**, 147–153

Haynes, S.G., Feinleib, M., and Kannel, W.B, (1980) The relationship of psychosocial factors to coronary heart disease in the Framingham Study. III. Eight year incidence of coronary heart disease. *American Journal of Epidemiology,* **111**, 37–58

Hebb, D.O. (1966) *A Textbook of Psychology.* Philadelphia: Saunders

Holmes, T.H. and Rahe, R.H. (1967) The social readjustment rating scale. *Journal of Psychosomatic Research,* **11**, 213–218

James, P. (1989) Dermatology. In: *Health Psychology: Processes and Applications,* edited by A. Broome. London: Chapman and Hall

Johnson, W.D.K. (1991) Predisposition to emotional stress and psychiatric illness among doctors, the role of unconscious and experiential factors. *British Journal of Medical Psychology,* **64**, 317–329

Kanner, A.D., Coyne, J.C., Schaeffer, C. and Lazarus, R.S., (1981) Comparison of two modes of stress management. Daily hassles and uplifts versus major life events. *Journal of Behavioral Medicine,* **4**, 1–39

Kiecolt-Glaser, J.K., Garner, N., Speicher, C., Penn, G., Holliday, J., and Glaser, R. (1987) Psychosocial modifiers of immunocompetence in medical students. *Psychosomatic Medicine,* **46**, 7–14

Kobasa, S.C. (1982) The hardy personality: towards a social psychology of stress and health. In: *The Social Psychology of Health and Illness,* edited by G.S. Sanders and J. Suls. Hillsdale, N.J.: Lawrence Erlbaum

Lazarus, R.S. (1966) *Psychological Stress and the Coping Process.* New York: McGraw Hill

Lazarus, R.S. and Folkman, S. (1984) *Stress, Appraisal and Coping.* New York: Springer

Levy, S. and Heiden, L. (1991) Depression, distress and immunity: risk factors for infectious diseases. *Stress Medicine,* **7**, 45–51

Llewelyn, S.P. (1989) Caring: the cost to nurses and relatives. In: *Health Psychology Processes and Applications,* edited by A. Broome. London: Chapman and Hall.

Maslach, C. (1981) *Burnout: The Cost of Caring.* New York: Prentice Hall

Maslow, A.H. (1943) A theory of human motivation. *Psychological* Review, **50**, 370

Mottram, E. and Flin, R.H. (1988) Stress in newly qualified physiotherapists. *Physiotherapy,* **74**, 607–612

McGrath, A., Reid, N., and Boore, J. (1989) Occupational stress in nursing. *International Journal of Nursing Studies,* **26**, 343–358

O'Leary, A. (1990) Stress, emotion and immune function. *Psychological Bulletin,* **108**, 363–382

Niven, N. (1989) *Health Psychology.* Edinburgh: Churchill Livingstone

Paris, J. and Frank, H. (1983) Psychological determinants of a medical career. *Canadian Journal of Psychiatry,* **28**, 354–357

Potter, J.F. and Beevers, D.G. (1984) Pressor effect of alcohol in hypertension. *The Lancet,* **I** 19–22

Ray, J.F. (1991) If 'A–B' does not predict heart disease why bother with it? A comment on Ivancevich and Mattesan. *British Journal of Medical and Clinical Psychology,* **64**, 85–90

Rathus, S.A. and Nevid, J.S. (1989) *Psychology and the Changes of Life. Adjustment and Growth,* 4th edn. Fort Worth: Holt, Rinehart and Winston, Inc.

Rosenmann, R.H., Brand, R.H., Jenkins, D., Friedman, M., Strauss, R. and Wurm, M. (1975) Coronary heart disease in the Western Collaborative group study. Final follow up experience of 8.5 years. *Journal of the American Medical Association,* **233**, 875–877

Schmidt, L.R., Schwenkmezger, P. Weinman, J. and Maes, S. (1990) (Eds) *Theoretical and Applied Aspects of Health Psychology.* Chur: Harwood Academic Publishers

Schuster, N.D., Nelson, D.L. Quisling, C. (1984) Burnout among physical therapists. *Physical Therapy,* **64**, 299–303

Selye, H. (1956) *The Stress of Life.* New York: McGraw Hill

Selye, H. (1974) *Stress Without Distress.* Philadelphia: J.B. Linnicott

Sharp, M., Hawton, K., Seagroatt, V. and Pasvol, G., (1992) Follow up of patients presenting with fatigue to an infectious diseases clinic. *British Medical Journal,* **305**, 147–152

Shekelle, R.B. *et al* (1985) The MRFIT Behavior Pattern Study: II. Type A behavior and incidence of coronary heart disease. *American Journal of Epidemiology,* **122**, 559–570

Slade, P. (1984) Pre-menstrual changes in normal women: fact or fiction? *Journal of Psychosomatic Research,* **28**, 1–7

Spector, N.H. (1990) Behavioral aspects of the modulation of immunity. In: *Theoretical and Applied Aspects of Health Psychology,* edited by L.R. Schmidt, P. Schwenkmezger, J. Weinman and S. Maes. Chur: Harwood Academic Publishers

Stone, A., Porter, L.S. and Neale, J.M. (1993) Daily events and mood prior to the onset of respiratory illness episodes: a non-replication of the 3–5 day 'desirability dip'. *British Journal of Medical Psychology,* **66**, 383–393

Sutherland, V.J. and Cooper, C.L. (1990) *Understanding Stress: A Psychological Perspective for Health Professionals.* London: Chapman and Hall

Thompson, J., Chung, M.C., Rosser, R. (1994) The *Marchioness* disaster: Preliminary report on psychological effects. *British Journal of Clinical Psychology,* **33**, 75–77

van der Gaag, A. (1988) How can we "start to succeed"? *Speech Therapy in Practice,* September, 4–5

Waal Manning, H.J., Knight, R., Spears, G.F. and Paulin, J.M. (1986) The relationship between blood pressure and personality in a large unselected adult sample. *Journal of Psychosomatic Research,* **27**, 299–305

Wilkinson, R.G. (1992) Income distribution and life expectancy. *British Medical Journal,* **304**, 165–168

Zigmond, A.S. and Snaith, R.P. (1983) The Hospital anxiety and depression scale. *Acta Psychiatrica Scandinavica,* **67**, 361–370

Zuckerman, M., Eysenck, S. and Eysenck, H.J. (1978) Sensation seeking in England and America. Cross cultural age, and sex comparisons. *Journal of Clinical and Consulting Psychology,* **46**, 139–149

Subject Index

Author Index